BY

WILLIAM GIBSON

WINTER CROOK   (*poems*)

DINNY AND THE WITCHES   (*play*)

THE COBWEB   (*novel*)

TWO FOR THE SEESAW   (*play*)

THE MIRACLE WORKER   (*play*)

THE SEESAW LOG   (*theatre chronicle*)

A MASS FOR THE DEAD   (*family chronicle*)

A CRY OF PLAYERS   (*play*)

AMERICAN PRIMITIVE: JOHN AND ABIGAIL   (*play*)

A SEASON IN HEAVEN   (*chronicle*)

BY

CLIFFORD ODETS *&* WILLIAM GIBSON

GOLDEN BOY   (*the book of a musical*)

A MASS FOR THE DEAD

WILLIAM GIBSON

A MASS
FOR THE DEAD

New York ATHENEUM 1977

Certain of the poems contained herein have appeared in *The American Scholar, Harper's, The New Republic, The New York Times, Partisan Review, Poetry, The Virginia Quarterly Review,* and *What's New.*

for their grandchildren

*Only take heed to thyself, and keep
thy soul diligently, lest thou forget
the things which thine eyes have seen,
and lest they depart from thy heart
all the days of thy life: but teach
them thy sons.*

CONTENTS

CONTENTS

CONTENTS

CREDO

GLORIA

ITE, MISSA EST

quare tristis es

Of All Such Earthy Melt

*Why art thou sorrowful, O my soul? saith the missal in my
hand. It is a little black tome, purse size; its pasteboard cover,
cracked and dogeared, is come apart from its text within, as
whose will not, and its loose pages of red and black matter are
thumbed soft; inside the husk of cover in a tight handscript she
has written* Flo Gibson, *and her last address. On my desk sits a
pair of rimless eyeglasses, with earhooks of pale wire daintily
figured, the lenses bifocal and thick. It was through these magni-
fiers that she read in this missal each Sunday at mass, and beginning,* I will go unto the altar of God, *glimpsed some enduring
rock in eternity. I am envious; I put her eyeglasses on, but the
words blur.* Why art thou sorrowful, O my soul, and why art
thou disquieted within me?

*The lenses are useless now, there cannot be two eyeballs again
like hers, a curious thought in so populous a world; but in the
small upstairs room where she died the eyeglasses, neatly folded
on a night table, so recreated her face I could not see them junked.
The missal I brought home from its own address, helping my sister clean out that always immaculate three-room apartment, and
carting back to my workroom here two armchairs and a boxful of
oddments. The younger chair dates from the summer my father
began to die, a springer of white-painted steel, which she bought
him so he could sit in the backyard sun; the other chair is half a*

3

century old, a formal throne of mahogany veneer with curved seat and floral carvings, the sole survivor of their wedding furniture. The oddments were from my father's pockets. For twenty-two years in her possession all these and more were used to being mementoes; I too think them good to have, they keep the leaf of misery green in a world so miraculous no bud of feeling is comfortless. I inherit not only them, but a habit of the heart.

I look in the other direction. Across the garden a couple of two-legged miracles are growing up like grass, boys, running naked and beautiful under our apple trees, after so strange a creation in the sewerage of the flesh, and never in all their running, to their last breath, to be out of earshot of their mother's voice or mine. Nor will their children be. In the hour of birth each of these boys was himself, infant scowler, infant chuckler; they grow, unalike, unique as her eyeballs, and each will alter the world minutely by some unpredictable touch, being man, the animal whose nature it is to alter nature and the world. Yet I see the older boy lose his temper at the sandpile, pounding with a rock on a toy derrick that is pigheaded, and I am bludgeoning an incorrigible spike ugly as a squashed snake into a plank of this studio going up, and my young father is grim over a talentless gadget he has brought home to my mother from a sidewalk pitchman, which ends up wrecked in our garbage pail, and it is some unknown grandfather of his whose fist is pounding sense with the rock into the toy derrick. The younger boy in a naked squat is maneuvering a chunk of old plank for a bulldozer, calmly making do, and in the garden my wife's father is erecting out of giant windfallen limbs a fence that will withstand earthquakes, but is only for peas to climb, calmly making do. The lives of these boys, so original to themselves, will be also as unoriginal as mine seems finally, a reincarnation of their dead.

In a wink now on these two sunlit bodies the hair of the monkey will sprout, and sexuality lay its jewelled cross, and the

4

acts of love, work, marriage, will be relived by both as I relived them under the dogma of my parents, in a long defiance, and deeply obedient; and to fatherhood each will bring his gift, his habits of the heart, inescapable as his bones. It is the only rock I see in the night that comes upon us, and how should my soul not be sorrowful?

INTROIT

I. Beginning Work

What worries
Is March; withindoors, in kitchen and nursery,
    Summer
In coinage like leaves and sons like cherries
    Is up
And over my heart, and tells its stammer
    Be still
In the talk of the loglight; dog days and sleep
    And love
Is enough.
              I see from the window the hill
    So hard
With winter the plot where the garden lived
    Rings
In the wind, lonely and bare as a board;
    It coffins
Seeds and sorrows in. Down in such wrongs
    Nights gone
I spaded to dig out my heart, as shriven
    Poor
As any foundling potato, but mine
    Had eyes
To witness, and more than sprouts to bear;
    For which,

As by day I wore it to market, the keys
    Of the house,
I mean love, and a rooftree over its riches,
    Came
In my hand; and a door on this windful of loss
    I shut.
It coffers my seeds and sun in. I am home,
    Let March
Be the mourner upon the hill.
                 And yet

    My eyes
Dog its heels. Interred in that patch
    Of toil
A sprout of me that no bed in this hot house
    Mothers
Is live, and uncurls, and cracks the world
    To be out
And green; its parent heart is what withers
    Blind
And tearless in me. Repletion and drought
    Mate
In the pith of my rooftree at summer's end,
    Its timber
Falls, with a heaven of leaves and fruit
    Decayed
Till its time is dug for again.
                Stammer,

    Be still:
It is in my bones I make love with the spade
    To the hill.

2. Now Let Me Conjure

I begin with her scrubbing at me. I am in a sunlit road at a clump of blackbrown balls, left by some almighty creature, gleaming, moist, delectable, and when I heft one toward the sidewalk at a moppet a flock of female cries is on my head, nasty nasty, and my longskirted keeper is kneeling to scold me and scrub at my fingers with newspaper. It is the earliest picture I have of the darkhaired girl who turned out to be my cheerful demon and mother. When she was born—late in the eighties, in a house on Broadway and 35th Street—she was named Florence Agnes, for bloom and purity; she grew to the names, no one I ever knew could touch her for brightness of heart or kitchen, she was a flower of steel wool. Everything in her character for years scoured me the wrong way, even after I saw it as a soulcleansing, of the disease and disorder in another childhood.

She was the last survivor of nineteen children, seventeen of them boys; all are melted into the earth again now, and some of their names even have blown away, but the juices of the flesh were rowdy in them once, a willful, clannish, hard-drinking, fornicating, blasphemous tribe. Their mother was a Mary Kane, who at fifteen had run away from a convent school to marry a song-and-dance man named Dennis Dore—pronounced as once written, Doré—because, my mother said, "she fell in love with his feet, dear." They carried him off much of the time; he crosses my mother's beginnings merely as a handsome man with white hair who "went with other women", and coming home drunk cached his money under carpets and atop windows, but in vain. The child my mother would climb after it, for Mary Dore was long practiced in spying on her menfolk when drunk. Nightlong she kept vigil for them—lifelong, I remember her at it still, a stubby old woman in black on a cushion in a window high in a Harlem tenement, peering down upon the overrun street, in wait for her boy Ben to come staggering along it on his forty-year-old legs—and when in the empty gaslit hours those blades lurched around the corner of the century with the drink in them, down the five flights of stairs their mother, in nightgown and shawl, went; she helped them up the stairs, and got them un-dressed and into bed with no falling over the kerosene heaters, and then salvaged what was left in their pockets. Sober, they would come and dump their money in her lap. Often enough she had an expensive banjo to help up the stairs also, clear of the drunken feet, for two of the brothers were leaders of a cele-brated banjo ensemble, variously trio and quartet. They dabbled in "heavy" music, dazzling the vaudeville circuit with a banjois-tic storm of a favorite Hungarian rhapsody, and played before the "crowned heads of Europe"; when Willy Dore died a show-business journal saluted him as "king of the banjos", the vaudevillians of the city sent a vast flowerpiece in the image of a banjo with a broken string, and fifty banjoists lined the stairs playing a hymn on strings muted by pennies while Willy's body in its coffin was borne down past them in its last triumph; and Ben in his grief took a great oath never to play the banjo again. Alas for grief, half a century later it came out he could hardly play: Ben chuckling told me how he was the quartet's fifth, when one of the true four was indisposed young Ben taking the banjo onstage would strum tempestuously away with the other three, his fingers unallowed to touch the strings. Willy's funeral was only the grandest of many, for Mary Dore saw fourteen of her sons die and their sire Dennis too. And the older daughter Minnie, who had buried a husband and a child, worked as a "hash slinger" in steakhouses, drank, and left again when she remarried; and Frank, who spent much of his time climbing out of bedroom windows, fled from one vengeful husband into the army and served fifteen years in the tropics, his mother not laying eyes on him again; and the businessman George—of whom she said not altogether benignly, "Everything he puts his hands on is money"—disappeared into the Larchmont Yacht Club, and never sailed down the Harlem. So out of her tenement window at last Mary Dore watched only for faithful Ben, who if he tasted one drink would not be sober for a week, but paid the bills, living with his wife and two daughters and itinerant cousins in a seven-room flat which was still "the old lady's".

Nurtured in the bosom of this men's club, the girl Flo saw "so much drinking and fighting, I just wanted to run away." When she was sixteen, the wish came true. After the death of her father, a bookie and his wife adopted her, with intent to improve her lot; she moved into their outskirts home, they entered her in a better school, bought her expensive dresses, and in the racing season took her off to Saratoga, Newport, "all those fancy places". Every week she stole time from her mandolin lesson downtown to sit in Mary Dore's kitchen, weeping to return if it "was only for a crust of bread", and after six months neither of them could bear it longer, home she came. She went out to work—her exile had taken her out of the final grade in her parochial school, so she was never graduated—and over the years rose from salesgirl in a five-and-ten to manageress of a confectionery shop; the next time she left home it was to be married. But long before she had devised an interior and immobile kind of flight, which is evident in her earliest photographs.

"I was pretty, dear," she said when I asked what she was like, "I had lots of boys." The photographs seldom capture the prettiness, but offer a fresh tidy girl—"and I dressed very nice"—whose body is tightening against impulse, awkward in a blending of timidity and discipline; it is not only in the archaic starch of dress, but in the inheld elbows, the stiffnecked head, the careful smile; emotion here is materializing in the tendons, turning to character. Her spine is a denial. The haunting image out of her adolescence will be how she stands screaming in darkness as something crawls on her breast, until the bookie's Negro running in with a lamp seizes a handful of her nightgown, and hangs on squeezing, and lets drop from within it at her bare feet a lifeless mouse; all her days she will be terrified of such creatures of the earth, insects, fish, snakes, of whatever is undomesticated, drunks and halfwits, and of thunder, the world atremble with instinct. Her young spine is stiffening, it intends to let no such nonsense out.

When she fell in love, it was with a youth whose temper was as impulsive as a matchhead. It is implicit in my first image of him, a crowd of home-from-work marchers on an el station, meaningless faces and feet, until suddenly my mother is waving and calling "Dearie!" and out of the crowd comes its meaning, in gray suit and straw hat, to catch me up and hang me over a shoulder; his spine was pliant with warmth, and sudden heat too.

They met over a legacy of music. Willy left nothing in his pockets when he died; this time Mary Dore salvaged his two studios for banjo instruction, with the lesser brothers teaching, twenty lessons for twenty dollars; it was here that my mother became mistress of the mandolin, and in time an instructor of it. She was just out of her teens when Mary Dore decided to add a piano teacher to the establishment, inquired of neighbors on street corners, and, hearing of a fellow who played, sent out word for him to come see her. The skinny youth who climbed the stairs to her parlor one evening was a postoffice night clerk, twelve days older than my mother, and had his own notion. He

would not teach piano, but remarked upon the gay musical
parties he often heard when walking beneath their windows, and
Mary Dore said yes, every Sunday night, it was her chief entertainment, and the young man happened to remember that the
previous night a girl with a mandolin was singing a catchy tune
named "San Francisco Bay", who would that be? Mary Dore
said it was her daughter, right there. The young fellow said hm,
and would the daughter play and sing it now, for him? The
daughter obliged, and he in turn made the piano rock with a
ragtime tune or two; Mary Dore then invited him to enrich the
parties, if not the studio, and bring the blonde girl she heard he
was keeping company with. The young man said he would be
happy to, and on the next Sunday arrived without the blonde,
who accordingly passes out of this history as not my mother. For
it was that midnight at the mail racks, with an eveningful of
mandolin-and-piano duets in his twenty-year-old head, that Mr.
George Irving Gibson said with customary promptitude to a pal,
"I met the girl I'm going to marry." It merely took him five
years.

He was used to having his way with more dispatch; somehow,
in a household of six boys and girls, my father had half achieved
the position of an only son. His mother was a massive lass, born
Kate Jennings, who rechristened herself Katherine for elegance.
She had been married at sixteen to one Gollan, a civil engineer,
first name Jim; she presented him with two daughters, Milly and
Ada, and a boy, hunchbacked from a fall in infancy, who later
succumbed to scarlet fever; eight months after Jim Gollan died of
pneumonia his widow was delivered of another boy, Will. She
fed herself and the children by sewing, making hats, baby caring. Her second husband was a cratemaker named Gibson, a
teetotaller who after marriage was converted to a drinking man;
his wife never called him by anything except his patronymic
—"You down there, Gibson?"—because her tongue would not

utter his first name, Jim. Over which gap she yielded three more children in a house on Eighth Avenue and 132nd Street, the boy called Irv, his sister Ethel, and a legendary brother named, in honor of some husband, Jim. In this double family my father rode to privilege on "the Gibson goat", his bestial temper, around which the women tiptoed: a "very snappy dresser", he would, upon finding in his drawer one of his detachable collars not ironed flawlessly, promptly rip it to shreds. It seemed such constructive criticism improved the distaff service, for he brought it to his courtship of my mother, with disappointing results.

It began with the Sunday evenings, where music was the food. Popular songs could be heard nowhere then except in vaudeville, and every amateur talent was valued; all the young folk who gathered round Mary Dore's upright piano could play or sing or dance, and passed the evening entertaining each other, with an interlude of tea and sandwiches, or beer in the kitchen where the men could drink it away from the girls' sensitive eyes; Flo sang over her mandolin, played a little tremolo piano, acted out songs in a man's hat, and Mary Dore had a grand time. Irv Gibson was seized upon by this flock. When at the age of eighteen months he whistled tunes his mother had declared he "had music in him" and would have lessons "if I have to go out washing"; he took to both the lessons and the practicing, and at fifteen had won a medal engraved "for excellence in piano playing". He could make the keyboard jump by note or ear, and once any gathering sat him at the piano stool they would not let him up. For several months he was a godsend to Mary Dore, then, having made the parties perfect, he disrupted them altogether.

Flo was waltzing with another youth when it happened, the piano ceased in the middle of a measure, and Irv Gibson rising put on his hat and departed without a word. It was a couple of days before he reappeared. He said he came on Sundays not to play for that gang but to see her, and next Sunday they were going to a show instead; she said oh, she couldn't do that, her mother loved the parties so; he said and another thing, he heard whenever a beau got serious her mother broke it up, this was one time she would not. Whereupon next Sunday they went to the show—Flo armed with a deadly hatpin, in case he "got smart", which he did not—and for two weeks her mother refused to speak to her. It was only a sample, for when at long last they married she refused to speak to her son-in-law for two years, and referred to him invariably as "narrow ass Gibson". I do not know that my father ever officially proposed; he would tease Mary Dore, "I'm going to get your daughter," and she would snap back, "You're not going to get my daughter," but the Sunday parties were ended; the weaning of Flo Dore was begun.

The ostensible use of the five-year engagement was to save up for housekeeping. Though her brother George had married on twelve dollars a week, and my father's half-brother Will on fourteen, both setting up house in furnished rooms, my mother was firmly minded to have her own flat and furniture. Saving for anything was not native in my father's relationship to money. One of his favorite sayings was "Get it and you got it," and the other was "Wrap it up." To the end of his life he dispensed cash with the carelessness of a man who had trunkfuls of it; I remember one door-to-door mendicant who hoped only to sell him a pair of shoelaces and departed with trainfare to Johns Hopkins for an alleged operation; no panhandler in the gutter ever bummed him for a dime but got a quarter, and when hooted at for his gullibility my father said, "Well, give it to enough, the right one gets it." He was always broke. At thirteen he had become a full-time worker, graduating from schoolboy to officeboy and the scant string of three or four jobs that were to tie up his lifetime; in his late teens he took a chance on a civil-service exam like a raffle and unexpectedly won the prize, his place in the postoffice at six hundred dollars a year, which for a youthful bachelor was affluence. Paydays he paid off this bill, that debt, and took his empty envelope home to fling down before the folks as accusatory evidence, demanding, "What am I working for?—work all week, I haven't a nickel to show for it!" and then borrowed a fiver to start him through another week. By wedding time he was making twenty-five dollars a week and had a flatful of furniture, bought outright, to show for it. But the rigor behind this accrual was the girl Flo's; each payday throughout their engagement he put his money into her hands and she budgeted it out, expenses, pocket money, savings.

Meanwhile they fought stormily. Most of the storming was my father's, who would bring his fiancée a box of candy and throw it out the window, or pitch his bag of lunch into her coalstove and walk the midnight streets instead of reporting to work, which meant less pay that week and a longer wait for the furniture. She tutored his contrition to be as prompt as his ire; her anger was frost, she had her mother's knack for punitive silence, and the thaw was slow. It took all his warmth to woo her out. When they made peace after one battle he went downstairs to buy ice cream, and she meditating in his absence froze over again and went to bed; returning, he sat innocently in the parlor with the ice cream melting, until her brother Ben invaded her darkened room to order her out of bed and back into her clothes, to "stop making a fool of that feller". It was a long learning to the bedtime rule of their marriage, never go to sleep angry, lest "something happen" in the night.

Often in the midst of his courting Irv she told me was called away to "quiet down" his father in some saloon, and their other houserule would be to let no liquor in. When they sat for a photograph together—two neat slim bodies, the girl unsmiling and her eyes astare, elbows and knees tight, hands clenched in her lap, immaculate to her throat in lacy white, and the young man with grin and straw hat both aslant, jaunty on the bench arm, one leg crossed, natty in his suit and tie complete with stickpin, his arm around her with fingers outspread possessively upon her shoulder—it was a portrait not only of contrasts, but of a nation's lower middle class coming out of its cocoon. However they fought, they were yoked by an aspiration to self-respect, down to the minutiae of unwrinkled collars, and a conviction, held before and since, that they could live better than their fathers.

So for five years mine like Jacob worked for his bride, and she withheld the instinctual gift of body to acquire not some chairs and dishes but with them that spinal erectness of independence which was to be the armature of our clay. It was a complex courtship, for they were put off by the contrarieties that drew them to each other, and what kept the flesh apart locked the minds tenser; I think the true use of those years was to house-break these two variant souls one to another for their lifework, marriage.

The ceremony was inconspicuous, performed in a city office by a justice of the peace. Her family was Catholic, his Protestant, and they had decided to offend neither by ignoring both; the young man was indifferent to religious matters, and the girl's conscience was satisfied by his agreeing to raise their children as Catholics; for herself, she thought the civil marriage meant excommunication. What both of them lived by literally was the language of the contract, whose majesty even in that office translated the event beyond local time and place into a wedding of everyman and everywoman: each took the other, to have and to hold from that day forward, for better, for worse, for richer, for poorer, in sickness and in health, to love and to cherish, forsaking all others, till death did them part. Having pledged this to each other, they went to dinner and a show and home to their virginal flat, where on a new bed they clove together, in the twenty-fifth year of their flesh.

My father's life was exactly half over.

3. Introibo

If resurrection be,
I pray
It trumpet forth my yoking flesh
Upright

Within a little grave
Of clay
Still hers. Eternity would hang
Unfelt

Upon my ghostly shrift
Of hands
Ungloved of lust; veins that mesh
Me in

Do carry half the tides,
And moon
She is, or mud like me, to whom
I lift

My moiety of earth;
Its head
So suckled on her cratered pear
Brides

3. *Introibo*

Half the world. Body,
Vulva,
Testicles, dying, covetous melt
Of gut

Together, skin, eyes,
Hair,
Brain, in these, where all of love
Is shut

And dying, is our bed
Of soul
To which I cling. I will not rise
Lacking

Her bowellage of love.
My wife,
It is to you, on impious knee,
This prayer

That resurrection be
I make,
Whose spousal ring of bone I wear
For life.

KYRIE

4. Green Hearts, and Stalker

I was born nine months and thirteen days after the wedding, and as a boy often wondered what was so funny about my mother's most reliable joke, "Thank God for the thirteen days." I was not born in the virginal flat because it turned out to be located over a whorehouse. Nights when my father was off at work his bride would lie awake baffled by a traffic of males on the stairway; when they began knocking happily on her door, their mistake and my parents' became evident. As promptly as was manageable the new furniture was moved into a flat a mile to the north, where I emerged unexpectedly into the Bronx. While the doctor, counting on a protracted first labor, was playing pinochle in Harlem, my mother and I were lying together in her blood with the umbilical cord still connecting us; the doctor strolling in found us attended only by a rattled neighbor whom my mother had called to via the dumbwaiter shaft; and the attack with which he set to work, severing us, knotting me, coaxing the afterbirth out of my mother's entrails, was explained by him with some apology, another hand of pinochle and we would both have been dead. It was not accident, but character, my mother setting me in my first hour an example in self-help.

I was fed on her breasts, and with paradox as much as milk. Christened in the neighborhood church, with her brother Ben and sister Minnie sworn as godparents of my soul, and held by her rigorously to the Catholic regimen all my childhood, I would not see my mother attend mass for twenty-five years. She commenced at once to work me to great expectations. She undertook my toilet training when I was three months old, holding me more or less on a potty while she hissed and grunted invitational sounds at my wobbling head. I mastered the matter, in time, only to find myself strapped in a highchair undergoing tuition from her in spelling feats—cat, dog, apple—with which I greeted such visitors as my uncles Will and Jim, amazed at this eighteen-months-old sage. Hardly was I out of the highchair when I was stood on my feet piping out a song before a congregation of Methodist sinners patient as saints. Her demand was automatic and insatiable: forty years later, when I told her a play of mine had sold to the movies for better than half a million dollars, she inquired, "Dear, will it lead to anything?" Yet she gave as she exacted, out of a spirit generous and tyrannical. It was my father who, in a fit of annoyance at the docile slumbers of his sister's infant, trained me to fall asleep without wailing by letting me wail all night, and forbade my mother to pick me up; if I bawled in my baby carriage she would halt it in a crowd, and, propriety-stricken girl, do a zany song-and-dance act for my gurgles. For twenty years she would plague me with "what people will think", and at the age of seventy be under the bed with my three-year-old, squealing like a piggy, some bud of childhood in her never nipped. Not in her lifetime would she relent with grace to "bother the doctor", and though we outlived my birth her stubbornness would in the end kill her; yet as a six-foot man I was urged by her to see a doctor every time I sneezed.

One of my earliest memories is of her rushing me to the doctor with a bloodily bandaged wrist, on which I still wear a three-inch welt of scar, incurred at two-and-a-half. En route to the store she entrusts me with two empty milkbottles, proving I am my own man, but warns me not to climb with them over those rocks, proving I am not, whereupon I climb over them, proving I am, and tumbling onto my face I see in the broken glass my hand leaking blood; though blood turns my mother faint she carries me home, stands me on the toilet seat, and rips up under-clothes to staunch my wound, which is soaking us both; she will often relate how, gazing down at her fumbling fingers, I say encouragingly, "I'll sing you a song," and do. The song tells me less about the boy's courage, which was to thin out much with experience, than about the kind of behavior he has learned his mother will approve. Yet her pluck, which surmounts her dread of blood, will not carry her into an unfamiliar office, and she takes me and my staining bandage out of the neighborhood by trolley car an hour down into Harlem, to the pinochle player. And here, to distract me while he sews into the heel of my hand the sixth or seventh stitch, my teacher of truth says gaily, "Look out the window, dear, there's a monkey!" and I look and there is no monkey; it is only a "white" and unforgotten lie.

After my birth, the doctor advised her to have no more chil-dren. She was always thin and frail, though in time we saw it was with the tensility of wire, and when she was twenty-seven she underwent surgery; it was for an exophthalmic goiter, the first of the many afflictions that were to bed her down in hospitals once, twice, three times a decade. What the doctor feared was strangu-lation in childbirth. The goitrous mass is ponderable on her throat in old snapshots, bulging at her open-for-breath collar, "big as a grapefruit" when the surgeon cut it out; even rid of it she experienced any agitation as suffocating her; it makes less bizarre the worst fear of her life, that she would be sealed in her coffin still breathing. She had deferred the operation to the last moment, unable to leave her baby, who managed in Minnie's hands, but when she survived the knife to reappear after two weeks her next to worst fear was realized, I failed to remember her.

In my third year we moved another mile to the north, in character. My mother's opinion was that the rooms needed re-painting, and in a half-year campaign she wrested the work out of the landlord; she could breathe again under the germless ceilings, until without warning he raised the rent three dollars, over which she went into a righteous freeze; she never paid it, and after a boroughwide search we journeyed forth to a four-room flat which was serenaded by a shattering el, much darker, much dirtier, and more expensive. In her latter years she would say with satisfaction that it "was foolish". We were now pinched for money and my father undid the pinch by his own budgetary principle, if your expenditures exceed your income increase your income.

It was a custom of the postoffice crew to pass around a hat when one of its members had a child; in my father's case it was passed around twice, for a "swell guy", and came to him brim-ming with a hundred dollars; but apart from this windfall, the postoffice yielded only the twenty-five a week which was no longer affluence, and a baby picture of me rearing far back in a heavenward gaze is captioned by my father as "looking for my old man's payday". Now he sat at the kitchen table to write out, in his large, clear, mistakeless hand, copies of a letter about himself, and mailed one to every bank in the city. Three banks in among the crevasses of Wall Street invited him to an interview; he came home to describe for my mother one set of offices so "light" he would "love to work there", seeing daylight as a privilege, and was delighted when asked to take the bank's medi-cal examination; he counted the days till the job was his. Their letter came, saying they could not offer it, he had a heart mur-mur. My father went again to them, as set upon their tidy establishment as he had been upon my mother, and so impres-sively in earnest about it that they hired him, reassured perhaps by his word that he "had never been sick a day in his life". Two weeks after he went on the payroll he was at the point of death with pneumonia, and embarrassment.

His new salary was forty dollars. His job was as clerk in the central mail department, through which by day and night letters moved to and from all sides of the globe, and he was to hold it for twenty years, surviving a merger with the largest bank in the world; he died as foreman of the department, at sixty-five dollars a week, with more than sixty "boys" under him. His hours were staggered, on alternate shifts. One week he left the house afternoons and came home past midnight, and the next week left after midnight and was home for lunch; it was a schedule which his body was never quite in step with, he slept fitfully, and often in the dark of the house he was seated in his pajamas at a window, smoking. Unpaid overtime was frequent, when a rush of countrywide mail was going out, or when the daily accounts were short by a penny stamp and everyone in the department, unable to toss a penny in the drawer, stayed for hours to track the error down. His first day at the bank my mother waited up half the night for him; he had told her of the great airless vaults, on timelocks that were unopenable, and she was confident he was shut in one. He came trudging up the stairs well before dawn, to say wryly, "I'm a banker now, these are banker's hours."

The pneumonia almost ended them, but he survived it in the bed at home, and his convalescence is impressed indelibly upon my behind. One morning I stood at the window in the dining room, wearing his old hat—of yellowed hard straw, he would strip the ribbon off and scissor the jagged brim away until I had a conductor's cap—while chugging a train of pencil stubs back and forth on the cement sill; finally I chugged them over the edge, a great wreck in the courtyard. My father was in bed, watching through the bead portieres whereby my mother had converted the parlor into their bedroom, and he called to ask had I pushed those pencils out the window? I said they fell out. My skinny father weaved through the portieres in his brawny bath-robe and said if I lied he would give me a licking, did I push them or not? I had no wish to stick to my story, but it stuck to me, it said they fell out by themselves, so my father said, "Don't you ever lie to me!" and whacked my behind until I bawled. It is the one spanking that lingers.

But the lie I remember next is not mine. My mother was sickly again, with the doctor at her bedside; my father removed me to his mother's house across town, a long day of which my eye keeps not a trace, though it dimly sees me retrieved, man and boy on the el stairs in a wintry night, then the shadowy room with my mother in bed, and in with her a little animal who cries. I ask what it is, and my mother says feebly, "It's a chicken, dear." I knew it was no chicken, it was my sister Jeanette, brought to us by the doctor in his black bag, they say, which I think is unlikely because it is full of bright knives, but "chick" she will be to my father the rest of his life. After this nine-and-a-half-pound baby, so toilsome a delivery that my mother's throat had to be trussed to sustain her windpipe, the doctor was emphatic, another birth would kill her.

My father was tender with her, as always, except when his temper broke out, usually from the jail of a Sunday afternoon. He thought the difficulty lay in my mother's being so punish-ingly silent against his angers; thereafter she tried reasoning with him, it made matters worse, he said it would help "if she just wouldn't say anything"; in their next fight, with silence and speech both forbidden, she went about the house singing blithely, "Tra la la, tra la la," but it was not the answer. She could at once touch him to penitence, with tears, but she had pride, and other tactics. In one of his umbrages, when he was washing the dishes and she drying, he smashed a cup into the sink; she considered a moment, and then smashed a clean one in; he smashed a dirty plate in, and she smashed a clean one in, and so they continued, dirty dish, clean dish, dirty dish, clean dish, he more irresolute and she obdurate, until contemplating the wreckage of half their chinaware in the sink my father said mildly, "Honey, I think we broke enough dishes for tonight." In another wrath he turned from her onto a bowlful of bananas and wrung each banana by the neck into a pulpy ooze, banana after banana, their innards squirming to escape through his fingers, until all were quite done in; my mother then said, "They're Billy's favorite, now he has no bananas," and my father washed his hands, put on his straw hat, and led me downstairs; we hunted without luck throughout the Sunday neighborhoods for an unpadlocked fruitstore, until we met a wandering peanut-wagon and my father bought two warm bagfuls, one for me, one for my mother.

His dudgeons always ended in a grace of giving. Castor oil was the remedy then for all that ailed body or soul, used also as a lubricant for aircraft engines, and one evening my mother decided a dose of it could do me no harm. She cornered me in the dining room to proffer it, a bulge of colorless slime on a giant spoon, and I would not open my mouth; my father took over the spoon and said he wanted me to take this, understand, and I nodded, but my mouth kept shut. Both my parents in turn thereupon swallowed a spoonful, and beamed horribly upon each other and me to show how tasty they found it, and my mother poured another spoonful to poke at my mouth, which was not open to reason. My father then said to put it in some orange juice, couldn't expect a kid to take it plain, but when my mother looked in the icebox there were no oranges. My father asked if we went down to the drugstore would I drink it in some orange juice, and I nodded, so he put on his shoes, and we descended the staircase hand in hand, pals. Halfway up the evening street under the el we entered a lighted drugstore and climbed on stools of metal scrollwork at a marble counter, where my father instructed the counterman to mix some orange juice and castor oil for me, and a black-and-white soda for him. The counterman set before me a glassful of inviting orange froth, and the instant his hand left it the mixture commenced to decompose, giving rise slowly to a membrane of colorless slime; my father said I wouldn't even taste it, believe you me, and sat spooning at his black-and-white soda while I shrank from my glassful of poison; when his straw had sucked up the bottom of the soda he said angrily come on now, and lifted the potion to my mouth, which I shut tight, and he bethought himself, pinched a nickel out of his change on the counter, and said if I drank up my medicine I could have the nickel, was that a deal, and I nodded; he hoisted the glass again to my lips, and they would not part. My father thunked down the glass, scooped up his change, and yanked me in his fist out of the drugstore, not pals, back along the street and up our staircase again. In the kitchen he told my mother to fix another spoonful, and while she was pouring from the bottle he said stubborn, stubborn, she knew who I got that from, and my mother said she certainly didn't, and my father said I didn't get it from him, and he thrust the big spoonful of slime under my nose; he said, "You take this right now or you get a licking, one or the other, take your pick." I quavered, "Daddy, I think I'll take the licking." After a minute of staring my father said, "By God, you beat the band," his mouth down in his wry smile, and he rumpled my hair, put the nickel in my hand, and told me, "You're some kid." And I lived, without the castor oil.

I sit over a battered album, black pages pasted with photos and captioned in white ink, and I spy on the love affair my father had with his firstborn. The captions are in his firm handprint; on the cover *Our Boy* is lettered proudly across a snapshot of a simpy babe, who on the pages within enters early boyhood to an accompaniment of "considerable kid" and "leave go I can stand alone" and "look out for me I'm pretty tough" and "a fighting pose" and "on the level folks ain't I some kid" and "I can't sing but you should see me fight"; an emphasis falls on valor, and I wonder whose. I think it was his brother Jim's, ascribed to me as my father's second chance. But I had no doubt then about the bravery of my father, who when I locked myself helplessly in the bathroom swung from our fire escape over a four-story drop to squeeze in the narrow window to me; and my own was lauded by him often enough, as when I dared the dark of my bedroom that terrified man and beast alike, except my teddy bear, or when coming home by trolley car the day I had my tonsils out I politely hemorrhaged in my mother's lap. It was their pride in me that was contagious, for a while.

I became king of the block, a predicament I achieved with one blow and a word from my mother. Four or five kids backed me up on the stoop yahhing while I swung my toy tennis racket at them, until I fled upstairs to my guardian angel, who informed me I must fight my own fights and ordered me downstairs again to my doom; when I ran to hit the ringleader in the face it screwed up like a baby's in tears, which constituted a knockout, and I inherited the kingdom. I then had to fight every new six-year-old who moved into the neighborhood. Perhaps it was the dethronement upstairs by my honey-haired sister, but a timid boy who moved to our block evoked my cowardice at sight, and after each of us skulked from the other for days we were pushed together by the gang; one poke from him and I bawled, which so disgusted my lieutenant, the ex-king, that he punched the new kid's nose for me, whereupon he bawled too, and the royal succession ravelled out in bafflement. I had failed my father's captions, not for the last time.

Valor however was the birthright of his kid brother Jim, who moved in a golden haze of it. He was a blond lad with a handsome mug, clear with soul outward, his figure stocky and mus-

cled with power; clothed, he stands in the snapshots with that
bodily serenity lent only by strength, and it informs his cocked
grin; beside him my father, two years older, looks brittle, and the
fact that Jim could always knock him about at will was one of
my father's few boasts. A natural athlete, Jim not only swam the
width of the Hudson but doubled back, and the swimsuit snapshots catch his hard beauty in the jackknife act.of diving, or
drawn up with mock heroic chest and a canoe paddle for a
standard, or tensed behind a catcher's mitt with his biceps bulging. It is a queer footnote to his legend that his job was as an egg
candler. The love my father felt for him he paid back to whatever was his big brother's, and the morning after the wedding it
was Jim who hoisted bread and a chocolate cake up the dumbwaiter to their flat, my father promptly invited him up, and my
mother hid in the bathroom till he left; and when I was born it
delighted him. On my first birthday, the gift he laid in my
diapered lap was an official football. The day after his country
declared war on a family quite unknown to him, the Hohenzol-
lerns, my twenty-six-year-old uncle enlisted in the army; he is
photographed that spring in uniform, toting a soldier on his
shoulders, guarding a railroad bridge with bayoneted rifle, pushing two soldiers in a wheelbarrow, sitting on a bench with his
fiancée and a little boy between them—me—to a caption of "not
yet but soon"; then he is gone, overseas, and the snow is on the
ground, and the boy instead is in a new soldier's coat and hat,
dutifully saluting. Letters for a year and a half went back and
forth, but not a word of my mother's second pregnancy, which
was to be a surprise to our corporal on his return. She was in her
seventh month when Armistice Day was celebrated in the streets
of the city, wild with horns and cowbells and all the Gibsons
among the thousands converging downtown to make a jubilant
noise unto heaven that their boys that day were alive; and my
father wrote to his brother in France a letter full of joyous
tomfoolery.

Two weeks later, around Thanksgiving Day, our doorbell rang in the night. My father unlocked the door, and my grandfather Pop Gibson walked past him into the dining room, where he stood with hat in hand, half bald, straw mustache sagging, his eyes in his spectacles confused; he offered out of his pocket a telegram, and mumbled, "They got Jim." Later we learned from a buddy that weeks earlier in October the son whom Pop called "my whitehaired boy" had peered over a hedge which he and his men had taken, and toppled back with a bullet in his heart; he "bled very little, it was all over in a minute," and the advance left his invincible body behind, never to be recovered; he was long in the earth, presumably blown apart, when our cowbells were clanking. I heard that night profanities unknown in our flat, my father blundering in the rooms and screaming, "Bastards, those rotten Hun bastards," in such a violence that next morning the neighbor downstairs came up to ask what was wrong.

The callow jauntiness went out of my father's face in the snapshots after that; it was gentled. For twenty years there hung on his wall a framed poem—"He is not dead, he is just away"—with a snipping of Jim's head from the soldier photos pasted on it, small as a thumbnail. In the spring of each year my father on Decoration Day would travel across the city, with his two children, to hang a wreath on a young tree which was tagged with his brother's name, one of a series planted along a Bronx boulevard as far as my eye could count; my father said the dead soldiers were not under the trees, but in a foreign land. And in his bureau drawer among his odds and ends—a silver-dollar brooch, a toenail shears, his piano medal, a cube of notched wax to mollify his stiff collars—lay the aging letter of tomfoolery he had written to his brother in that land, which had come back undelivered.

With this death, and the birth of my sister several weeks later, our family was complete: we were now four and a shadow, stalking. My father, as though ridden by some inarticulate sense

35

of this, soon attempted a year of not losing his goat with his wife and children. He circled the day on the calendar we kept tacked up in the kitchen, and that page stayed; week succeeded week, and month, and season, with no explosion; in those hot moments when he was at boiling point he reached for his hat and the doorknob, and marched about in the streets of the Bronx until the steam was out of him. It wore out much of his shoe leather, but when the circled day came round once more he could look back and be content, and all of us marvelled: that year he had mastered his temper.

But afterwards he lost it again, many times; he was flesh, alive and imperfect, even in a world whose matter around us was unravelling as fast as it was created.

5. October End

Blood is in the leaf,
    It glows
Hemorrhage red on black arm oak
    To preach
    Elate in winds;

        Its life
        Hangs by a hair.

    Fever in a green day
        Prose
Fans the grass to holy folk
        Golden
        In its speech,

        So gay
        Its deathbed air.

    Purpling on the sky
        Is smoke
The tapers of the crematory
        Bogs
        Exhale in praise;

KYRIE

By rote
Glory, glory

Is the flagrant cry
Of hills
Tubercular in blooms of untold
Tongues
One raindrop kills

And clogs
My prayerless throat.

6. Kyrie Eleison

Our first death haunted my childhood. It is with me again now, each generation its shadow is deeper; this fall every child born to the world plays in a fickle shadow of murder and mercy.

Here, where our boys run in the drifts of the maple leaves, we are newcomers with squatter's rights in a very old cemetery. Death was always underfoot, no stem of grass but is a tombstone, the topsoil is rich with its forgotten bones, billions of hands that in vain clung to the air, and went under; and each mouth filling with earth cried out its lonely eleison. And my boys, who know they too must someday die, ask me why.

Have mercy upon us, saith the missal: that outcry of woe, is it anything but the primal wail to let us live? live in the hour of the flesh, another minute another mercy, and in the hour of its death emigrate into eternity with undamaged wits. In a prayer I had by heart when I was as green as my boys I pledged my somewhat inexperienced belief in the resurrection of the body, and life everlasting. In my orphaned forties I walked again in the church my mother had me christened in, and sat alone amid its acre of pews below dim lamps on long chains in a quietude which was a simulacrum of God's mind; high in this alabaster skull, birdlike above the altar, hung a replica of the carcass they said was his beloved son, crucified, sword-pierced and naked, but clad in a monstrous dream of triumph over death. It was this dream which had reared a thousand hundred thousand such temples around the graveyard of our planet, like lookout towers for some after-life, and brought mankind to its knees in them, that death might be a beginning.

I am poorer without this dream and paradisiacal answer for my boys, as my father was. I had often heard him say, "When you're dead, you're dead," though the framed poem that hung by his bed all his life said his brother was not, he was merely away. It was not all poesy. I was to learn that only death as generality is inevitable, individual death comes always as an accident, and what we mourn is in part the oversight—a diagnos-tician seen a month too late, a highway crossed a second too soon—so easily undone, undone, undone in imagination, whose stammerings are another way of saying let us live; my young uncle in truth was "just away" by the distance of an accident called war. And it is not their deaths I would withhold my boys from, but that abortion of their lives.

For it was murder, the abortionist, who haunted my childish head. When I was ten I undertook an elegiac novel; in a thick notebook with a marbled cover I inscribed in ink the title *Jim*, and at once ran out of material. Not of motif, that handsome boy's death as a gratuity of war was to be a cornerstone in a lifelong suspicion, rising like a monument in me, of society as a gigantic trap, and of all its dedicated rulers, whose talents so invariably end in murder. In the estate which I devise to my boys I include that monument; it is a more practical lookout.

Yet I was mistaken: three and a half decades later I saw the murderer's face. Exhuming my childhood among the family mementoes I came upon a letter scribbled in a dugout "some-where in France". It was a long letter which, among its chitchat of marching and combat, said casually, "We didn't take many prisoners, as it is easier to kill them. They certainly are a bunch of cowards. Just as soon as they see they are caught they come running up to you with their hands in the air yelling, Kamerad! You would hear one of our boys say, Here is your Kamerad—bang!—a shot and it would be all over." The letter, written to his mother shortly before he died, was signed "your good boy, Jim".

Came running with their hands in the air yelling, Have mercy upon us; and the murderer was my uncle. All that my father loved and admired in him was true, and insufficient. The war was not an accident, it was a failure of the human tissue, preserved as on a microscope slide in the letter of a hero.

It is my uncle's shadow that falls upon my boys. The sense of mortality irks them at odd moments, and sleepless at bedtime one boy invites me to "figure out a way" he need not die, and I think how the animal wants to live; sitting at his hip I say he will be immortal in his son as I am in mine, which satisfies neither of us, and by his bed I see the toy rifle to which he has lashed a rubber knife as bayonet, and I think how the animal wants to kill. The shadow which overlies our roof is sprung from the light that bred the two-legged beast.

But when he is asleep, and I am out on the hill for my nightly count of stars, I think is this townful of roofs not a miracle? I can tell my boy how we have dug for the forgotten hands, and surmised a million centuries that crept by the beast living isolate in caves; only yesterday he perceived that in bands he might overcome the mammoth, and changed from claws to tools, and overnight changed wildernesses into cities; and did he not change himself? It was outgrow or die, and he outgrew. He forbade himself rape, homicide, plunder, incest, cannibalism; he laid down another imperative, it was the tool he invented chief of all tools, and it moved the earth. He called it conscience, a knowing together, and I can tell my boy it is our warranty of human life, which houses us under the hope of these roofs. Humankind alone of the beasts upon the earth is so changed.

41

Squatter yesterday in a bone-strewn cave, and tomorrow a voyager to the brightening planets, man the fantastic, we are the electric stuff of creation, and the earth is not a graveyard but our seedbed; and in my boy's loins is a billion years yet to come. I must tell him this romance, for it is true, and insufficient.

Tonight the wind is contaminated; on other roofs in each country men are measuring the fall of the shadow, strontium, carbon, cesium, across the loins of every child born to the world; and nightlong in mountains and deserts the atomic foundries are roaring, a knowing together of armageddon. Murder enough is around me on this hill, mole, snake, owl, and I make this eleison to the stars, but whatever moves them is not mercy. Mercy is what lets live, and is nowhere but in man. Distances of stars, ages of rocks, millennia of nations, these other paradises, other dreams, dissolve like the mists of our pond and leave me with two hard pebbles of fact, the small heads of boys, and all history is for me only the size and time of my hand upon them: where is man but in me, and in them? Now, as before, it is outgrow or die, and every man is the murderer. And faint in the roar of the foundries I hear again the feet of my father walking the streets of the city that year, with his brother dead, when, sparing the lives of dishes and bananas, he marked on the calendar for the wife and kids his vow to outgrow, and taught me the animal wants to love.

It is his eleison I make, Have mercy upon my increase. And thus saith God himself that formed the earth and made it; he hath established it, he created it not in vain, he formed it to be inhabited.

7. After a Quarrel

How in the dusk of its boneyard swamp
  My frog of a heart
Is squat, and black in its bad blood, and sulks
  To croak its pomp

Of grief. Behind in the house my lights,
  I mean wife and boy,
Are dark, and this bog is devoid of mothering moon
  And star. All night

Its mud will boil in a gloat of trouble,
  Grief like a heron
Stalking the green small hearts in a sunless world:
  Mine is a nibble

Of gnats, and fireflies worry my head.
  Croaker, leap to!
Here are your lights of old in a winking of ills
  To tongue and feed

And burn with: mourning now not one,
  Hop, and for three
Be light, in the roof of house and heaven, I mean
  Its fathering sun.

paternoster

8. Forever Mutely Drown

It is night, and my father is up.

Three floors of wooden house around his head, above, below, are settled into darkness and sleep; the gas mantles on pipes, which hiss when they light up the rooms, now are quiet, and little in our newly occupied flat is visible except the windows, open to the yard in the rear and in front to the streetlight. At one window a cigarette glows, where a wordless silhouette, the figure who will overhang my life, sits in the dark with his thoughts.

At his back are the five rooms of a coldwater flat, familiar enough in his mind. First is the rear kitchen, where shadows are soft on the bulk of coalstove, slate sink and washtub, and white table that his half-brother, cabinetmaker, has joined to outlast us all; on it is stacked the week's wash, damp twists of towels, clothing, sheets, which my father as always has scrubbed for his bride in the washboard suds, rinsed, wrung, and piled for her to hang in tomorrow's sunlight on the clothesline from the window to the yard pole; and in the dark something is dripping, our icebox, the ice hunk is melting within and drop by drop falling into the pan underneath, money melting away. Second is the dining room whose furniture, no older than the marriage, glints in the starlight like the bride's mind. It is a suite of oak veneer: round table, with cut-glass bowl of wax fruits on a doily, straight chairs tucked equally around it, china closet with glass doors keyed to lock the "good dishes" in, and buffet whose lengthy drawers hold silverware, stationery, linens, sewing basket, child's games, in such methodical order that any drawer opened is a showcase. Third is the middle room, where no starlight comes, there is no window. In a double bed here a young woman lies half asleep on her back, thin and hyperthyroid, her throat disfigured by its recurrent knob of goiter; the long pale face with its narrow brow and straight nose is set tight-lipped and uncomplaining, and over her too large eyes is laid a "cold rag" soaked in icewater. A board closet obtrudes wide alongside the bed, and in it our assorted clothes hang tidily. Fourth is the front parlor, with its bay of two windows, at which my father sits in a rocker with his spark of cigarette and his thoughts. A hard cold piece, the rocker is of mahogany veneer like two other pieces that almost match, a formal curved chair and a lamptable with scrolled legs, but the warm soul of the room is the upright Horace Waters piano, its face a litter of sheet music; its top is loaded raggily with the popular songs of a decade and, mute in its green felt sheath, a mandolin. Fifth is the side bedroom, where the streetlight via ceiling and wall finds two children who sleep soundly, in a crib a chubby babe, in a small bed a pompadoured boy. And around us all the house is safe, sleeps, is furnished for our comfort and self-respect, with food in the icebox, clothing in the closet, shelter overhead from the night's weather, money melting away, and made good again by the work of my father. But my father is sleepless, and sits up at a window, smoking.

He lets himself forward, his finger taps ash into a saucer on the sill, then he leans back with his bare feet up, cigarette in lips, hands clasped behind his head. It is the head of a young man of thirty-two, a little gawky with ears; the face is gentle, the upper teeth evident and somehow fragile in the sad mouth, which yet is so easy to smile with a self-deprecating turn down, and the sparse brown hair is already giving way to bald brow. He is in his pajamas, his body is narrow and boyish in the rocker.

Now in the obscurity of the middle room his young wife sits up groping. My father at once is on his feet and in the dark among the furniture to her bedside; taking the tepid cloth from her fingers, he squats to poke it into the pot of icewater on the floor, and comes up with another cloth, freshly squeezed; when she lies back he folds it across her brow, fingering it in to ease her eyelids, but her own fingertips take over. He leaves her quiet, and after putting his head in to check on the sleep of the children, he sits again to his bay window and cigarette in the saucer.

It is one o'clock, and he gazes down upon the deserted sidewalk, along which in another hour he will be walking to work. Fifteen feet from his window he sees a thick old poplar; under it the sidewalk is slabs of slate, uneven, heaved by its roots, and the road is rural with dirt, pebbles, tar, leading somewhere into the other life he might have had; and across the road is the massive lift starward of a hill that always after, in the heart of his sleeping boy, will be like the hill of heaven.

The boy is bedded in the slumbrous innocence of childhood now, where now is forever. But all the while, in the windowless bedroom, a cheap alarm clock ticks, and in the kitchen something is dripping, time the present, melting away; the child's games in the buffet unseen are turning slowly to dust, and unseen the iron turns in the earth that will make the steel that will make the trucks that will cart the hill away. Over its hump the stars are awake, so distant that, scattering by millions of miles each night, they keep one fixed design in all the history of the human eye, and this family is less than a blink. Upon the hill the field crickets tick the night away, and the clock ticks toward its alarm, and in the mortal cage of his ribs my father's heart is ticking. The cigarette is lifted to his lips, and glows again. What is he thinking?

It is night, and my father cannot sleep.

LAVABO

9. Survivor in Orchard

In winter ground
Each abject tree a gallows fraught with ghosts
Of better times, of fruit and roosts,
Is of my mind:

Bled is its loin.
And still, within my tree of bones, one dupe
Hangs on. The workmanship of sap
And sun is down,

Why is this loth
Depleted apple, here, a heart, still clinging
To its bough? Let go, unstring,
Come down to earth,

Be laid and low.
What does it look to in this fruitless time?
And still it hangs till kingdom come
Back to each tree

With bird and bud,
And round this apple, old in knowledge of green
Love, cry me tidings I'd foregone
Of song and blood.

Hang on: hang on.

10. The Plot Where the Garden Lived

The neighborhood to which we had gone back was a part of the city not easily come to, moated by the Harlem River along the west and unentered by the el to the east; between them it rose like some backward green garden of hills, original rocks, grass, trees, small cornfields. It was known as Highbridge, after a footbridge high over the sewery river. In its midst was a broad barren of hill, which went rollicking down to a tar road under a rank of old trees, and in their shade stood a handful of narrow wooden houses yoked together, three families high, each house with its grace note of picket fence. In one of these we had the middle floor of five rooms, and it was from this flat that my father was soon to claim at the city morgue the body of his other brother.

I had been born on this street six years before in a better tenement with steam heat, from which my mother's quest for justice had unhoused us; she was dissatisfied in the four rooms with the el, they shrank as my sister grew, and my parents were eager to move back to the old neighborhood into "any kind of a dump" with a fifth room. The postwar pinch in housing had brought my mother low, she was gratified that the landlord charged nothing to let her rehabilitate this flat with her own hands. She, my father, and his brother Will worked nights on it together, peeling off eight layers of wallpaper, scrubbing floors, patching plaster, painting; only the ceilings cowed them, so a cousin-in-law who was a fireman painted the five ceilings, earning twenty-five dollars and a familial acknowledgment from Will, who called him a "cheap sonofabitch".

Family and craft both mattered to my namesake uncle, who had little of one and a good deal of the other. Will was the child begotten a few nights before the death of his father, and not until weeks after the funeral did his mother, Katherine Gollan, widowed at twenty-three with two girls and her little hunchback, discover she was pregnant; though she swallowed irritants and jumped from the bureau to bring on a miscarriage, the boy clung to his twig of life, and would eat his portion. Helped by her mother, Katherine kept the family together, but the hunchback died, and the mother died, and Katherine then boarded the children out so she could work, the girls in one institution and Will in another. Her second marriage reunited them, and Pop Gibson taught the boy his trade of cratemaking. Will grew into an excellent cabinetmaker, and it was about the time he was reclaiming our flat that he studied with a craftsman's eye the disappearing feats of an international celebrity, Houdini, who allowed several carpenters to erect a massive box around him onstage and then materialized in the theatre aisle; Will wrote Houdini a letter promising to build him singlehandedly on any stage a box he would never get out of, meaning never, and understandably received no reply; it was a famous if somewhat unclimactic incident in the family. But the furniture Will fashioned as gifts for every relative was still in daily use half a century later, and the white table at which I ate ten thousand meals survived in my mother's kitchen after her death, unshakable as iron.

So in the new flat I think it was not his plastering but the boy that was imperfect: I soon had an excavation in a wall which was my "telephone" to a crony in the next house, and privacy was insured by a cushion. We had no other telephone, but in time several other holes, debouches for squads of cockroaches that my mother drove back with squirts of green powder and rats in for potluck whom my father pursued around the furniture with a broom, until he packed every crevice in the flat with broken glass; and one day my crony and I overturned all the rocks in the fields roundabout, loaded two cigarboxes to the brim with petite snakes, and stored them in the earthen cellar, whence they vanished, only to reappear peeking spitefully out of rotted floorboards and riding up and down in the dumbwaiter. "Snakes now," my mother said brightly, but nervous, "rats, roaches, snakes, my goodness, this house is a regular menagerie." It had no electricity, we read by gaslight, but its chief lack was heat; with the first huff of cold weather we set out the kerosene heaters to taint the air of the flat, sealed off its front half with newspaper wads around the doors, and saw we had enlarged our lot down to three rooms. In these we huddled each winter for the next three years, burgeoning into the front rooms every spring. It was low point in the climb to our middle-class lodestar, we never again lived in so primitive or infested a house, and thirty years later my mother still spoke of "the old days in Highbridge, when we were all so happy."

The garden was not of local earth, of course, the clemency of its climate was off the flesh of my parents; some loving touch of their courtship was upon them always. Afternoons when my father left the flat for work my mother would be half out the window to watch him walk down the road to the corner rocks, where before disappearing he waved back and cried, "I, L, Y!" and she waved out and cried to him, "I, L, Y!"—their unbreakable code for the three bedrock words in the language—and the climate between them filled the block. It was more than figurative. At Christmas my father would bring home a bonus, a sum varying with the bank's profits but usually a couple of hundred dollars; he spent it to the last penny on gifts, and a generation later I was reminded by a girl who "never forgot it, there wasn't a kid on the block who didn't get a present." Children not his would run to meet him when he came home from work. In the summer nights half the block would gather under our streetlight while upstairs my father, having pushed the piano to the bay window, banged out tune after tune for the roadful to sing and dance to. The neighborhood was itself a family, a skein of friendships that tied school, church, street games, holidays, into one knot of living.

It was here my mother first led me to school by the hand, two blocks around the hilltop and across a cobblestone street, where the iron-barred yard and graystone walls engulfed me instantly in a slumber; I see no detail of three years within it except a classroom storybook and a twisted ear, two hypnotizing pities. My parents lurk in both. The twisted ear was on a boy otherwise hale and hearty whom I saw only in the schoolyard, but at each encounter I delivered to him like an automaton whatever I had on me, pennies, candies, my lunch, a little ape of my father. The fat print of the storybook told the adventures of the gingerbread boy, run, run, you can't catch me, a gleeful rebel whose tragic end, to be eaten up, was inexorable once he had run away from his matronly maker, who wished only to eat him up. I had no outer eye then for the small tyrannies of my matron, and I did her proud in school; I was twice "skipped" into higher grades of slumber.

It was a public school because my mother was convinced, by ample evidence in the Dore family, that Catholic schooling resulted in illiteracy. On weekdays she ascribed this to "too much time spent on religion", though her folk were not notable for saintliness either; on the Sabbath however she pointed me forth through hailstorms to nine o'clock mass and Sundayschool. Here with gummy eye I sat in a candle-lit dungeon through years of total gibberish. The priest wandered before the altar muttering in Latin to himself, now and then turning to lift a bored hand in blessing, and at long last ascended the pulpit to announce in unmistakable English that my stingy offerings had caused a shortage of coal in the church; two altarboys in skirts rang bells, genuflected, and decanted wine for the priest, a pair of angels, tarnished only by my knowing I would soon be shooting immies with them and hearing of their struggle to free the decanter from the priest's inebriated clutch; I sat, stood, knelt each time enough of the congregation sat, stood, knelt, all of us erratic and at the mercy of some confident soul in the front pew, until that late moment when it was not quite sinful to leave—perceived by all with infallible unison—and whatever prayers remained were drowned out by hundreds of hasty feet, mine among the first. The interlude of fact in the daylight was shortlived. A herd of children soon trudged up the cobbled alley that led to the Sundayschool shed of corrugated tin that sat dark green on the rocks above our backyard; inside a multitude of folding wooden chairs was grouped for buttocks according to age, but even the youngest now much the worse for wear, under the tutelage of unmarried ladies of the parish with no duties in their kitchens; they drilled us for another hour in our catechism, and rewarded the diligent with picturecards of the saints in sepia. The hailstorms were real enough, cackling on the tin overhead, and it seemed a fit setting for the odd chant with which we concluded, "Hail, Mary, full of grapes"; it was the grapes that seemed irrelevant.

Every seventh day my head was stuffed to the ears with this quaint cosmology, and my mother was happy. Its reward was not in the hereafter, but in the here: I was at one in tedium with the neighborhood gang, all named Murphy and O'Brien, and every grown-up I knew on our block I saw in the church, except my mother and father. Home at last, I would find them still living in sin, with my sister at her doll cut-outs, my father at ease behind the sports page in his pajama tops and the pants he had worn downstairs to buy the newspaper, while my mother in a crisp housedress darted about the kitchen in the midst of the roast with four vegetables which was her Sunday act of devotion. And instantly I was on my belly with the gaudy funny-pages, for my delight in which that particular newspaper was chosen by my father, and I would inveigle him into joining heads with me over the "red magic"—tricks with matchsticks and cards and tumblers of water, all printed in diabolic red—which never quite worked, but cleared my brain of other devils until the next Sunday.

My father's indifference to the deity was a male prerogative in his family; the womenfolk were all strict churchgoers, but Pop Gibson had preferred saloons. And Will in his youth was "full of fun" with his pious sisters. Much embarrassed by their stepfather, they were dismayed one night to overhear Will stagger in muttering to himself, and spied upon him trying to hang his clothes on a non-existent nail in the wall; after he was snoring Milly stole in to smell his breath, but in the dark her nose inhaled only his whisper of glee, "Go to bed, you nut." Ada's churchgoing was a profession, which presently took her off to Africa as a missionary, and always she sat discoursing of the word in a rapture, with gestures; when Will put a book in her hand it would end unnoticed in her lap, and she preached on while Will in passing handed her a towel, a sewing basket, a pipe and pouch, a shoe, until coming out of her sermon with a broom in her glorifying hands, her broad lap brimful of junk, Ada cried in exasperation, "Will, you fool!" At his jauntiest twenty my father was the recipient of a Bible inscribed to *George Irv Gibson from Sister Ada,* not with love, only an admonitory *John 3–16* if he wished not to perish, but he steered a steady course between church and saloon behind the Sunday sports page. The one time

I provoked him to a statement of faith was on the question of where all our rats came from; I said they came "from the Protestant church" on the hill, and he said irritatedly, "What's Protestant got to do with it? I'm a Protestant myself!"

In fact the Catholic church was nearer, its green shed almost touchable from our kitchen window, and much in our family life was implicated with it. Once a year the tin hall blossomed into a weeklong bazaar, whereby the church augmented its coalpile. Here, at a booth with a variety of prizes and a wheel of chance, my sister fell in love with a china doll as big as herself; it was not for sale, but all that week my father led us up the path among the rocks to the shed, where night after night he played against the wheel for the doll and never won, dollar after dollar coming out of his pocket, the week dwindling, the coalpile growing, the doll paid for several times over out of my father's three-o'clock-in-the-morning labors; on the last night he put his money down until they dismantled the booth, and then sought out the priest, laid upon him the tale of his tot's love, waited while the arrangements committeee dug among invoices for the cost of the doll, paid it, and brought the doll home to my sister. The day came when she dropped it, and half the night lay moaning—"Daddy: I broke my dollie, Daddy: I broke my dollie: Daddy, I broke my dollie" —while my parents in their bed listened in that grief for a child's grief which the child cannot suspect; love like water tumbles downhill between generations.

It was this tin hall which also bred the minstrel show, a yearly venture by parishioners, at which my father played piano for any neighbor with a voice or a delusion. When my sister was a plump four my parents rehearsed her in the words and gestures of a song about a little red schoolhouse, my mother attired her in a brief red frock and hair ribbon, and with my father at the piano our sprite topped the show; I had promised her a dime if she sang without mistakes, but on our arrival home I presented her with my entire bank, and was also applauded. My parents had made a point subtler than they knew, that generosity was the gayest conqueror of envy. And it was from this tin shed that I took home as a Sundayschool prize the first book I owned, its jacket overcome by a young daredevil in goggles riding a motorcycle straight at me; I thought it a dud of a prize, books having no value in our house, but I gave the motorcycle a try and on it rode into all literature, and out of my family's arms.

But most haunting was a summer afternoon, queer as a twisted mirror, in the parish house. It was a weekday tea of the Sundayschool teachers, with my mother and me prim in our good clothes, and hovering at a piano a favorite male countenance, my uncle Will, out of work for reasons of health and brought along because he had dropped in on us in the midst of a lonely walk. A fine tenor, he seated one of the teachers at the keyboard and entertained the tea party with a ballad, which all the ladies enjoyed, so he sang another, his eyes closed in his good face with its pitted chin and boyish spill of gray hair, and all praised his third song, so he sang a fifth, and the ladies were more than satisfied, so he sang a seventh, and his grim hand would not let the lady pianist escape, and they rollicked into a ninth, and the tea broke up in a scurry of purse gathering and bobs of terrified hats with Will chanting at the top of his voice and "talking queer"; and my mother, though mortified, waited to guide him home. This was the summer I first spied the snake in the garden—when on my belly beneath a communal oak I feasted upon a bared inch of knee, the property of an adolescent girl who sat above me in a nest of baby carriages and mothers, and I lay all the idle afternoon adoring it, bland under my mother's distrustful eye—and unknown to me its venom was then writhing in the limbs of my uncle, forking into his skull.

In happier days he and his wife would stand singing to my father's jangbangling piano, two of the dozens of relatives, friends, neighbors who "loved to visit", as one recalled, because my parents were "so cheerful". My mother had a gift for hospitality which was radiantly semisuicidal. She had entered upon marriage able to cook only toast—which went unnoticed for a while, since my father's invariable meal was a charred slab of round steak—and the first dinner they gave saw her in a panic in the kitchen, beset by mutinous potfuls of unknown matter, until one husband venturing in hastily donned an apron, asked only that she "keep the guys out of here", and subdued the entire meal for her. But panic was an old acquaintance, the motor of my mother's soul, and her genius was for turning it into useful activity; she soon became an extraordinary housekeeper, studying the households of my father's sisters, and so outdoing them that he said teasingly he expected her next to "wash the coal before using it". It was literally so that visitors could have dined off her kitchen floor, and their numbers made it imminent, anyone dropping in at once found himself captive at the table to too much good food, and Sunday nights were festive with gossip and music in a resurrection of Mary Dore's parties, with ten or twelve in for an improvised supper. The wives helped clean up and put away the dishes, each couple left the flat feeling like the choice light of our world, and my mother and father sat in exhaustion, pondering how to keep from being eaten out of house and home.

All dead, the faces of those grown-ups return to me quite unlike ghosts, laughing and boisterous, full of news of my parents, but under the fixative of time, deaf to my questions. The neighbors ambled in from upstairs, downstairs, adjoining houses—lettercarrier, printer, el gateman, each with his missus—into friendships that were joined for life; their aging faces reappeared at my father's wake. Other friends were inseparables out of his youth, my mock uncles and aunts, all with their troubles. The most successful was a man who had entered the postoffice with my father a dozen years earlier; authoritative as a hammer, he rose in his official career to the postmastership of the city, but his unofficial career was wandering indecisively with his household from neighborhood to neighborhood, some thirty moves in a decade; his wife was so sickly my mother would routinely visit her to do her housework. Two of my father's buddies were musicmakers like him, a pair of bricklayers, one a dapper johnny with fingers so nimble on the keyboard my father acknowledged him as "a star", the other a giant with a baritone roar that he loosed at the ceiling, one hand cupped for amplification behind his ear; in picnic snapshots the three stand with interlocked arms, their straw-hatted faces majestic with cigars, captioned by my father as "we smoke but we don't buy", and again with their young wives, six grinning heads together, "married but happy"; one buried his wife and took to drink, the other lost his life-savings in a lapidary shop he bought into a day before the great depression. My mother's own pal from schooldays—"my oldest and dearest friend, Nelie"—was a placid spinster in an auburn wig worn since a childhood fever, who dwelt at her elbow, loyalty incarnate, and outlived her like a severed shadow. I brought her my questions, but in old age she had no memories other than my mother's, eerily echoed in my mother's very words, so vicarious her life; she summoned up the young Flo as vaguely—though emphatically—"lovely, like she always was"; then I asked if among the seventeen brothers she had any recollection of Alfred, dead at twenty-six, dead for more than half a century, and she said, "I was engaged to Alfred." Others from the old postoffice gang straggled into the flat, on shore leave from the navy or back from drifting in the west, wistful fellows who had also missed the turn into family life. And we had a breadline of unmarried clerks from the bank, the most memorable of them a piano-playing cockney, a tippler who composed hundreds of popular songs, though not popular

63

enough; he spent much of his week at the heels of music pub-
lishers and songpluggers, his life going to seed for the "break"
that was never to come, while over the years he appeared with
each fresh manuscript to sing it at our piano for his only public,
my father, who admired him. My mother admired his accent, she
thought it English and refined. My parents' capacity for friend-
liness was exhausted only by one avuncular character who, together with his wife, was banished from our flat. A curly-haired
runt with a missing finger, he was an heirloom from my father's
bachelor days and that rarest of souls, a person my mother disliked, though he was widely travelled, shipping out as a strike-
breaker to scattered cities, and clever, talking compensation
boards out of sum after sum for his finger lost in honest labor
ten different times, and devoted as a tick to my father, who in
periods between strikes and prestidigital amputations kept him
in handouts; my mother tolerated him for the sake of his wife, a
fruity woman, childless, who was genuinely fond of my sister
and me and often cared for us when my mother was sick in bed,
at which times the household money, in saucer and pennybank,
showed an odd tendency to evaporate. But it was not until the
winter that Will's widow after one gathering reclaimed her purse
from the bedroom where coats were heaped and missed sixty dollars out of it that heads were put together, and tales, of other
shortages graced by the presence of the couple. My father that
week led a few complainants to a shabby flat in Harlem, where
his unemployed pal, coming home warm at last in a new overcoat, and his wife, pale in the cheer of a new floorlamp, said
their purchases were nobody's business; and my father invited
them not to visit us again. Thirty years later the woman, dying
in a county hospital where a cousin of ours worked, still asked
how my sister and I had fared. Dead with her, all dead, that
phantasmagoria of grown-ups whom I could not wait to be like,
rich, wise, lucky, they seem so to me yet; they lie coffined in

possession of a treasure I can never come by, in their earfuls of the small talk of my parents, and their eyefuls of those two ordinary faces in the years when I was too busy with my tops and marbles to look at them.

Yet even around our street games the figures of all the parents, looked at or not, lent a benevolence to the neighborhood. Its heart was the hill, and our games came up with its seasonal changes from outbreak of weed grass to burial drifts of snow; but it was one changeless flock of families upon the hillside in summer and winter, and time hardly moved, the children grew no older, the parents were as durable as the big trees of the street.

In spring, when we were digging dirtholes with our heels for immies—marbles, imitations—our fathers were in view digging with spades, until the field next to the end house was a crazy quilt of little vegetable gardens; here in the evenings the grown-ups would cluster in twos and threes, the mothers in aprons talking, the men on their knees in old pants coaxing along their tomatoes and stringbeans. In the untended afternoons these garden squares, staked and roped off, made ideal sites for their sons to stage mock prizefights in, a sport which resulted in some baffling crop failures. The true sport was baseball on the plateau of our hill, a trodden diamond in the rough, alive all day with a scatter of players, the gang I was in and the teen-age giants who chased us off and after supper the young fathers in collarless shirts, home from the bondage of offices. At a bottom corner of the hill was a dell with the communal oak, where in late spring the "strawberry festival" with its free ice cream was sponsored by our wardheelers for a pandemonium of neighborhood children and our mothers, who had recently received the vote; their purity was expected to redeem the world, a hope which was not quite realized, it succumbed under my eyes to free strawberry ice cream.

Summer opened officially the day my mother let me out barefoot—my soles gingerly among the fallen catkins of the poplars, so like the caterpillars of her terror—and was a long contentment of dirty toes. Out of our parents' eyes we cavorted on imaginary steeds over the hillside, vying in death leaps from its ledgerocks, elevation three feet; we bellycrawled to its far side in high weeds, to spy on the walrus-faced caretaker of the Protestant church, and sprang in the air with cries of "Kaiser Bill! Kaiser Bill!" until in frenzy he lumbered after us halfway down to our road; we scavenged for the stubs of holy candles dumped back of the true church, and bore them away to the hut of slats and cardboard which was our unfinished lifework; we watched the iceman stagger under his load into our cellars, and then clambered over his horse-drawn wagon to pilfer ice for sucking, cautious not to swallow the cloudy "pneumonia" it was made with; we trekked down to the sunken Harlem, and watched the older boys dive bare-assed among a drift of feces and mystifying number of white balloons, and charged up to the footbridge above, climbing outside its iron railings to execute skips which, elevation one hundred feet, would have given my mother a heart attack to witness; we knuckled our immies along miles of gutter, and gambled on curbstone and stoop with picturecards of leaping ballplayers and menacing prizefighters that came one with each penny's worth of gum; and gum lacking, we waited by the fire barrel of the roadworkers and chewed the ebony nuggets of tar leavings, which were "good for" the teeth they did not pull out. And under my father's eye I feasted on hot dogs and sodapop in the grandstand at the big-league ballgames he took me to. Once he instructed me to "never forget" I had seen a no-hitter, so I never did, and another time at the players' gate I shook hands with a second baseman beloved by him for sliding into base head first, a practice I thereafter followed, luckily without serious brain damage, and one dawn we stood together on line for half the day to get into a World Series game, which canonized me in the gang.

But that was in autumn, when my mother had shod me again for school. To the sill outside our kitchen window my father now wired the orange crate that was to be our winter icebox, and my mother encased it prettily in figured oilcloth, which would keep the snow out. All along the block the front rooms were abandoned, and children slept in kitchens, dining rooms, parental beds. Up from the cellar bin came our kerosene heaters, stovepipes on squat legs, glowing in the dark with sizzly pans of water set on top to replenish the oxygen; and when in the morning I scrambled from the sofa I found my schoolclothes on a chair at the lively coalstove in the kitchen, hung there by my mother to make them inhabitable.

It was the season for fire. On the hill each night the kids with permission to "sneak out" congregated at cookfires of scrap boards borrowed from buildings in construction, and crammed a few brands into tin cans punched with nail holes and reined with wire, to whip them round and round as personal ovens. In them we roasted mickies—potatoes, stolen on the gallop past the sidewalk displays of grocery stores—until they were as inedible as charcoal, when we ate them. Potato thieving was only an exercise of neighborly rights, but one night I and another fire worshipper climbed a fence into a "dago" contractor's backyard, toted bundle after bundle of his laths over the hill, and cooked our two mickies in a ten-foot conflagration of the neatest firewood ever. The irate contractor next day tracked our fathers down; mine, the other being needier, paid for all the laths, and punished me only by convoying me to apologize to the foreigner and advising me next time to "use my head", at which I felt more stupid than piratical. And each fall there was a towering bonfire which belonged to the grown-ups. For a week the neighborhood contributed to it, piling on the hillside the unwanted articles from every household, bundles of newspapers, cartons and crates, seatless chairs, wobbly tables and bureaus, disgraceful mattresses, until on Election Day night two or three of the fathers climbing over the edifice sprinkled it with kerosene; when they touched a match to it, every family on the block was present to cheer this gotterdammerung in honor of our brand-new leaders with the same old strawberry ice cream.

Winter came with the first snow in the night that stuck—the trolley cars stuck on the bridges with it, and in one blizzard my father labored home with me in his arms for better than an hour—until in the sunlit morning the hill was transubstantiated. It was heaven, a whiteness of packed slope trafficked by hollering boys, girls, young parents, and a host of sleds tugged by figures uphill, tots on wee sleds inching down, youngsters streaking past on slim racers, big sleds loaded with families spilling into the road, and battles of snowballs flying between the igloo forts. Here I charged with my racer in a bellywhopping delight while below a moving-van rolled toward us, and I shot out into the white road; a fingersnap earlier and my sled would have been under its doublewheel, but I struck the tire and was thrown back into my life, and tugged my sled uphill again into a company of merrymakers intact in our magic skins.

And the earth emerged as always, into Easter; another year of holidays was begun. Holidays were the hinges of the seasons, remote from their origins, and Easter signified only the terminus of the six-week lenten fast during which, for some adult kink of reason, we had survived without candy. It collapsed in an orgy of jellybeans and chocolate bunnies, hidden by my mother in odd nooks of the flat, where after church my sister and I hunted them out; they baptized gummily the pockets of our new "good" apparel, good for nothing but to stand around in on our sidewalk all the holy afternoon like awkward manikins in a storewindow, stuffed with jellybeans.

The holy day of summer was the Fourth of July. Miniature

explosives had been accumulating throughout the week in every household, but none to equal ours; my father would bear home from a store downtown some twenty or twenty-five dollars' worth, half a week's pay, which bought a great deal of noise. It took me from breakfast to dusk, and fifty trips up and down our stairs after fresh pocketfuls, to exhaust this arsenal. There were baby firecrackers, wads of a hundred fused together, which were detached and lit singly by me, though in a royal gesture my father would set a wad off in one wild spitting mass; and torpedoes, which exploded when hurled onto the sidewalk, preferably at somebody's heel; and pellets called snakes, which if touched with a match gave birth to a writhing gray serpent that strove along the ground and perished at last in a crumble of ash; and sulfuric patties which were ground underheel till they crackled away to a smoking scab; and the larger firecrackers, the two-inchers I lit with my stick of punk and fled from, and the six-inchers I was not allowed to play with alone, but watched my father ignite under tin cans, which flew up over our heads; and pinwheels, nailed to a tree in twilight to whiz their colorful life away, and sparklers, the dipped wires that hissed a thousand white sparks, desirable only after dark came to the hill; and into the night my father launched our showering rocket, price one dollar, the climax of the day. Only our sparklers then, glittering in all hands, were left to star the hillside with constellations of families, until at the last quarter-inch we slung them skywards to die out like falling souls.

Autumn came with two holidays, minor and major. Though decorum was her staff, my mother was a gay participant in disorder that was institutional, and on Halloween she prepared for my sister and me the socks full of flour with which the neighborhood smallfry belabored one another, until by suppertime we ourselves looked ready for the oven; and in the evening her laugh shrilled like a bird above the shenanigans in our flat, where neighbors and their offspring joined us with hands behind backs to tongue pennies out of her platterfuls of flour, spewing, and over a washtub we stalked with dribbling noses the apples my father had turned into treasure islands, tipsy with buried silver. And on Thanksgiving Day it was my mother who with a burnt bottlecork dirtied up my sister's face and mine, and sent us downstairs in rags. Our lives that day were inverted like the jackets we wore inside out, whites turned black, boys in their mothers' skirts and girls in their fathers' pants, cherubs in false-faces with depraved noses, and all, in a travesty of that poverty our families were two jumps ahead of, begging alms, swarming in threes and fours like a plague of mad dwarfs through the houses to every doorbell—"Anything for Thanksgiving, mister?"—and choiring in the courtyards until the coins in newspaper twists came plummeting through the clotheslines, and voices pled with us to sing no more. Late in the day my sister and I would straggle home, our pockets burdened down with the neighbors' fruit, candies, and loose change, to find my father at the door handing out to the neighbors' kids a countersupply of fruit, candies, and loose change, the flat made aromatic by the pipe of my uncle Will and genial with other relatives, my mother in command of too many cooks in the kitchen, and her silverware impeccably laid out for the turkey dinner all had come to share.

And at last the earth turned toward the holiday for which the year existed. The month that intervened was somehow lived through, with its character-building threats in Santa's name, its letters mailed confidently to the North Pole, its visits to the lanky geezers with slack beards in department stores and my suspicion that something was much amiss, perhaps with my mother's eyes; and one evening my father took us all to pick our Christmas tree out of the mass on a sidewalk rope at the grocery. I helped him lug it home, and it slept that week on our fire escape. It was not set up till the night before Christmas, after my sister and I were tucked in but hardly asleep, and that Santa himself ornamented it was the first fact to crumble, for we could hear our parents long at it in the frigid parlor, wrapped in their overcoats, hissing instructions at each other. Quiet then took over the darkened flat, and my sister and I lay awake with all our senses alert for Santa's entry through our coalstove. It was an endless night, when every rat scratching in the walls promised to be him, and we started up fearful that we had missed him or he us, calling was it time to get up, and our parents fumbling for the alarm clock groaned it was two o'clock, go back to sleep, and so with every half-hour as the night wore miserably on; and before dawn they staggered out of bed, my father to light the gas mantles and plant a kerosene heater in the parlor, my mother to bundle us up in sweaters and bathrobes and bring hot cocoa to us all where, in a tiny cheap cold room, we sat again under the tree of paradise. It was broken out in a winter bloom of jubilant fruits, angels, birds, stars, and around the cotton snowscape under its branches all the floor was a windfall of riches that dizzied our eyes, the big gifts standing bare amid a mob of brilliant packages that we tore apart, crawling and yelping and backtracking from tricycle to doll carriage, from trains to scooter, from baseball mitt and toy house to sewing machine and soldiers, to sled, to dolls, to trucks, to games, to books, all of my father's bonus lavished in an unthinking lesson that, in its wink of light, the time of man was a horn of plenty.

But in the new year the tree was stripped of its miracle. My father forced it out the bay window to drop into the tiny snowyard, and I dragged it across the road to the hill, where in time some hand set fire to it; half out of the snow, its charred skeleton pointed to something. High above it the misshapen snowman with coal hunks for eyes saw nothing of his drippage in the raids of the sun, time and the hill melting away. For now, like the clock that ticked in the night at my parents' skulls, the charm was running down; in the new year my uncle Will lay dying, and I was sprouting into myself.

It was evident the summer I pondered not only a girl's knee, but two lessons about money. I sold a half-dollar's worth of my fireworks to another boy for a penny or two, and sat on the curbstone happy with myself as an enterprising fellow; my father said nothing, but when my mother told me how I had hurt his feelings an utter desolation overtook me, I was an eight-year-old miser, I had violated his work, his code, his love, and that two-cent transaction would always seem one of the worst mistakes of my life. My father observed that when he was dead they might say he "spent a lot of money, but he had a heck of a good time," and the pursuit of this ideal took me into the second lesson. When his own uncle slipped a dollar into my palm I treated myself to some penny candy, and, with a vision of buying up the world, hid my handful of change on the darksome sill of a window high in our hallway which let neither light nor air into our bathroom; I had to leap to it from the banister, it was out of reach of all normal life, but my mother was led by her angel of cleanliness even to that altitude, with chair and dustrag, to discover my crime; and my vision and coins ended up permanently out of reach in my piggybank. The first lesson taught me not to live for money, and the second to put it in a safer hiding-place.

The crime was secretiveness. It is the first evidence I see that I was finding my mother's hand steely upon me; in my father's laxities of live and let live the chores of disciplining us fell to her, though in any circumstances she could not but invite them; matter not in her control made her nervous. It was by reflex that, when my sister in her baby carriage had bitten somebody's finger, my mother bit hers back. I came home sooty-faced from a mickie roast on the hill and my father said I "looked like a real boy", but my mother flew for the soap, her amulet against the devil. One afternoon a pubescent boy from upstairs backed me against our picket fence and fed me nonsense syllables; he said, "Say shit," and I obliged, and he said, "Say fuck," and I obliged, and he then stopped in to tell my mother the words his devout ear had been shocked to hear me utter; that evening I came home for supper and found my mouth being scrubbed out with soap instead, frothing with human justice. Much of my mother's energy was devoted to contesting nature on the battlefield of my scalp. My hair grew forward, but she soused and combed it back in a pompadour which, though it brought out a certain bulgy-browed idiocy in her child, she was fond of and determined to "train it" to; for years her hands drove at it pistonlike, with water, brushes, vaseline, combs, lard, nightcaps, until when I was graduated from elementary school not a hair in that pompadour was rebellious; she could not see my soul.

It sprouted, though the days in the garden were growing chill; it was that autumn my father's brother disappeared. Much of Will—his humor, his skill with his hands—had in any case been fading into his past, and his renewal in the flesh of four children had disappeared more than a decade before. The twins his wife conceived first had died in the womb, and were removed surgically; in her second pregnancy she bore a daughter who a few hours later died; the following year she gave Will a son, christened after him, and in his fifth autumn the boy died of a brain infection. It was not mischance, the children could not survive the inheritance of the syphilis that commingled in their parents' flesh.

When it was contracted, nobody knew. But Will was little more than twenty when he began marriage, on his fourteen dollars a week in that room furnished with hope, and before he was thirty the four children were dead. Much later the surgeon who excised the twins told Will's mother the disease was "of long standing" in the girl, but misdoer or dupe, it hardly mattered, two creatures were caught in the coils of the snake, and wherever his finger of lust had appointed him, to whorehouse or peccant bride, Will held his tongue; though he and his wife were to separate more than once, he "never said a word against her". Will was something of the family intellectual, a voting socialist, reading man, owner of a few operatic records. His tenor joined with my father's piano at many a church or bank supper, and the two half-brothers were "very close"; the married sisters had moved out into New Jersey towns, taking the old folks along, and with only the brothers left in the Bronx our flat often echoed with my uncle's voice. The lonely walk that brought him to our door the afternoon of the parish-house tea was not unusual, after a quarrel at home, but his breakup of the tea was the flare of disaster: the illness exploded in him that summer.

Taken in by his mother and half-sister Ethel in Jersey, he found work as a carpenter on rooftops. The sun beating on his head was "the worst thing for him", he was moody and would not join company at the table, but chiefly his head was "burning", and he bent by the quarter-hour soaking it under the coldwater tap; when the fright of an imminent "spell" was on him he would ask his mother to pray with him, and they knelt in a locked bedroom together, my whitehaired grandmother of sixty-five and her son with the boyish spill of gray hair, praying for the help that could not stay the microscopic worms now festive in the brain. Its signallings were awry, he "made the screens wrong" that he planned as a gift for Ethel's new house, and they were left unfinished. One autumnal morning he climbed down from his roof, and at noon turned up at his flat in the Bronx looking for his wife, who was not at home, and he distractedly made his way on foot north to Mt. Vernon, where he arrived by evening at the house of an uncle dishevelled and wild with inarticulate talk "about everybody, not like him"; the next day he was taken in custody to the penal hospital in the East River then known as Blackwells Island.

My father visiting him there would come home shaken with the sight of his brother in a straitjacket. It was not long since I had bought myself a pencilbox for school, my father with one glance at its underside said, "There'll be nothing in this house made in Germany," and escorted me and it down to the store to get my money back; now the death of a brother was in his nostrils again. He was ravaged by the bruises he saw on Will's face, which the burly guards blamed on falls, but in our kitchen my father demanded of my mother, "Why did he flinch? He flinched from me!" All winter in the violent ward Will lay in the bonds of worse than death, but before the first leaf of spring he was unsouled of that straitjacket of flesh, his lungs filled with pneumonia and he died. His body, delivered to the city morgue, was spoken for by my father and removed to a mortuary in Harlem; in a coffin it reposed in familiar clothes again and a new necktie of dark blue with white dots, his favorite pattern; my father had hunted the city for it, and said to a sister, "I bought the tie, and I tied it on him." The body was buried in a grave with the children, the one-day-old girl, the five-year-old boy, the forty-two-year-old man.

So went out that light, unwanted in birth and in death, the boy who never knew his father's face, grew in no garden, and for half his years had lived with the taste of himself as his children's killer. His sister Milly was haunted by one memory of him, peering from behind a fence along the road on which she and Ada, eleven and nine, trotted from school to lunch at the home where they were boarded out; the fence was around the other institution that held Will, then four, and each noontime without fail the diminutive boy was there, waiting in silence, his face between the white slats, to see his sisters come and go; that face through the fence peered after her for seventy-five years.

In the summer after his death we moved out of the flat that his hands had helped make livable. My mother's goiter again was thickening in her throat, the doctor told my father she must have rest, and the throngs of company that dropped in for a cheerful evening with my parents drove us half into bankruptcy and altogether out of the state; we followed the van filled with our furniture across the river into Jersey. We were the last of the family to leave the Bronx, and though we were to come back to it, my childhood was no longer there.

We could not find the garden again. In better neighborhoods our life was enriched by radiators, electricity, radio, telephone, refrigerator, car: but we had no hill. And of all the sounds in the world, none was to fill any other room so plangently as the music I ignored in that parlor, evenings, when I lay on the floor teaching my sister the rules of parchesi, at which she cheated, while my mother in the scrollwork chair with her mandolin and my father in his collarless shirt at the piano, both playing, gaily sang out "their" song of first encounter, "Oh by the Golden Gate, that's where I first met Kate, she stole my heart away: on San Francisco, oh you Frisco, San Francisco Baaay—" Even in manhood, when I stood again before the house and saw it ugly, cramped, defeated, and the rollicking green country gone, carted away with the poplars and the hill, and everything around me bronxed over with cement sidewalks and brick apartment houses, it could not touch my image of a half-wild garden in which I still spied the bay-window house as it was, the bellybutton of a world to come, and its tar road under a hanging mercy of trees, and its hill populous with knots of kids and parents, seated, standing, in the calm of the summer evenings: we were happy as the day was long.

That time, that neighborhood, thousands of miles ago and thirty-odd years behind me, scattered with its folk, was to live only in me, a green haven I could never find my way home to, until by the grace which is in our bowels I crossed a threshold, in the night around me all the house again was safe, and slept, and checking the beds of my unwitting boys I perceived I was back in the garden.

11. Family Tree

Is all in the eye of the sun
Undone?

A gay
Snow fell childlike in the night
To our agony tree;
Its wrangle of dieback arms
And torso,
Cracked in old grief from foothold to throat,
Awoke full of calm
Today

Unhealed,
Being live, but its sores redressed.
My children, stay.
Limbfuls I see the sun divest
Of love
Down to the bark, and that obdurate coat
By wind unbuckled
Yield

11. *Family Tree*

Its dung
Of crotch, heart wood, will,
To blow afield,
Dust out of dust, in this acid
Light.
Rib of me, stay. Who will stifle the shrill
Lesions of my knuckled
Lung

If you like a windfall of snow
Go?

12. Lavabo inter Innocentes

Several days beforehand the boys and I trudge with a saw into the snow of our woods; it contains no balsam fir, the Christmas tree of my childhood, but white pine by the tens brush our eyes, and it is one of these we are after. The boys usually want to fell a giant, but I talk them into a young stem which needs weeding and will fit under our ceiling, and they divide the dozen strokes of the saw into shifts, a two-man job. After they yell their warning "Timber!" I have to draw the tree down out of a clutch of other branches, and with the help of my sons, who impede me no more than I did my father on the sidewalks of the city, I carry it homeward across the snowfields; we pass their hill of heaven where in winter they sled and in summer dig forts, their tilted acre of playground with swings I hung under the apple boughs, a tree house the three of us nailed in the hemlocks, a sandpile I bounded by ten-foot cherry logs, all in a silence of snow, and make for the dark green house below.

It has thirteen rooms and a sun porch, six of which are in part or whole a warehouse for their toys, and now we open a seventh. The young pine in a room no longer called a parlor stands in the crook of another piano, whose tongues will resound forever in their ear of childhood too; they and their mother hang the gracile branches with a winter bloom of fruits, birds, stars, and underneath we heap its harvest, the brilliant packages, a tribute

80

of rebirth from friends and relatives and grateful parents; the scene is set. It will be another Christmas dawn, another town, another time, and in a bedlam of giftpaper torn apart two other innocents, crawling and yelping and backtracking in the spill of a world which is a horn of plenty: nothing has changed.

I will wash mine hands in innocency: so will I compass thine altar.

Their other grandfather observes that "what we owe our parents, we pay it to our children," but this Christmas my eye is preternaturally clear, I see I am in debt to both generations for life. I am home only for the day. All its festive time I dote upon the boys, whose lift of an eyelash is unbelievable to me, the noise of their bratty combats is a music blessed in my ear, back from its death vigil in the city, and misdeeds is a word I have lost the sense of, doing is being, being is beauty, and my brats are the wonder of the world, living flesh, which my mother now is not.

Sixty hours ago I heard the last exhalation out of her body with which my mother vanished, into nowhere, for the evil manikin with the dropped mouth in her bed, instantly yellowed, was not my mother, but matter stopped, my mother was its motion. In a coffin this day her body lies, its eyelashes forever moveless, its lips forever shut; and the scrambling of my boys among their gifts fills my eyes, some of them being from her. No mystery is in her matter now, it is plain as a chair, the sitter gone, and soul is a word which, derided in my teens, I have found the sense of again. It is not death, but life, that dazzles me with enigma, the lightning that forked soul out of the bare earth, and put the eye in my clod of head, and I am privileged to see, suffer, know, who might have been born a luckless stone; almost I can believe that creation is what I was born to see and praise. And it was out of this habit of marvelling that three days ago on her deathbed my mother struggled upright, seventy-two years of workaday bones, and so simply thanked God for her life.

LAVABO

I have loved the habitation of thy house.

Tomorrow I will see the tenantless body lidded, and lowered into the earth, to lie once more with my father's; perhaps in time, when the boards rot, two particles of their dust will again touch. Neither will know. I, my wife, our boys, today kneel at the gayest of trees in a windfall of gifts, mine being knowledge of them. Now that I have no maker I am dumb with my debt, but to the three in this knot of family, my resurrectionists, I owe it again. For in Christmas week too my father died, and I ignored this season till our boys restored it and him to me, I felt him reborn in my flesh, they created me father, a giver of life; and my mother's tireless hands, that for years I dodged like enemies, made friends of mine again over their diapers and pins, and I was recreated as son, a color that was happily in her living autumn. Throughout the short light of this day, while the yelping boys crawl in its plenty, their innocency sets me a table in the midst of death. I think, what do I set for them? and out of my own backtracking under other trees in another boyhood, brimful of all I had from parents and would repay to sons, I pray for them first the gift of marvelling, which is love. I was drunk on it at my mother's breast, and in the bounty of my father's pockets; in the charmed life we led in our garden it was their gift to each other, and because of it even the crooked way I grew in their hands was a promise I knew in my bones; the sky would never fall. Night falls, but in it the children come forth, like stars.

I would give them my debt. Tonight my wife and I will lie again in each other's arms, where, forsaking all others, we re-created this garden of seeing, in which each boy is sprouting into himself, that bean or eye compounded of familial earth and his breaching of it. Hard times will come, tomorrow.

My foot standeth in an even place.

MEMENTO

13. Tobias's Prayer

Dog and angel of skills
Who barked and chimed me a progress
Sweet in the sour, air of sewer hung, carious
Tenement jails

I grew in, beast and boy,
Toeing me strait in a clubfoot ring
Of lockstep and stumble poor, by snarl and song
Beset me free.

I being come to my troth
And devilled bride, the opulent
Hip of the world, great bullion teat, metropolis,
Divulged in her pith

Where, all inroad, she lies
Cobbled with spice and skulls of good men
At my feet, do fear, I do fear, nor dare devil in
Upon her lubricities

Lacking the hobnails of grief.
To my wedding feast now let me conjure
All souls, misbegotten and damned, if I am a stranger
To ills, or deaf

MEMENTO

To cries I turned into songs
When song was my turnkey, and only toil
To go with my saviour angel and dog, in a world
Of gifts, and wrongs.

14. Or Mud Like Me

Death could not halt the tragicomedy of untidy living in Mary Dore's long gas-heated flat, it merely changed the characters. Relatives young and old came in to take over the beds, drawn by her tough heart like a lodestone; while it beat, the seven rooms would be rowdy with the flow of life my mother "just wanted to run away" from. A froth of lesser figures came and went—a boarder who was a "boy friend" until he died of cancer, and a migration of cousins, caretakers and coachmen from the estates north of Hastings-on-Hudson where Mary Dore had been born, sixty years after the Revolution—but the hard core was of immediate kin. Even my mother ran only a mile, and not a week passed but she was back at the door of my Catholic grandmother, a pudgy bulldog of a woman who meant to be reckoned with to her last breath.

Until we left the city my mother led us like clockwork under the Eighth Avenue el to the corner tenement at 139th Street; high overhead was the seven-room lair which the old lady, besieged to her doorsill by the "boogies" she scorned, was obstinately holding to the death. In the flow of my childhood that flat in the thick of Negro life was the ancestral rock, and in it I imagined all the family tales, though many antedated it. From the Bronx my mother had pushed me to it in my baby carriage almost daily, until my father forbade it because she "didn't have the strength"; thereafter she visited weekly and in time with two children, my chunky sister in arms, me at her hand, climbing in dungeon dark up and around the five long stairflights to a skylight landing and her mother's embrace, for the old lady "adored" her; and over the years my father—periodically demanding, "Why do I have to go to your mother's every Sunday?"—shepherded us there by trolley car, and made restitution to Mary Dore for her lost parties by laboring at her defective piano all the afternoon while the clan sang, my grandmother trudged about in a glower of pleasure, and over everyone's lap clambered a joyous little poodle named Trixie, said to be white, grimy from the coal bucket and raw with mange, odious and beloved. Trixie in some way seemed the soul of the flat. Never destitute, the old lady would slip my mother in hard times the money for emergencies like my Easter outfit, but the household too had a mange upon it. The piano keys had shed some ivories, the sofa cushions were flaking off their painted scenes of canoes and palm trees, the carpet in the long hall was worn with the footpaths of the dead, and throughout the flat its curiosa—the bead portieres, the interior shutters, the marble washstand so agreeably alcoved in the hall, the sliding doors, the belly stove on its zinc square in the dining room—were leftovers of better days; the oleographs of dead ducks and fruits had umbered on the walls. The old lady kept the rooms scoured, but a must of dying came out of the groin of the building. Yet I was happy to be there, and munch in her kitchen at the slabs of bread-and-butter sprinkled with sugar that she plied me with, and gawk out of the window over rooftops at a fairyland castle whose towers soared in her sky; she said it was some kind of college, and neither of us knew that in it I was to hear such siren voices as would make her daughter weep.

Into her flat the old lady had taken first her sister, everyone's Auntie Aggie, a spinster nursemaid, superannuated by a stroke because she "acted peculiar", particularly for a nursemaid, she had a habit of wandering off and getting lost. It was a family custom for all in the flat, from Mary Dore down to the young son-in-law my father, to scatter out through the streets of Harlem in a hunt for her, until one spied her in a store and led her home; but when in my fourth year she was missing for a week—detained in a furnished room by a couple no less peculiar who told the police she "had a cold"—the family decided to put Auntie Aggie behind locks in a state hospital; here she took to walking backward when she meant to advance to her kin and, bequeathing us all this symbol, died.

Her fate overhung another head in the flat, too handsome and lively then to dream of it, the son who never left, Ben. Good earner, fast spender, talented chuckler, crony of priests, police captains, and Tammany wardheelers, Ben had all the instant affability of a drinker, which in his first career as salesman for a dairy firm made him "the best outside man in the city"; he was so finicky in his garb they dubbed him "Gentleman Ben", a dubious compliment, but one he dug out for me with a flicker of smile in the ruin of his later years. Often enough as a child I saw him beginning upon that ruin. After a week of whiskey he would sit unshaven and bathrobed in Mary Dore's rocker at the belly stove, drinking the coffee she brought him by dribbling it from cup to saucer and slurping the saucerful in, a touch of glamor which, when I aped it, my mother whisked from under my nose. In her teens my mother had seen Ben move his pregnant bride Kate into his room—one way to smuggle a family in, for in Mary Dore's eyes if one's name was not Dore it was mud—and increase the clan by two daughters; the old lady gave her son's wife little enough house, and so indomitably took over the rearing of the children that Kate escaped out to a lifetime job as cashier in a steakhouse.

A denizen of another room was my mother's sister Minnie, a frowze with a loose mouth and hair like dyed straw, our "goodhearted slob", always ready to give any of us the shirt off her back and to excoriate whoever declined it. Long ago married to a soldier, and widowed by the Spanish-American War, Minnie had moved back into the flat with her small boy, to leave him in the old lady's hands while she went out working as a waitress; one evening she came home to find the boy was dead, he had fallen into the cellarway and opened his skull. For years afterward when Mary Dore was watching the night, elbowed on her cushion and half out the window high above the streetlamps, it was for Minnie's homeward lurching as much as Ben's, and indeed a night came when Minnie, drunk in the street with another waitress, saw her sidekick hit and killed by a trolley car. With Minnie in and disrobing her fortyish charms, the stubby old mother would shuffle around in her nightgown and shawl grumbling—fine hour of night to be out, fine thing not knowing where a daughter was or who with or doing what, fine condition to come home in too—until Minnie would say, "Shove it up your ass, Ma," and topple into bed.

It was Minnie and Ben who, as my godparents, were responsible for my spiritual education, and furthered it by teaching me all the four-letter words. When my mother scrubbed my mouth with soap she was reaching far back after other tongues, for Mary Dore's was no less spicy, and she undermined Minnie's engagement to a cockney because the English were "pee-noses". Minnie's amours were a confusion—she once entertained a second caller in the parlor while a first was huddling on the fire escape—but in her late forties she remarried and took a flat downstairs with her husband, a swart day laborer with sleek hair; this son-in-law Mary Dore always identified with enthusiasm as "the nigger barber". But by then she had elevated my father from "narrow ass Gibson" to "dear Irv", and drawn close to her daughter-in-law Kate upon common ground, the turf.

My grandmother was very fond of playing the horses. The

steakhouse in which Kate worked was a hangout for racetrack touts who gave her tips, and the two women would empty out their changepurses to lay bets; the old lady was in the habit of passing her inside dope on to a friend, a police lieutenant in the precinct, who in turn shared it with his men, good thus spreading out in ever wider circles. Kate once brought home a hot tip when there was not a penny in the house to bet, and Mary Dore could not bear it, kept demanding now was Kate "sure" the horse would win, and at last looted her son's bureau of his diamond ring, gold watch, ruby ring, and gold cuff links, which she took down to the avenue to pawn, and, having stopped in on the lieutenant with the good word, placed her bet. The police force placed theirs, and the horse lost. Ben came home to the flat to dress for a grand Knights of Columbus dinner and could find none of his valuables to wear; his womenfolk were as baffled as he, and helped him search through all his drawers, and under the bed, and in his clothespockets in the closet, until Mary Dore was inspired to recall she had come down from hanging out her wash on the roof to discover the door wide open, there had been a robbery. Ben said that was a hell of a thing and had she notified the cops, and she said it had slipped her mind, and Ben marched off for the precinct house with the old lady crying down the stairs it would do no good. The two women waited in the disgruntlement which in the clan was expressive of all suffering, and Ben marched up the stairs again to say the lieutenant himself would be over soon. What delayed the lieutenant, nobody's fool, was taking up the second collection of the day among his troop of little old New York's finest, now in the nobler cause of motherhood, and when in due time he knocked, saluted the glum ladies, and surveyed the flat, his professional opinion was that the valuables had not been stolen; Ben said they had to be, he always kept them in his drawer, but the lieutenant crawling into his closet emerged with a shoe wherein lay the diamond ring, gold watch, ruby ring, and gold cuff links, all fallen out of Ben's hanging pants. Ben said it was "the damnedest thing he ever heard of".

Yet the granddaughters whom she raised would remember Mary Dore for her dignity. True, she would sit with Kate at a table in a saloon drinking her beer, but very dignified, she never left the flat without her corsets on, and the girls helped yoke her into them whenever she was thirsty. When her gentleman boarder took her to Coney Island, lost her in the crowd, and returned up the five flights of stairs without her, my grandmother was awaiting him at the top with the bawling-out such treatment of a lady called for. The second time Ben's girl turned up after school with lice in her hair Mary Dore donned her corsets and sallied out to "raise hell with the nuns", saw to it they paired her grandchild with a less populated seatmate, and back in the flat so scoured the girl's head with kerosene she gave it "a second-degree burn"; now out of the dark backward tangle a line is luminous in the likeness of my mother. The old lady commenced each day by putting on a fresh starched housedress and her earrings.

The earrings, black ovals with a hued mosaic of a Greek temple, I found among my mother's mementoes, her keepsake of Mary Dore; from that disorder of low life she had chosen solely and unerringly the tokens of self-respect. My mother at heart was, was not, of the clan. Of my grandmother she said, "She had a very hard life, dear," and her judgment on the family was not condemnatory, only regretful; she had scrubbed her way out of it, and stayed her soul with principles like the whalebone staves I recollect in her own corset, just as removable, for she was on lifelong call to her kinfolk whatever their troubles; indeed, nothing on that merry-go-round of drunkenness, lies, illegitimacies, so offended her as her brother George's breach of manners when, disgusted with them all, he retired to a house in Larchmont and "went high hat". My mother "stuck to" her folk, but half her heart went out to another family altogether, my father's.

It was into the Protestant bosom of his clan, and a climate of seemliness, that the moving-van led us in our venture across the Hudson. There we stayed less than a year; my father's hours at the bank were always eccentric, and he commuted in deserted times by a concatenation of bus, train, trolley, ferry, subway, until his misses by the minute and hangings about by the hour—on his first midnight the train broke down as well, and he had a five-milk walk to his bed—so enraged him that he packed us back to the Bronx. But in that year the divergence between his folk and my mother's as two ways of life was to illumine the end of my childhood.

At the woodsy edge of a hamlet named Bergenfield my aunt Milly's house sat on a wide green knoll, and into it the moving-men carried our furniture, to mingle with Milly's and overflow into her cellar and attic; we were to live with her family, a husband ten years her junior and their boy, three weeks older than I. In an adjacent town my aunt Ethel, with husband and small daughter, was in occupancy of her model new home, built with a bedroom for my grandparents Pop and Katherine Gibson, its screens rectified by a hand other than Will's. It was a far haul from the nuptial flat, with its waterpipe and toilet in the court-yard, where my father was begun; now all his folk, having es-caped piecemeal out of Harlem "before the Jews and colored came in" and across the Bronx and onto the lawns of New Jersey, were together again and firmly ascendant on the trellis of the mid-dle class, well-housed, well-churched, and, with Will's memory scabbed over, wholesome as honeysuckle; only sister Ada was errant, and she was in Africa persuading the unclad natives to wear proper clothes.

Though differences between my two aunts' households were perceptible—matters of income, for Milly's husband was a clerk like my father and Ethel's a prospering actuary—they vanished against the backdrop of my mother's kin festering in their tenement; the charm of my Catholics was their alacrity to forgive themselves every sin, and my Protestants lacked their advantages, being sinless. One of Ben's girls visiting had much mortified my mother with her new in-laws when, four-year-old cherub scratching, she piped up, "Where in hell'd you get all these mosquitoes?" My aunts' husbands were both church treasurers, and in their homes the strongest language was "for goodness sakes" in an uncle's mouth; infidelities and illegitimacies, like earthquakes, occurred only among foreigners; beer, wine, whiskey, had last been heard of years ago before Pop Gibson grew too tired to drink against the wind; the theater was the devil's roost, and when Milly first set foot in one at eighty-two it was to see a play of mine, full of goddams, though Milly said stoutly, "If Billy wrote it, it's all right"; even tobacco was of dubious morality, and one uncle expiated his borrowings from church funds by forgoing his pipe. Now among these exemplars for the better part of a year my mother tutored herself to the marrow in happy decorum, and developed an ulcer.

It was a cry for help in heaven. To my eye a country homestead, Milly's was actually a rented, comfortably worn, six-room house; ample enough—its crowning glory was its attic, where on rainy days I played with my cousin and sister among occult trunks—it was delicious with the currents of cookery floating out of its kitchen, Milly and my mother forever at work on meals for seven. A decade back, the chocolate cake that Jim hoisted by dumbwaiter to my newlywed parents was of Milly's baking, and my mother had apprenticed herself to her in a sistership that was to endure half a century. Milly was fifty, good-humored, vital, her big girth teased by my father in a snapshot caption as "falling away to a ton", an apronly woman used to living with doubled families. My grandmother's firstborn, she had talked Ada into pardoning Pop Gibson's irruption into their midst—"Ada, there isn't many men who'd marry a woman with three children"—and helped raise his issue, Irv, Jim, Ethel; at thirty she yielded to a suitor who was twenty, but had a mustache, and now three families shared the roof. Under it she bore her own child, a girl. After six months her young husband broke the news, withheld for the sake of her milk, that their daughter was a "blue baby" with a chance of living if she survived a year; at nine months the infant was dead. Milly was forty when her womb bore again, a last seed, and this time a boy "red as a beet", but she lay in her fears until the lady doctor swore at her, "So help me God, as far as I know this child is healthy!" and three weeks later it was I instead who almost expired of pinochle at birth. Separated by thirteen years, Milly and my mother thus had contemporary babies to talk about, and that conversation once begun grew into the wonder of the family; they would "rather chew the fat than eat", and, despite the damage all the menfolk foresaw to their tongues, their days together were a bliss of small talk.

My mother was no less friendly with Ethel, then in her late twenties, though removed by more than the ten miles between towns. Ethel was not only the family's baby, but its scholar and beauty, the gentle heir of its middle-class accession; my father proudly captioned her formal photograph—a highschool graduate with diploma cradled along her forearm, blonde, lovely in white from her shoulders to her shoetips—as "this is my sister she has big feet don't you think"; trained as a schoolteacher, she was flung into action against the little ruffians of the lower east side, a class of fifty-five boys from whom she came home in tears every night, until her fiancé arrived from the other war to rescue her. A few years after marriage they broke ground in Jersey for a house which, with its new bricks, new furniture, new grass, my mother was somewhat in awe of.

On Sunday visits we travelled to it by bus, or, in their touring car with isinglass sideflaps, Ethel and her family brought the old folks to Milly's. Here on the porch Pop Gibson would lie jack-knifed in the hanging bench with the newspaper in his fists, my mother and two aunts would initiate a pantry clatter of dishware and tongues, my two uncles would stand at the mantel worrying about their church mortgages, my father at the piano would throw in a quotation of "Onward, Christian Soldiers" in ragtime, and my whitehaired grandmother, immobilized by her bulk in a sofa with her needlework, would call in half-mock alarm, "Now let's not have any arguments about religion!" It was a land of sabbatical peace and plenty. Outside the kitchen windows lay a rurality my mother loved, clean sunlight, tame green copses, tidy houses, a small town not yet become a suburb; inside, the oven sang with its roast, the stovetop was live with vegetable simmerings, the pantry was a pungence of coffeebeans ground in a handmill, cheesecloths hung pregnant and purple in a straining of jellies, and the windowsill simmered with the freshbaked breads set there to dream. Withal, my mother's stomach commenced to digest itself.

The tensions were subterranean. In the unfenced backyard my sister and I had a favorite game, oddly poignant, we laid fieldstones together in a floorplan of rooms, and loitered in these confines as "our" house; my mother too was in exile, no longer monarch of her sink and curtains. Her hands so inventive of tasks—when my cousin and I "took piano" my mother sat daily with each of us at the keyboard to unravel the lessons—never lacked business, but in their bones were as imperious as Mary Dore's, and in this joint household were under a great strain of politeness. Disconnected from her mother for months, she was also quartered among churchgoers of another stripe, and was not made happier when the Catholic priest, known all over town for his denunciations of his vicious flock, was carted away in the midst of raping a nun. Milly's husband, to whom my mother had not apprenticed herself, had his own crotchets, such as forbidding the children to speak at the table, and at every meal criticized my glass of milk as interfering with my nutrition, it took up room in my stomach intended for solids whereas water would not; my mother paling would murmur, "Drink your milk, dear," as another drop of acid trickled in her gizzard. Mealtime in spite of the precedent grace was not the children's hour—Ethel's husband was so strict about "finishing the plate" that his daughter habitually left the table with food tucked away in her socks—but worst were the evenings when my uncle instructed his boy with a steel ruler on bared buttocks. The boy's rebellion was a furtive kleptomania, money and pocketknives and rings would disappear from bureau tops, and the beatings that ensued were dreaded by son and father alike, but a duty to which both submitted; my uncle would wait at the stairs till the boy called down winningly, "I'm ready, Daddy," then ascend to him with ruler in hand, and the blows were audible with the boy screaming, screaming, and my mother sat tightlipped over her darning-knob as my uncle descended again in a sweat; after several years of this, my cousin became a missionary. My parents seldom laid hands on me, and then obviously more for their good than mine. I used my beebee rifle in the woods to shoot a sparrow, my cousin reported it, and my mother was so abased by my misdeed she snatched up an umbrella and in pursuit of me all around the house swatted me with it until her character was improved. Most rare, such unexpected lapses into the Dore manner were not the least of her worries, especially west of the Hudson, and her apprehension of doing the wrong thing was lifelong; from girlhood on it dwelt under her carapace of good manners as "nervous indigestion".

Now its spasms were acute, a pseudonausea rising in her until it found release in a convulsion of saliva. I see her in a telling moment, all of us in our Sunday clothes disembarked from the bus en route to Ethel's, awaiting my mother's "sick spell" to climax while she stands over the curbstone, my father supporting her by the arm, till she drools her mouthful into the road, and her nausea subsides; these attacks took her finally to the doorbell of a local doctor's house, and she learned she had a duodenal ulcer. The doctor sent her forth on a punitive diet, milk, dry toast, poached eggs without salt or pepper, and in the midst of our holiday feasts—the gathered family round the table devouring the turkey, cranberries, candied yams, assorted vegetables, mince pie that my mother's hands had cooked—she would sit to a plate of boiled spaghetti bare even of butter. When in due time she sampled other fare her spasms revived, and then, armoring herself in all her inflexibility, which the family characterized by saying there was "nothing Flo makes up her mind to do she can't do", she lived in obedience to that prisoner's diet for two unbroken years, and was cured.

But she was long back in the city in our own four-room flat, shared only with cockroaches, and it was a briefer but deadly illness that we returned to. My mother never lived again under a roof not hers; in her widowhood the tiny apartment she occupied for nineteen years would, like her mother's, shelter many a stray—spinsters, widows, my sister with her baby during the war—but the indebtedness was theirs, and she declined all invitations later to move in with my sister's family; no comfort could equal her "independence". Its roots were deeper in her than decorum, the illness that lay in wait was her mentor's, and even in death Mary Dore's taste was averse to collaboration, she arranged every detail of her funeral herself.

The old lady was then eighty-three—the records said seventy-six "on account of the insurance companies", her practice being to pay less and collect more on her ten-cents-a-week policies—but indestructible until the end, with all her teeth and not a gray hair; old fighter, she ran her house still, and only her legs went back on her. She had "terrible varicose veins", which hemorrhaged and ulcerated, but she ministered to their oozings with salves and rubber bandages, and ignoring the doctor was never off her feet. No one in her household could do the cleaning, clothes scrubbing, cooking, ironing, to satisfy her, and in truth the females were not of her kidney, my mother had inherited it all; the old lady was picking up after her brood constantly, and Minnie's dust of facepowder left on the marble washstand sent her into "spasms of anger". She kept body like house, bathing and creaming her face nightly. No doubt the varicosity hurt in more than her legs, for she was always young enough to be vain, and in her last snapshots still outdressed all the ladies; and everyone knew that when in youth she undid her hair it touched the floor. The floor was not far, she was hardly five feet tall, but now formidable as a boulder. She was most proud of her small foot, a sign of gentility, and when suitors appeared for her granddaughters she judged their characters by shoe sizes, giving short shrift to the "clodhoppers"; she always spoke with respect of her dead husband's feet. Her own shoes, like her corsets, my mother still bought for her in a shop downtown where they had lived thirty years before, she would wear no others. But it was a rare favor she allowed to be done for her, she had no confidence in the performances of lesser souls, and none of them was surprised when she went shopping at the undertaker's, picked out her casket, paid for it, and then instructed him in where she wanted it to stand in her parlor, the placement of flowers around it, and the garments in which she was to be laid out, down to the black velvet throatband which she wore on all formal occasions. She left it to her survivors only to notify the undertaker, a consummation she could not see a way to take care of herself; but then Ben's daughter said the old lady "wouldn't trust anything to that bunch, she never knew if they'd be sober."

It was not how the old lady spoke, her contempt was for outsiders. She had three sons left, one an army bum halfway around the world with an affinity for the guardhouse, his rank kept climbing to sergeant and collapsing to private, and one a country gentleman, the family success, who not every Christmas bethought himself to send her five dollars that made her meditate if he "could spare it", and one as likeable a companion as any man could wish for, whom many did, and if he was ten minutes late for supper the old lady was on her window cushion in a fret praying to Jesus, Mary and Joseph, and the saints preserve us that this time he not stagger into view on the drink. Yet her voice still preened with "my sons", she had seen nothing to equal her sons, and of the Broadway producer who married George's daughter she said curtly he was "not a patch on my son's ass". It was Willy she meant, long dead, but none of them was out of mind, and my mother would remember the old lady plodding through the cemetery "in the ice and snow with her bad legs" to the graves of her boys.

Ben was now in the chips—he had taken over from his brother George a Harlem ice company whose team-drawn wagons clomped through all the streets of Manhattan—and on holidays would load the family into his new tin lizzie for an outing; and Mary Dore invariably said, "Let's all drive up to Hastings!" In that township Ben would brake to a stop so she could ponder the brick house, empty and dilapidated, in which she had been born the better part of a century ago. Between the rotted doorsill and the old pugface at the car window lay a dark woods no one else could see, all the memories of that "very hard life" which to little in female experience was a stranger.

She remembered parents who "had some money" but died, and relatives who took the child Mary Kane in, educated her in a convent, and disowned her when, as docile at fifteen as she would ever be, she eloped with her song-and-dance man, first

encountered as a banjoist at a ball. It was not the only memorable
ball in her life, for a tintype in her later teens has her seated in
the gown—striped, voluminous around her trim figure, with
severe white cuffs and collar, and above the throatband a black-
braided head as lovely and firm as a tulip—that she wore to the
Astor House festivities for a Mr. Lincoln, en route to a fateful
inauguration. She had already commenced on her career of
childcarrying, which was to span the years from the Civil War
to the eve of the Spanish-American, and would say that "all I
ever had was one in the carriage, one coming, and one hanging
on my skirt"; she bore her nineteenth child when she was fifty-
three. Throughout she was a quasiwidow, her touring husband
"only came home to make babies" and pregnant women kept
withindoors, so she went nowhere much of the time. Yet she had
the honor of once dancing with General Grant—"quite a
rumdumb," she confided to her grandchildren—and her son
Willy was to bring to the flat such eminences as Lillian Russell
and Diamond Jim Brady; their huge photographs, yellowed
under glass, still hung in her parlor in my childhood.

It was long gone then, that heyday in the dying century when
her Willy led what "may safely be counted as the foremost
Banjo Trio of the age" in tours from San Francisco to Europe,
not omitting a stellar engagement at the Metropolitan Bicycle
Academy for the Midnight Fancy Bicycle Ride. Willy too was
much absent, but Mary Dore managed the studios in Manhattan
and Flatbush where the brothers had an overflow of pupils, she
looked after their bookings and tours, and she missed no New
York performance—from Tony Pastor's elegant restaurant to
their Annual Grand Banjo Concert with "an orchestra of one
hundred banjo and guitar players" at Chickering Hall—in her
eavesdropping duties as gleaner of every audience criticism. Her
daughter Flo was born into this ado, when Mary Dore was
forty-six. Seven decades later when daily my mother was scissor-

ing into the newspapers for her scrapbook about me she advised
me to take a screenwriting job because "Hollywood is the place
to get well-known", and tonguetied with several angers I advised
her she "knew nothing about it"; she replied, somewhat hurt,
"My family was in show business a long time, dear." Mary Dore
was fifty-five when that time vanished in three days. Willy playing at an outdoor resort took cold and died, of pneumonia, of
touring, of drink, of the women he "was a devil with"; he was
twenty-eight years old, and not the first of her fourteen boys
that Mary Dore saw into their graves. Without him her doughty
body kept the studios in business for another dozen years, but it
replenished the earth no more.

The preceding year she had buried her lastborn, Stevie, aged
six months. More than one son died in his beginnings, Paul at one
month, Artie at ten months, Percy at nine months, Freddy at one
year, and others in their young manhood, Harry who drove the
horsecar, Alfred the ice-cream salesman, Johnny the actor,
"handsomest man in the Tenderloin", and the four whose names
are lost; tuberculosis, diphtheria, influenza, rheumatic heart, cut
them down, and the three-year-old Wally screaming "held his
breath" until a colored scullerymaid to prompt it threw him into
a vatful of water on the coalstove and scalded him to death. In
her early sixties Mary Dore accompanied the coffin of her husband Dennis into the great Catholic cemetery where so many of
their family lay, and said goodbye to his faithless but beautiful
feet. Nineteen times her womb had opened fruitful to his seed,
and nineteen times carried its burden for most of a year, and
nineteen times delivered it to the world in blood and hurt; the
bosom in her bulged corset had for nineteen toothless mouths
filled with the milk that became the bone, entrails, muscles, hair,
fingers of children, and been suckled empty and old; nineteen
times she had lived up to her elbows in their urine and feces,
boiling and scrubbing ten thousand diapers by hand; a thousand

nights she had walked the floor with sick babies and fallen asleep in her rocker at the bedside of sick children, nursing them through colic, measles, croup, "summer complaint", chickenpox, mumps, whooping cough, scarlet fever, and mopping up the vomit of nineteen stomachs, piling blankets on their chilled limbs, spooning warm oil into their infected ears, laying "wet rags" on their fevered eyes, had eased their misery with medicines, enemas, hot water bottles, alcohol rubs, steam kettles on kerosene heaters, and in their boredom of a thousand convalescences she had been picked bone-dry by the plagues of peevish demands that only mothers suffer; and fourteen times she had sat by sickbeds and impotently watched the flesh of her flesh, of her labor, of her love, die. And she endured, but at a cost, the worse part of a century had changed a tulip of a girl into a fortress, the wistfulness in that flower face long gone under, and her old countenance at the car window, staring at a ruined house, was plain as rock, massive and defiant.

Of all nineteen it was my mother, the sole heir of her fiber, who was at her bedside in the night of her dying. That day Flo had teased the matriarchal face into a smile by asking how she could bear to "lay in bed so long without corsets", though it was not long, forty-eight hours after the old lady contracted pneumonia sitting on her stone stoop in a nightwatch for her boy. The priest visited her—she was a weekly communicant who journeyed five miles each Saturday to a confession in the old neighborhood where she had borne my mother, the family joke being that she would not let the Harlem priests in on her sins—and her last confession was made in bed. In the teeth of extreme unction the family doctor was bluff in praise of the old lady's vitality, he had "seen her pull through worse than this", and in the kitchen undisturbed were the pies she had just baked for a Halloween party, and a day before she had, bad legs and all, helped Ben's teen-age girl carry a two-wheeler bike as usual down the five stairflights to the sidewalk; nobody believed her capable of a weakness like death. But at five o'clock in the morning my mother, seated hand in hand with her, heard the rattle in her now obsolete throat, and presently woke the older girl, and said, "Momma's gone."

My grandmother was laid out as she had dictated, in the parlor, in her black lace dress and throatband, and my sister peeking with me through a keyhole asked why flowers were being "planted" around her; and three days later she was buried with her husband in the double grave he had purchased seven years before my mother was conceived. It was full of her children, and would receive yet one son more. As long as she lived my mother visited the grave two or three times a year to pretty it with flowers, and at seventy she said, "I suppose when I'm gone no one will keep it up"; when I went in her stead I could not find it. No headstone had ever been bought to mark it, and in a wilderness of other slabs I walked somewhere across it in anonymous ground that held the bones of my tiny uncles, the dancing feet of their father, the music unplucked in Willy's fingers, but chiefly what remains of an old lady with a bulldog heart, to mark which in lieu of more durable stone I leave my wreath of words.

She is not done with us yet. In our kitchen I stand displeased that someone has done me a favor, made my coffee wrong, and at the sink my mother's ghost pours out half of my favor to her, a cup of tea too dark, and the old lady's croak is out of another century, "I'll do it myself": now that I am a grown-up too, and can do whatever I like, much of what I like is somehow what she liked. The doctor who saw my own mother through the pain of her dying months said she was "like a pioneer", but the voice of my grandmother was in her from a day when the land was young. Even the old lady's low jinks with money in that long-ago flat are still rippling out among us. Inquiring at the cathedral offices about her grave I was told of the arrears on the upkeep, the last interment was of Ben and his Catholic daughters were billed alternately by the archbishop for seven years in vain, each mailing the bill on to the other, and when I espoused the archbishop's cause, their father's grave, four dollars a year, one daughter said lightly to forget it since she'd "never use the grave" and the other said indignantly she was "not for God's sake responsible for a grave somebody else bought", and the archbishop has given up on the old lady's granddaughters, the bill is now mailed—in vain—to me.

15. Memento Famulorum

Burned is the city wherein I
    Mourn.

Half is my house of old wood and
    New
Between sleep and daylight fallen in
    Two,

Done is the fire, and

Dead is my rooftree an ill wind
    Blows
Bare of its relics: a new leaf
    Grows.

Done is the fire whereof I am
    Tongue.

Charred is the stairway I time after
    Time
Go down among graves: and up again
    Climb

To ashes and strangers, and

15. *Memento Famulorum*

Vacant the bed where I twist ten
    Score
Of my listening bones: to feet at my
    Door.

Strangers and ashes whereof I am
    Born,

Hard is the knock at my body and
    Soul
To which I unlock: and the house is
    Whole.

sanctus

16. To All Their Blackened Ears

Holy, holy, holy, the earth is filled with thy glory, hosanna in the highest, and in the lowliest too, the voiceless choir of whom I think while I take a breath now. I pause not only because I have so much yet to put down before I am light of my burden; I have come to a part in it I am less than eager to look into. So I permit myself a look back instead at the host which is blackened in the earth, unsung, lives too commonplace to have been newsworthy, and all, though their graves are lost, the nourishers of my children, and who is to celebrate their miraculous number?

Of those who have gone before us, thy servants and handmaids, be mindful: thus also the missal, and to aid me in my observance of the injunction my father's sister has sketched out for me a family tree, rooted in Staten Island. Its matriarchal bole bears the names of her own grandmother and grandfather as the begetters; out of them arises a multitude of branches, some broken off, some proliferous, writhing into the forty-three lives of my greatuncles, grandmother, aunts, uncles, father, sister, nephews, cousins, sons. On this tree of worshippers I am an incidental twig, not easily located, and the sense of myself as the nucleus of consciousness around which the world lies is abashed.

In my youth these who went before were nothing to me, my own twigdom was all, but now that I have more past than future I turn toward them, I am of them, I feed on and further this earnest oak established by William Jennings, shoemaker, and his bride Susan. I know little of them more than their names, but when I saw a tintype of Susan Winters I felt a prickle of the eerie, it was my father's face that in the lanky tresses stared at me. Susan was his grandmother, dead before his birth, a thin six-foot girl who married the widower Jennings, reared his two children, bore him eleven others, buried him at forty-nine, watched his patrimony leak through the fingers of the sons, and in penury until her death worked to support her daughter Katherine, young widow, and her brood; Milly in her eighties remembered her grandmother Susan from childhood as "a wonderful woman". Except that she was "New Jersey Dutch" I cannot see back of her, that trickle of sap comes to my twig from a parentage unknown. But Susan and William were not the begetting trunk, and I can follow the Jennings limb downward two generations earlier to John, waterman, and another William, "yeoman" under the king; that trickle is from England, for it was there my greatuncles sent their brother Len to collect an inheritance, though he returned with only the news it was nothing, and thereafter lived in inexplicable comfort, buying up the Staten Island dwelling-houses of the Jennings males scattered into Ohio and Michigan. This limb was the proud stock of my father's womenfolk, who had not been informed it was of "pee-noses". Yet with the grandmother of my grandmother, the waterman John's bride, a trickle comes in from a different soil; her grandfather Richard Skerret, also a shoemaker, was a Frenchman, who when the colonies won their war settled on the Island and raised nine children with a Mary Hegor, of German parentage; and with her a rivulet out of another country feeds the tree, unsuspected by my father in his boycott of the Huns.

And I am mindful of more than these: it is only the Jennings tree, and three other massive boles must be sketched in their conjugation of branches to engender my twig, now lost to sight in a tangled forest of lives. The dark has closed around all three, but the blighted earth of Ireland lurks somewhere below each. On my grandmother Katherine's limb our Pop Gibson appears from nowhere, in-law, without antecedents; and in truth his tree is anonymous, with sisters as ghostly as his mother and no given name for his father, who in some year of famine prior to midcentury landed in New York from the Protestant north of the emerald isle; thence the roots of my second bole wind back in time, not indigenous, to farther soil. And the branchlet which is my father bears the name of another in-law, Florence Dore, rootless here, but one of nineteen branchings of the mighty tree founded by Mary Kane and Dennis Dore. The Dore bole which antecedes it is also unknown, with all its brethren; in one family tale that song-and-dance man is offspring of a colleen and a schoolteacher in France, in another an Irishman who improved the spelling of Dorey to share the fame of Gustave the illustrator, but in either case the third bole has a taproot in the ould sod. As for my fourth, Mary Dore warned her brood often enough that if she had "a drop of Irish blood in me I'd squeeze it out of the whole bunch of you, I'm a Yankee," but she was surrounded by innumerable cousins named Donnelly and Doherty, and Ben with a twinkle told me she was untainted Yankee "from County Cork"; in Hastings, where a century and a quarter ago she was born of a Shepphard girl to a Kane who "built houses", the family papers lie in the ashes of a fire as extinct as the souls that thrived upon that unremembered tree.

So the hybrid juices of five countries climb in the intertwining branchwork of names, Skerret, Hegor, Winters, Jennings, Gibson, Shepphard, Kane, Dore, up through a multitude of children fed by the daily labor of watermen, shoemakers, vaudevillians, cratemakers, to the limb which is Flo Dore and Irv Gibson, bank clerk, and along their twig Billy, family bookkeeper, into the two twiglets who are my boys.

And of those who have gone before, the boys must be mindful

of twice my multitude. For they bud also out of an exotic tree which, via their mother, born in Colorado, bifurcates back through Russia across unknown lands a thousand years into Judaea. In the streets of Denver a miller's son and sometime teacher, her young father, having emboldened his shy hawking cries by practicing them in an empty lot, vended fruits and vegetables from a pushcart to support his bride and newborn daughter; his way to those streets lay through lumbercamps in the north by way of Galveston to the south, from Bremen, and backward over mountains he crossed on foot in the night to elude conscription by the Czar. His bride-to-be, a merchant's daughter, emigrated more conventionally through New York to their rendezvous in the Rockies. Their birthplace was a town in the Ukraine, Proskurov, where the ghetto was many times expunged in pogroms, and Jews not uncommonly amputated the thumbs of their male children, who otherwise would vanish in the recruiting raids of the Czar's soldiers, kidnapped into a twenty-five-year bondage to defend his world of Christian ideals; and back of that ghetto, obliterated from historical record by the pogroms, generation after generation of homeless roots anterior to my sons wander away over country and country into the ancient hills where Abraham tended sheep.

Holy, holy, the earth indeed is filled with thy glory, though the graves are lost, and I can tell their tales only in my own, but where and who is the begetting trunk? The bedrock in which my aunt's sketch roots her bole is a stratum of cloud adrift at an inconceivable altitude; our oldest patriarch was in his time too only a twig on a tree like none known on this planet, whose married torsos divide as they descend, multiplying as prodigally downward as upward, into all humanity, air plants never rooting in terra firma; for homeland and anchorage there is none, the stability of the tree is in its interlocking of limbs, man to wife, mother to babe at nipple, grandfather to toddler in hand, and all that multivarious yoking of boles in antiquity to twiglets in time to come, rooted in nothing, is purposeless, its own beginning and end. The ancestral juice that nurtured the crowds of children, grandchildren, greatgrandchildren somehow kept alive in migrations, famines, pogroms, epidemics, wars, is one with the flow from the arms of my parents, through me, to the skinny arms of my sons. Sprig of this bottomless forest, I no less than any am the begetting trunk.

Yet in a dream I climb again a long stair toward a skylight landing and a door, on the other side of which my grandmother waits with a sugared piece of bread-and-butter for me, and halfway up am bewildered, it is the right tenement but the wrong year, the old lady is dead, I must go through the streets of Harlem in search of the flat where her son Ben my godfather now lives, but again tricked by time I turn in confusion, for Ben too I know is dead, his daughters no longer walk these sidewalks, and amid a traffic of strangers, directionless, without home of my own, I awake to the dark bed of reality in which I lie, orphaned, a fearful child of almost fifty, until manhood comes back in my limbs with remembrance of my bedmate and boys.

So the twig is the pith of the bough, live within, and though I am loth I must go down again into my own twigdom, upgrowth heedful only of its self, seeing it as neither singular nor past; that writhing out of a family's arms is history far older than mine, and more prophetic than I could wish. The decade of enmity between generations that I lived once, and now take breath to live again, lies in wait for me a third time, next year or next. But I too say holy, hosanna, blessed is he that comes in whosever name; when in my boys the sap of green wisdom is cruel, let me think twice that they relive me, as I relive my parents, and every twig is the tale of the tree. And if I suffer myself to confess that time, so mindful at last of those who are gone, it is partly for those who are come.

PREFACE

17. Is Live, and Uncurls

In the year that followed Mary Dore's death I knelt at the altar rail and stuck out my tongue for its maiden wafer of confirmation, the smallest boy I knew, swathed in a doublebreasted blue serge suit with my first long pants on legs so nervous that afterwards I could not stand still in the street, I kept sprinting around the block to flee the neighbors' eyes. I was twelve years old, the land was full of spies, and my long pants and I were a fraud.

At six, familial earth was my world, and I was a giant in it, I rode forth as king of the block, and smote my playmates, and alongside our house sought out the dragon, who was disguised as a shy frockling of five, but I said I would show her mine if she showed me hers and eventually she consented, so we denuded our middles, bowed in reverse to display our respective behinds, and there I left her lightly and forever. That derring-do had deserted me. My sexual education had been brief—it occurred in a dialogue with my mother over a rudimentary sketch of a man when she said in alarm, "What's that, dear?" and I said proudly, "It's his weewee," and she said, "Oh, that's not nice"—but to the point: the sketch went into the garbage pail, and by nine I had learned not to expose my weewee or hand.

Love and fisticuffs no longer were simple matters. In the school to which I walked a country mile from my aunt's house I was overcome by devotion to a girl with a pale face and loose black hair; that beauty was never out of the corner of my eye from the bell which bade us in to the bell which parted us till the morrow, but I was now such a master of vent" in a blackboard game wherein boys chalked up the initials of girls by whom they wished to be pursued around the desks my hand would not write hers, and cunningly each time substituted those of a horselike creature two feet taller than I, who then pursued me around the desks, the school grounds, and most of the town, a worshipful pest. In that schoolyard a boy who came to my chin also gave pursuit to me, for no reason except my fearfulness. I would hang back in the morning fields until the bell let me in to safety, when it expelled me I outran him like a stricken rabbit for home, and for weeks I skulked along the roads with my eyes swivelling five ways at once; whenever we sighted each other the chase began anew, and only ended when one afternoon he and another boy sprang from behind a tree, I begged him not to hit me, and he most amiably agreed; for him a game was over, but I bled with the indelible stain of my cowardice. Much of that year, beset by love and hate, I was out of breath. I had none for the adults around me, my mother, my father, their kinfolk, in whom I would not—but in my own voice I hear what a windbag a grown-up is, encouraging my boys to the heroisms I fled from—confide these failures: unworthy of them, I was blown back into myself.

I had begun school so literately for my mother, who tutored me a jump ahead of the teachers and kept every relative informed of the grades I skipped, that I was always a year younger than my classmates, and inches shorter; over their heads I spied a more manageable world in books. In the Bronx at eight I was an idler in the Shakespeare Avenue library, staid with works for the young chosen by some board of educators for their lack of interest and newly dead from the city bindery, but in the library of our Jersey town I was in an opium den. Like its police force of two constables, who took turns on one motorcycle, and the fire department, suspended in a great iron ring above our road-side weeds with a hammer to summon volunteers, the town's fund of books was homely, all donated as rummage by house-wives, ending their days under one roof with the motorcycle; however modest in quantity, their quality could not have been worse. I ran upstairs to that office each week for my aunt Milly's book—so dependable a saga of sheiks and captive virgins that two-thirds through she habitually sat with it pondering, "Didn't I read this one? I think I read this one"—and there my hands scrambled along a shelf glutted with dreams no less paradisiacal to me, of lads whose surnames rang with their timbre, swift, rover, sturdy, who invented flying machines and found lost cities of gold. So now had I. All winter in my uncle's morris chair I flew away; so eager a nose in a book was a flattery to my parents, and each inhalation took me deeper with their blessing into a landscape where they had never set foot.

It was to the common ground we had left that we reverted in my tenth summer, but the magic had closed behind us. A dozen blocks from our heavenly hill my mother located a fourth-floor flat—like Mary Dore she had a taste for rooms that were "high up", lighter, and two dollars cheaper—which overlooked trolley tracks, a firehouse, and clustered roofs. Yet only its roaches were reminiscent of former days; we could not enter them again, and the treks I made to play with the old gang, the visits my parents paid on neighbors, told us we were outsiders to that streethood and its sidewalk spontaneities under the trees. My parents still tried, moving us and the furniture a few months later into an-other building over a grocery two corners distant from the hill, but the corners were not to be got around.

This aerie on the fifth floor, with steam heat, a downstairs door that unlocked to a buzzer, and a mirrored wall in the tiled vestibule to check one's fitness for the street, was our first "apartment"; our fortunes were on the rise. The bank in which my father worked was now a colossus with a hundred and twenty-five vice presidents, of whom he was not one, but in some lofty office he braved the personnel chief to request a raise, the chief asked why, my father said he had two children to bring up, the chief said that was no reason, my father said and he deserved it, the chief said that was a reason, and my father's semimonthly paycheck was invigorated by five dollars. It paid for the luxury of high "dutch shelves" around the dining room, which my mother decorated with souvenir plates from expositions and steins with hinged lids that never saw beer, but not for a fifth room. Kitchen, bedroom, and parlor completed the flat, my sister and I shared the bedroom, and my parents bought a couch for the parlor which every night they pulled out into a bed for two, disjointed and skimpy; they slept on that creak of wires for the next seven years, for the two bedrooms we could later afford were given to my sister and me, and when my father's labors earned him a true bed it was the one in which he was to die.

Death brushed past the window there too, though his next appointment with us was not for a year, to take our matriarch Mary Dore; but for three days the doctor held out no hope for my sister. Day and night my mother sat in the bedroom watching diphtheria strangle her child. A quarantine sign was fixed on our apartment door, and I, barred from school and sickroom both, shared the couch with my father, while our goodhearted slob Minnie came in to run the household. My mother was sickly enough on her ulcer diet, with the goiter again clogging her throat until she "couldn't catch her breath", and the vigil left her frayed, but the child's life hung on keeping her supine; my father insisted on taking a night watch, albeit so sore from serum shots he could "hardly go to work", and my mother said he would doze off, but he said he would not, and in the early hours she was drawn by a misgiving to the bedroom to find him asleep and my sister climbing out of bed; thereafter she kept watch herself, trusting no one. The small buttocks had been injected with a massive dosage of antitoxin, and my mother, warned by the doctor that paralysis or stoppage of the six-year-old heart was not unlikely, sat in the night with her dreads. The day the doctor saw the child choking to death he "went in with his fingers" to dig the membrane out of her larynx; holding her, my mother was drenched with blood and sputum, but assisted while a tube was inserted in her daughter's windpipe, and then, infected, fell ill too. All month the life of the household tiptoed past their ominous door. But in time my sister was out of bed, playing with her dollhouse beside the radiator, and my mother lived to tell me in later years no detail of her own diphtheria, only her child's.

For I was oblivious to much in the house: dearer to me than mother or sister were the newsboys of the Bowery who, in another body of tales I had come upon, try and trust, sink or swim, do and dare, grew overnight into railway presidents. These foundlings, born before my father and out of print, too noble for the library, survived in bindings as ragged as themselves, itinerant from boy to boy like legends. I was most alert in cornering schoolmates said to have this or that bracing title, and inseparable from it when borrowed; I slept with it under my pillow, and in faint dawnlight read on and on before the sorry world awoke, at whose stir I ceased being rough and ready, put away luck and pluck, and rose from riches to rags.

The competence of those manly waifs eluded me. Deprived of their chance to sell newspapers in snowstorms, I undertook a dozen times to vend from door to door such household staples as sachet powders. According to the gaudy ads in the funnypages through which I ordered my stock, I would upon completion of sales receive a dirigible as pictured, aloft with full crew; always a bit uneasy about where to keep it in our flat, I was not inconvenienced, for within a few days the packets were too grimy to be shown to any housewife, after which I lived in weekly terror of the firm's duns and impending lawsuits, until my father would bail me out, buying the shabbiest and mailing back the remainder. Such enterprises were not my only avenue to wealth, we had a school bank to inculcate habits of thrift or, in my case, theft. I was given ten cents a week to deposit, of which I spent nine, and led a sad life in candystores half the term until my mother confronted me with my bankcard and its sickly entries of ".01" instead of ".10"; the alibi I had rehearsed for the first, teacher's carelessness, was somehow less convincing for the fifteenth, and my mother in two minutes had the truth, which grieved both of us. I then asked, "Will Daddy give me a licking?" and she, misunderstanding, promised he would not. What he gave me, soon enough, was a dime-a-week allowance. But I had meant it as a toadying request, to ally myself with her view of me, and the residual shame was not at the pilfering—two years later, desperate for lack of a bimonthly magazine about to vanish from the newsstand, I hijacked her pocketbook—but at the temptation to that alliance: to pretend to feelings was a serious dishonesty. And true feelings I could find no tongue for. In a party game of postoffice a strange girl called me into a bedroom for a kiss often enough that I was in a fond swoon for a month, but she heard from me only on St. Valentine's Day when I mailed her as an anonymous gift a giant mockery of my heart scissored out of the newspaper ads; it was cousin to my father's captioning a snapshot of six of his womenfolk as "gee what an auful bunch"—so spelled—but more malignant. Even my fistic retirement in triumph was less than confident. When a stickball game with the old gang broke up over a disputed decision I called a boy a "sawhead", he called me a liar, an older youth laid a sliver on my shoulder and pushed the sorehead into knocking it off, and a fight was ordained; the gang marched us off to a level lot, where the boy and I poked at each other until he tumbled backward and wept, thus losing, though he sobbed he was hurt on a stone; to me his stone was likelier than my fist, and I was the only witness who believed him. His downfall at my hands assured me I was unequally matched with the world.

I was beginning to lose my way in it, and in the sixth grade took pencil to found my own. In the evenings at the dining room table, cleared of its paraffin bananas for my schoolbooks and ink, my mother or father would often see me through the difficulties of homework; when I had to write a composition on fire prevention my father at my elbow waxed enthusiastic and together we forged a clever piece, ABC, always be careful, which as mine so awed the teacher that I was asked to read it to the school assembly. From a stage usually reserved for such dignitaries as the principal and the "health clown" who demonstrated how to chew our milk thirty-nine times, I read my father's work to the entire student body, while the lintel over my head in carved letters advised all present that knowledge is power, and so it seemed was the writer's life. This success inaugurated my scholastic decline. I was soon busy on a first novel about my uncle Jim, a distilled work consisting solely of his name, and in spare hours I indited other narratives in the notebooks with marbled covers that I loved to buy; each opened on a freckled newsboy in a snowstorm crying his wares, wuxtry wuxtry, and closed therewith. Yet in these minuscule fancies I drank blood, all the autocracy of my grandmother which was excluded from my household diet by the autocracy of her daughter, and the taste was addictive. While I lolled in a classroom dream of reading and writing, arithmetic marched across the blackboard and was erased, and its only ripple in my consciousness was the monthly subtraction I saw in my report card; geography, history, everything slid past my eye, from that year I was done with high marks to gladden my betters, and in my head the edifice of my life loomed up on the cornerstone of my father's goldbrick.

It was at this turn that my parents, abandoning hope of the garden, moved us away from its outskirts forever. Twice daily my father rode on a trolley car that groaned to a stop at every other corner between our door and a subway entrance in Manhattan, and my mother, to save him that hour a day, set out in search of four rooms within a walk of the subway; she found them across the river in Washington Heights. She then made ready for moving-day, and the family toiled for weeks to meet it to her satisfaction.

I was sent to remote stores to beg empty cartons—"ask for a good strong one, dear"—for packing, a hard choice for my mother, who hated to ask a favor where she was not a customer but expected her grocer to shortweight her the second he discovered her intent to move; invariably when she had me "run downstairs" to him she adjured me to rivet my eye on the scales while he was knifing a hunk of butter out of the tubs, and by ordering a piece of steak first to conceal that hamburger was my ultimate wish lest he substitute chopped cat, and to make him slosh the cream up and down before he ladled our portion out of the deeps of the milkvat; there was always a hidden war between my mother and her grocer, though more hidden from him, and she cautioned me to sneak my cartons past his window unseen. From the bins in the cellar, where each family padlocked its odder belongings, my father struggled upstairs with the two proud barrels which were part of our estate, for sole use on moving-day, and stood them in the dining room. In them our dishware was to travel, and nightly they commenced to fill, my sister and I swaddling each cup and platter and glass in newspaper, my father tucking them with care down into the barrels; my mother kneeling at ten cartons segregated clothes, toys, linens, groceries, pots and pans, all our unbreakables gathered in reverse order to our need for them in the new house, trimly packed, and dustless under newspaper. For a month she was washing shelves and scrubbing floors, scouring everything from the exterior of windows—seated outside them on sills above five stories of clotheslines in tight-mouthed fear, until my father came home to take her place—to inside the oven, leaving the flat immaculate for future tenants. Down from the walls came her nineteen-cent pictures of flower arrangements, and the bric-a-brac of shepherd-esses in white porcelain from the dutch shelf, and the dimity curtains from kitchen cupboards and drapes from the parlor arch; the clothes closets grew barren; my father rolled up the rugs against the wallboard and the house was impoverished. Item by item we withdrew from it our taste, colors, textures, love, and by breakfast time on moving-day, when my father unjoined the bedsteads and my mother hurried to pack the last dishes into a barrel top, the rooms were like the empty husk of itself a locust leaves behind. I hung out the window to see the van back up to our sidewalk—it was raining, a family custom—and soon the men were clumping upstairs and into the flat, three huskies in workclothes, who surveyed our knots of worldly riches, propped the door open, and hefted everything out, singly and in grunting pairs; when my father spoke to them he would roughen his voice and drop in a pale profanity, to undo for a moment his whitecollar fate, and sealing mine. Least intimidated by their brawn was our upright piano in the parlor, but it went too, swathed in mats and ropes. Dollied to the window hole and hooked to a tackle rigged on the cornice of the building, it was cursed and shouldered out, and for a dreadful instant swung in the air uncertain of doom, until a man on the sill steadied it with a hand, the sidewalk man began to pay rope out, and slowly the huge and precious instrument, the family's soul, descended; and the grocer saw in one minute our piano floating at his window and my mother at his door politely telling him goodbye, she had decided to move.

With my sister she then boarded the trolley car for the new flat, to see our furniture set down in it by the huskies as prearranged in her mind and by nightfall have her house in order again, but my father and I stayed as overseers to the final suitcase. When the floors were bare of every echo of us my father locked the door, neither of us knowing it was the last flat in which I was to be my parents' child, and he went downstairs with the keys and a two-dollar leave-taking to seek the janitor in the cellar; the half-filled van labored away from the sidewalk into the future, but the drizzle had stopped, and when my father with his umbrella came out of the cellarway he agreed to hike into the new borough via the footbridge. Halfway across its redbricked span we had a last look at the neighborhood named for it, Highbridge, with its green bluff and the diadem of family houses along it and the grayed sky above it all, then turned our backs, and over a river stagnant as Lethe walked together out of my childhood.

For beyond the bridge my unwitting body had a rendezvous to keep, that year, where a rope dangling in a skeletal church under construction awaited me. I was to come to it in a dusk after school-hours, and jumping to climb, with my thighs clamped upon it, feel a tickle in my glans that sent me down to urinate at the brickpile, but no urine was in me, so I tackled the rope again, felt the same tickle, again stood urineless, and was convinced my penis had lost its mind; in its eleventh year my body, hanging on a rope with the first itch of lust in its bud, was speaking to me of desires, decisions, disasters, all the imminent disease of manhood, with which I thought I could be done by relieving my bladder. This expectation marked my crossing over into the adult capacity for error, and the church promptly made the rite of confirmation available to me.

The slap on the cheek with which the visiting bishop welcomed me to it signified the blows I must be prepared to sustain for the church, but nobody thought of one to fortify my parents against my self-contempt. It was not the neighbors on that first day of long pants I kept sprinting around the corner to outrun, it was my unworthy self, who lived in my parents' house. Almost everything they put their hands to, from my father's sorting of letters at midnight far downtown to my mother's three-day kneading of dough for the brioche rolls I loved, had at heart the growth of the two children who were their chief business in life; now mine was to escape them. Though once a month I would kneel to confide myself to the priest's jowl in the dark of his booth, an instinct was at work in me to devise my own kind of communion, and all he heard from me was that I had said two damns since my last confession. The secret I could not name, or know, was that I was forsaking my parents.

18. Growing

When I was childish
Daylight lay over my city, dusk I had none,
    I grew in the eye of my father
        Blinded by sun.

    Sunset I saw by
Shivered my tenement, yet in a widow's town
    I had the moon for a day.
        Her eye is down.

    Now I grow manly
My lights are behind me, a humped and malign
    Shadow falls over the city:
        Look, it is mine.

19. In Personis Proprietas

Distinction in persons, oneness in being, and equality in majesty, this the angels do praise, or so saith the missal in that prayer, known as the preface, which, after the celebrant's varying petition that his gifts be acceptable, introduces the canon wherein the offering is fixed for all time.

It is a thanksgiving, not to the unity of a single person, but to that trinity in unity which I could not understand in large on Sundays, but lived with in small on weekdays. In the flats of my childhood, father, mother, offspring, our being also was one; each partaking in the nature of the other, though distinct in himself, was inconceivable apart, child entwined on parent, parent entwined on child, equal in a sway which, if less than majestic, at least prefigured the kingdom of this world, and haunts it forever. So was each of my parents haunted, but of this too I then understood nothing. When in the space of eighteen months my mother sat in her deathwatch at the bed of her mother and my father went to another of the city's islands for the body of his father, I could not know how much of themselves my parents saw in those coffins; nor till death unfathered and unmothered me would I look in myself for the leavings of our oneness. In my trinity it was the distinction in person only, the creation of self, which concerned me from eleven on, and in the flat on Washington Heights the deaths of my grandparents went by me as not my business.

A string of four rooms on the fifth floor back, the new apartment was of good light and cheer, but in our second month there Mary Dore died and some innocence went out of our lives, which took on a darker edge. In odd hours and corners for years to come my mother would encounter her loss, though her practice, as with her headaches and stomach upsets, was to "work it off" by attacking the household with dustrag and carpetsweeper. My father in his piano playing kept his fingers off all lovelost ballads. Piano, furniture, the bric-a-brac up again on dutch shelves, made the flat hardly distinguishable from its predecessor, but the two novelties in it significant of our rise, a wall telephone and a table radio, conspired over one such ballad—"All alone, by the telephone, waiting for a ring, a ting-a-ling"—to call tears into my mother's eyes at every broadcast; my sister or I would dash to switch it off. Though it was no grief of mine, after the old lady's death I kept a rosary under my pillow, greeting night and morn with a fingering around it which spared me each time another hundred days of hellfire, until I lost count, but guessed I was safe for at least half of eternity.

My mother was comforted that I lay thus in her company of angels, but it was only above the bed, I would lie underneath it when more mundane company heaped it with coats so I could study the ladies' legs. My image of the female anatomy was derived altogether from manikins in storewindows; though my sister and I inhabited one room, sleeping with our hands clasped across the gap between our beds, my mother was indefatigable in steering us out of each other's sight at clothes time; and my first glimpse of a young nude the summer I was thirteen—she was two, in somebody's yard—was a shock. I worried about that frontal cleft for years, believing my angle of erection was malformed. I saw each of my parents unclothed only once, on their deathbeds: my father was near comatose when, lifting his pelvis to change his pajamas, I averted my eyes from the modest digit that had sired me, for in the earlier weeks he "didn't want Billy to see" him, and one of my mother's last breaths, as I ministered to her fleshless flank with a hypodermic needle, was of regret that I had to "see everything". The law was bodily reticence.

Yet under it I had no boyhood rights, my mother scrubbed at me in the bath every Saturday night until I was pubescent, and when I was on my belly to practice my swimming stroke she blurted, "What are you doing?" in alarm that I was copulating with the bathtub. My parents each had a hollow try at preparing me for the other sex. In my eleventh year my mother told me posthaste that girls lacked a weewee, which corroborated the manikins; later, prone with schoolmates in the weeds of the Harlem bluffs, I spied on a couple parked in a car below, but could not see why, and in the excited aftertalk of beholding her "cop a feel of his and boy him with his hand on hers" it was on the tip of my tongue to cry out in a triumph of news, "She hasn't got one!" This datum was more than I gleaned from my father, who sat me down, advised me he "hadn't missed a thing", ran out of other advice, was inspired to suggest I bring him my questions, and assured my mother I "probably knew more than he did". I brought him no questions, though my ignorance was pansexual: I was into my teens when I walked by a policeman on a mount with a meaty dangler, and only my timidity saved me from warning him the horse had a dangerous leakage of entrails.

It was outside the flat that my education moved into higher gear, but not in school. I was a lusterless pupil, and of note in the classful only when, on a dare, I rang the deskbell in the teacher's absence and was put in the clothes closet, or had my jackknife confiscated while notching away at my desk lid; after some such lapse my mother, summoned to confer with my teacher, was chagrined to be told her son "does just what he has to and no more". I was unmoved by the indictment. The fact was that, once taught to read, I saw little further of interest in my school-

books or teachers, except down young Miss Fanning's neckline
when she bent over her desk; I was in a simmer of curiosity
about much, but none of it was in the curriculum, and I learned
nothing in school, from the parsing of sentences to the population of Thibet, that my bowels could make use of. I memorized
what grown-ups wanted me to memorize, sensing they were no
longer my helpers but adversaries. For true learning I was on my
own, and I was schooled in living matter by the boys I knocked
around the streets with after three o'clock.

In seventh grade I met a young worldling into whose light I
was to lean for years; that friendship fluttered up, not without a
shadow on my parents, in evening visits by the boy with his
violin and mother to our flat and piano. My parents had kept up
my lessons, conveying me from a young housewife in Jersey to
an old housewife in the Bronx to a young old maid in a brownstone conservatory on Washington Heights. I chafed under the
practicing my mother held me to, an hour a day by the alarm
clock she set atop the piano, and shortened it by advancing the
clockhands after each arpeggio; nonetheless I was soon promoted
by the director into the care of a male teacher with a behind-
the-hand whisper that I was "a whiz". I made my debut in a
students' recital before a pride of mommas, albeit so groomed by
mine that throughout my élégie the sole of my brand-new shoe
skidded regularly off the pedal in a percussive obbligato unantic-
ipated by the composer, and, hearing from my teacher that great
pianists never wore new shoes, I registered another black mark
against my mother. Of my musical flair, everyone said I "got it
from Irv", and it was true. While the mandolin to my mother's
hand was a kind of social escort, my father came to the piano as
to a mistress; every payday he "blew himself" to a thirty-
five-cent treat of whatever song hit was current, and up the stairs
made eagerly for the keyboard to "try it over"; this had been his
habit for two decades, and our piano top was burdened with a

tattered stack of sheet music on either side of the ten-volume set of salon masterpieces, complete with bookrack, that my parents had just purchased on weekly payments. It was this body of melody, from snappy foxtrots to artistic gypsy dances, that my new acquaintance with his fiddle and I at our upright struggled through in duet, two eleven-year-olds beamed upon by our elders in a weekly tableau of refined childhood.

In the streets we were less refined. I tailed after him in a clump of his cronies, a few classmates of twelve and thirteen who were self-chartered as a five-f club, findem, foolem, feelem, fuckem, forgetem, and to whose dialogue I could add nothing because I understood so little of it. We prowled the city, and in the subway they identified all the young women who by their gait had the clap, in the art museum they judged the sarcophagi would be good places wherein to jerk off, in the public swimming pool they were on the lookout for some schoolmate's pussy, and every term to me was a brainteaser; their vocabulary of strange sonorities, dong, twat, hump, hard-on, whoor, muzzle, muffdiver, bewildered my ear, but month after month I listened to their wit—"This kid sees his grown-up sister in the bathtub, points and says what's that, she's bashful, covers up with her hand, says well when I was a itsybitsy girl there was this bad man with an axe came and hit me there, her brother says jeez he hit you right in the cunt didn't he?"—and, laughing imitatively, took home from each opaque joke another crumb of fact about the world I was growing into. Too vain to risk questions, I waited for a fifth enigma to clarify a third. When the oldest boy left us on a streetcorner because he "had an appointment to jerk off at four", I tucked the mot away; another month, on my young friend's roof I climbed the ladder of the unused water tank to find him within dabbing toilet paper at his penis, and he said briefly he was taking a leak; the explanation cast no light on his being prepared with toiletries, but a good deal on the mot.

Why toilet paper was needed was a new enigma, to which my body offered as yet no answer.

My friend had a rare gift with a pencil, his drawings made him a celebrity in eighth grade, and with a gangful of our chins over his shoulders he created a throng of pantied doxies, all legs, bellies, breasts, buttocks, whose like I looked in vain for ever-after. Although too aristocratic to lend himself to raw fact—the arching phalli and vulval offerings on public toilet walls which I studied in lieu of my textbooks—he evolved a cartoon symbology in flagpoles, fire hydrants, chimneys, of the genital property of each boy in our group, excepting mine, a blow to the heart. He, they, I, tolerated me as a hanger-on. In winter we all journeyed eighty blocks to an indoor pool where they swam while I floundered in the shallow end; my sense of physical competence was in any case much cut into by a brace my parents had bought to correct my stooped shoulders, which I wore secretly to school every day under my shirt and in that locker room had to expose to their eyes; but it was my babyface groin that most humiliated me, the nudest in the shower, and I looked on enviously as each boy searched in his sprouting pubes for possible "crabs". Social rank among us was more or less a corollary of genital riches, and the idol of the flock, a golden athlete of fourteen whose portly penis was our bellwether, made it a custom to begin his day with a plunge in a cold tub. That winter my mother, who each night distributed my schoolclothes among our radiators to warm them, was incredulous to see me at dawn fill our bathtub from the coldwater faucet and spraddle on all fours above it for a quarter-hour of dread before I sank shudderingly in; I arose to my agony every morning throughout the eighth grade, hoping so to double my capital, though the evidence was obvious that it worked in reverse.

I was upborne to my friend's apartment by an elevator, and in his society I grew as alert to class as to sex differences. I was uneasy when I broke bread with him and his international parents, a French governess and an Italian chauffeur whose decades in service had endowed them with all the attributes of wealth except money; of uncertain income, they lived in a more expensive neighborhood near the Hudson, and my mother would dispatch me to it in my best suit from Wertheimer's, though the boy's was from Rogers Peet, and everything she rehearsed me to say was silenced by the worldly banter over my head at their table, and her instructions on how to eat my supper turned out to be unequal to what they called dinner; drilled against doing the wrong thing I ate in the sweat of my mother's brow, anxious from the first sip of cold soup, surely a mistake, through a gauntlet of unfamiliar forks and foods, to the last incomprehensible fact, cheese for dessert. In imitation of some actor the boy had practiced the art of lifting one eyebrow, and under it many of my pursuits turned gauche. I was deft at shooting immies with the kids on my block, winning fistfuls and selling them by the nickel's worth, a source of extra pocket money; each Thursday I lugged a canvas bag of five-cent magazines from headquarters in an older boy's flat to doorbell after doorbell; for a season I hawked chances to my schoolmates on punchboards I bought in the candystore, happily taking in and seldom paying out pennies, nickels, dimes on a hierarchy of ballplayers' names, and invested the profit from each punchboard in a grander one until, admiring under my schooldesk a two-dollar colossus, I was wiped out in one swoop by a teacher who expropriated it. In such ventures I felt my friend's eyebrow upon me like a princeling's upon a fellow in trade. I saw none of his cronies in a stir after pocket money, they all dwelt in apartments with elevators, to which I was not invited, and when on a call with him I spied in one youth's bureau a drawer brimful of nothing but socks—I had four or six, which my mother scrubbed on her washboard as I dirtied them—I thought it a practical joke; in a split second I guffawed, heeded their blank eyes, and grew older.

My parents were not insensitive to my growing pains. One summer afternoon my father, on encountering me alone at the corner, asked where everybody else was; I said they were in the drugstore over fifteen-cent marshmallow sundaes, which was true enough, and I was not because I only had a nickel, not true enough, I felt unwanted; but when my stricken father dug into his pocket and flipped a quarter into my catching hands, I raced off to the sundae. My mother perceived me as so vulnerable that she alluded to me always, even in the thick of fame and fortune, as "poor Billy". Throughout our childhood she confided to all how sorry she felt for me; my sister, watching her spoon into my open mouth most of the delectable "blood gravy" from the roastbeef as one of the boons I was favored with, could not see why.

A hundred times my father said, "Anything that's mine is yours," sharing with me whatever my eye fell upon, from his neckties to his last forkful of the lemon meringue pie my mother baked to his delight. When he flipped me a quarter it was out of his own pocket money, two or three dollars a week spared from the household for his cigarettes, sheet music, coffee at work; though my mother never in her life "hung up" a landlord for the rent she was no more than a dollar ahead of any payday, and reached many a first or fifteenth of the month on a fiver borrowed from her friend Nelie. It was a family disaster when in that flat my father came home from the mail-department boatride to break the news he had lost twenty-three dollars in a crap game, and he never again touched dice. For a few months he took on a second job as a salesman of fuel coke, spending in alternate weeks his offwork mornings or afternoons in a canvass of building owners to solicit orders, loathing it, and faring so little better than I with my five-cent magazines that my mother prevailed upon him to quit. Yet I never lacked my allowance—now a quarter, and in highschool a half-dollar—and however insolvent by Saturday noon I missed not one of a hundred chapters of movie serials that drew a bedlam of kids in a weekly rite; while there was a dime in my father's pocket, I had money.

Any chat with a salesman at the door revealed my father had more talent for buying than selling, but all my life it was truest of both my parents with wares intended, like the ten volumes of pianoforte favorites, for me. At nine I was smitten in a far store by a replica of a doughboy's rifle as tall as I, and my father hearing of my plight made a trip to buy it, bringing home a child's popgun, and I thanked him in a despair, the error seeming irremediable; he observed me, asked into the facts, herded me with the quarter popgun on a bus back to the store, and paid a dollar-fifty for the rifle I pointed out. At twelve I was smitten by the glamor of the Boy Scout uniform, and after I joined that sacred band was like to die until my parents took me shopping downtown at national headquarters, whence I emerged in official khaki from head to toe—scout hat, knotted scarf, double-pocketed shirt, canvas belt hung with five-bladed knife, pants tapering into wool stockings—and returned by subway to the tenements of Washington Heights with wilderness hatchet in hand; my mother "never bought herself clothes until something wore out". At fifteen I was smitten by the miracle of type, and on that passion they spent sixty dollars, more than a week's pay.

Their "spoiling" of me was a counterweight to my opinion of myself; when I ran with my father's quarter to the gang I felt of no account with, I was enriched not only by his coin. I took their love, gifts, homage, for granted. I was worthless and precious, was nothing, was all, and in the growth of my distinction in person their bequest of vanity was the bread I lived on through the lean years of self-distaste. It led me each year further from them into a cloudland where I was supreme, the solitude of books.

I was now so rapt a reader that my mother would advise me in Dore parlance to "get out and blow the stink off" me, though with misgivings. I played stickball in the gutters with neighborhood kids in between autos—thrilled with mystic power when one of my uncle Ben's ice vans with its team clopped through—and shot checkers on the sidewalks and ran in the connecting cellars until the janitors charged us out; this neighborhood was dense with buildings, and the kids included a species new to me, called jooz. Of these my mother was suspicious, she told me that in spite of all appearances their underwear was dirty. Her model was a gamin named Izzie who inhabited our stoop, eating the pickings of his nose; one afternoon in a chase I leaped down a stairflight and opened my scalp on the steps overhead, and with my family gone it was Izzie's momma who took me in, cleansed and bandaged my bloody skull, and sat me still until my own mother, home with groceries in a dismay, rushed me to the doctor for stitching; thereafter she took a brighter view of the underwear. On mine, she cautioned me often that I never knew when I might be hit by a car and taken unconscious to the hospital, as though to be seen in soiled underwear there would be the climax of the disaster. Yet she had reason to worry, in streetplay I did much more than "just what I had to", and not infrequently was in the doctor's office as a by-product of my enthusiasm. Ben's daughter recalled me as "a pain in the behind, you'd no sooner go out the door than you were in trouble"; in football I tackled not necks but legs and harvested a faceful of heelmarks, I impaled a lollipop stick in my palate, more stitches, I caught baseball directly behind the batter and regularly got hit in the teeth with the bat, and I dashed over an idle tricycle in a sidewalk landing that broke my wrist, on which I wore a gallant cast for weeks. When I abandoned these small adventures for the grand ones in books I was equally headlong, and read in my corner deaf to mother, father, sister, visitors, and every summons to supper. It was not now a flattery to them: my mother had a dream that while seated outside a window washing it she lost her balance, screamed to me to save her, and I mumbled from a book, "Wait till I finish this chapter."

I see now it was intolerance of myself; I was not reading so much as laying upon this pimple of my smallness, that bruise of my cowardice, this boil of my asexuality, the unguent exuded in every chapter by the puissant souls I put on for an hour. I acquired them for fifteen cents in the candystore, pulp-paper magazines of western, sports, "amazing" stories, a dime extra for interplanetary travel. I lent and borrowed a hundred paperbacks about a Yale athlete who was world's champion of everything, and so baffling a pitcher with his "doubleshoot", which curved twice around the bat, that the tales turned only on whether he could make his way onto the field through the gamblers who daily drugged him. One of my father's bricklayer buddies told me I had "a very imaginary mind" and put into my hand the initial book of a cycle in which I kept company with the most inspiring creature yet, an English lord who was reared as an ape, combining the best traditions of each. My young worldling introduced me to a first hero of the intellect, the rational sleuth of Baker Street, plus other detectives who constituted half the population of London. I worried over the persistent plots of a Chinese fiend to destroy the world, spent much of my school-time in retrospect among dinosaurs at the earth's core, and happily would have died as a beau geste in the French foreign legion with my heart broken by my seatmate Edie Finkelstein but for her eyeglasses. I became aware of style over an author I delighted in, but hard to come by, who chronicled in slang the rise of various prizefighters dubbed "leather pushers", and that Christmas under our tree I was stopped in my knee tracks by a pile of glossy books, his complete works, from my father to his "bookworm".

Yet his ambition was to see me distinguished as a big-league ballplayer, and he too ordered me to "go downstairs and play like a regular kid"; I took to the roof. I pursued my reading first on the top steps above our landing. My mother smelled me out and directed me down from there; my habit then was to squat with my book in a roof corner out of the wind, but my mother would search among the chimneypots till she uncovered me, and directed me down from there; finally I scaled the wall of the skylight housing, and unseen on my private roof above the roof lay in gravel reading throughout all her reconnoitering. Possibly she was so intent on having me in the street because she suspected I was masturbating, which I was, though in some innocence. In my desire for muscles I used a clothesline brace on our roof as a chinning bar, writhing my body up in a shudder to lift my nose triumphantly over, and the strain at my loins invited the same itch that had kindled in my glans upon the rope, but fiercer, until a convulsion liberated it in a sweet if wordless utterance; I would stagger back to my book more worn out than built up by this physical culture, and day after day my chinning improved. The rooftop was my hideout, gym, reading room till winter closed it down, though I remember even then huddling at the skylight in my sheepskin coat with a magazine on my thighs, fists in pockets, blowing into my fingers to turn a page.

So it was that my grandfather died unnoticed by me. I had little to do with him in any case; he was rarely with my father's mother on her annual visit to us for a week—a respite for my aunt Ethel, a doubling-up in beds for us—and it was she whose image lingered in the rocker afterwards, obese, whitehaired, massively handsome, rocking, rocking; my grandfather was somehow without echo in our four rooms. My father captioned a snapshot of the aged couple seated on a bench as "best in the world", but he was a minority in that opinion of his father, the old man was a stranger not just to me.

He was head of the family in name only, Pop Gibson, and in name too he had his difficulties. As a widower in courtship he had been "Mr. Gibson" to his intended and "that man" to her daughters Milly and Ada, then pubescent; my grandmother-to-be at twenty-nine was making chemises by hand for seventy-five cents a dozen, her three children were boarded out, and the girls crammed their mouths with Mr. Gibson's ice-cream cones and candies indignantly—"he only wants us to like him"—until he moved them all into a Harlem flat; his new wife then addressed him intimately as "Gibson" but for weeks the girls refused him all name. At last she ordered them to "call him something", and in their recoil from terming him father they grumpily settled upon "Pop". The poverty of widowhood had not impaired Katherine Gibson's sense of coming from good stock, her first husband had been an engineer, and my cratemaking grandfather thus began the marriage against odds, outnumbered by females and a ghost; he never overcame them, and seemed "not part of" his family, a humble man fallen among good women.

Brooklyn born, he was then thirty-seven years old and a member of a temperance society that fortified itself in military uniform, but he changed his mind. The saloons notwithstanding, he was a "good worker" and provider, with his own shop; the cratemaking he had learned as a child from his immigrant father. Orphaned at thirteen in the midst of the Civil War, he had grown to manhood both self-sufficing and in some way dwarfed. He drifted out of touch with his sisters; his two children by his first wife lived with in-laws, and he never took a step to see them, though when they came to his shop in need of a pair of shoes he was "terribly generous" with money; he spent most of his second marriage behind a newspaper with pipe or stogie, and none of his children sat on his lap. Not unkindly, he lived with some indifference in the region of his heart which I felt when he visited us, but I had missed him in his lost loves, his whitehaired boy Jim and his stepson Will, whom he taught his trade and was "crazy about". What he taught my father was his placation by generosity—established early, for at eight the boy Irv's first act toward the newborn Ethel was to bring her his piece of bread as a present—and in his middle years of salooning he would come home repentant with cakes, like his son later after a tantrum; my father too was the legatee of his looks. But Pop Gibson was fierce with a fanged straw mustache which belied him, no one was to remember him as other than "quiet, a very quiet man" even in his illness.

Its sign was a bloody discharge from the anus, not a middle-class symptom, and voices were lowered when mentioning it after thirty-five years; it was no fitter for conversation then, and the hemorrhages went on untended for a year or two, the old man was dying without a word. He was tired, and at seventy-five put away his hammer. He had been nailing crates and boxes for sixty years, and throughout our own stay in Jersey was a watchman for a sugar refinery on the Hudson, leaving Ethel's house at five-thirty every morning to make his way there; but he was losing blood, and though in the snapshots his hands were beautiful as ever, bony, lank-fingered, loose on a hip, the toll was in his slack face, the old pate bald, eyes sunken behind the rimless spectacles, his stogie and piratical mustache in a listless droop. He quit the refinery to rest, his only income now the monthly check which the government mailed in recompense for the life of his favorite boy. When Ethel's husband conceived of moving to Trenton without his wife's parents the crisis took my father back to Jersey for a tribal parley, and the old couple waited while their children decided what to do with them; they were given to Milly.

There in his stepdaughter's house, while I was chinning myself into birth, my grandfather went about his end. Duller each month, he slept on a couch most of the day, and my grand-mother would say impatiently, "Gibson, get up and do something." In the mornings he still arose early, to garb himself in a dark suit and collarless shirt—on Sundays he put on a wing collar, but by afternoon it was always unbuttoned and flapping loose at each ear—and after breakfast he shuffled downstreet in his high shoes, bought the newspaper, shuffled back, and retired with it to his couch, where he "thought he was reading but he was asleep"; a chronic inflammation on his wrist bothered him, and the rest of his routine was dosing it with a liniment he prescribed for himself. My grandmother said, "All I hear is Gibson's snoring and all I smell is Sloan's liniment," and off she went to Trenton for adventure. Days later Pop would say to Milly, "When's your ma coming home?" and, being told, mutter in a rare moment of demonstrativeness, "Be glad to see her." It was evident now that ignoring his hemorrhages would not discourage them, his womenfolk felt they should "do more", and Pop was brought across the river to be examined in a New York hospital a trolley ride from our flat; here his illness was diagnosed as cancer of the rectum, and two weeks later he was dead.

The two weeks were an indignity like a mock crown on that old passive skull. In the middle of the night Pop lost his way in the corridors between ward and toilet, and was frightened into confusion, and next day found himself in an ambulance that debouched him into a more bewildering labyrinth; it was Belle-vue, he was there for psychiatric scrutiny and confined in isolation from the family because the inflammation on his wrist was contagious, erysipelas, so no recognizable face appeared in the dusk of his perplexity; he was moved next to Ward's Island, a nook for the insane, and as soon as my father set foot upon it a doctor advised him the troublesome hand should be amputated. My father in disbelief said, "The man is dying and you want to cut off his hand?" As the family's city man my father "did all the running", watched the old man in bed through the glass of a door, and came home that week in a distress I overheard in his talk with my mother, but thought less noteworthy than my book. Immured on this alien island, suddenly, as if by consent, Pop Gibson, who had yielded so much of himself into other hands and lay now among madmen, died.

The funeral arrangements were made by my father. The wing-collared body awaited visitors in the mortuary in Harlem where, three years before, the black gathering of family had been in leavetaking of his stepson Will. My whitehaired grandmother said, "See if they took off his hand"—a whispered question, submissive, born half a century earlier when as Kate she had aspired to Katherine and that worthy deference to authority which was become the backbone of the family, middle class, and nation—and my father contemplated in the coffin the cadaverous fingers whose splayings upon boxes and crates had fed so many children, our last workingman, and told his mother the hands were intact. On the third day the corpse was placed in a hearse and taken by ferry back across the river, late April, and all the cemetery unbudding, while my father stood and saw the long box with its contents, once his father, interred in the Jersey clay.

What my father's thoughts were, his feet at the edge of that pit, I never heard; eleven years later I would know. Disappearing under the shovelfuls of loose earth was mind that had created him, it had been before him, it had dwelt over him year after year like light at every opening of his eyes, surely it was immortal, and all between father and son, past, present, future, was therefore alterable, and in proper time the trinity would be restored when the young angel who had fallen from it to be distinct in person came to redeem the lost oneness with a crowning word of love, and instead my father stood in a cemetery where nothing ever could be altered, the word unspoken, as the shovelfuls of dirt covered a dead ear in that last and utter alienation. A portion of my father, nurturing only in that mind, was buried with it, yet henceforth he would live too with an accession of mind, deepened, haunted, enriched, and more father now. Not all the light that had been the mind, flesh, soul of Pop Gibson was gone, some in descent was flickering in his son, and through him, like the flicker of Mary Dore through my mother, had been lit again in me, and as a bequest through me to my unborn boys it would descend the twigs of our family, burning, a poor immortality, always in change and dark to itself, but indestructible as the buds of the cemetery that aboveground were opening, and is yet to be among the flickerings in the heads of my children's children; and so runs this world without end, free souls all.

Two months later I graduated from elementary school at the head of the line, though in a ranking only by inverse height, and moved a summer deeper into that escape from the household, and dream of escape from the authorities, which was my adolescence.

20. Burning Bush

Of winter's kill
Shrieking
Primal as the unlit air
Is still
At last. Twigs
Bone
Brittle, and every bud
Stricken
Dead black as a
Blown
Matchhead, this, a bare
Gray
Stick in the mud
Of April
At our road, is done.

Red
Maple it was, a
Cry
Up from the burial floor
Growing
Bright as a stain,
Bog

Wild. Its rooted clot
    In my arms
   I with its small
    Green
Pith and scarlet head
    Brought
   Live for a fall
    Candelabra
Home; it would in my whim
    Burn
   Huge in our chill
    October
Night and knock of limb
    Going.

   Well, it will not.
    Half
Of summer ends, its garb
    A mood
   I—almost—buy
    Of dust
To dust, and some I love
    Rot
   Eyeless to sun
    Or dark;
Breakdown in our flare
    Is all
   I now discern,
    A drift
To ash. In time this dried
    Bean
   Earth will drop.

Almost.
Down at my doubting thumb
Thrust
Into its side
To lift
Out of our eye this barb,
A snuffed
Straw in the wind,
Dumb
Founded I see the wit
Flowing
Under the world
Sweat
Its will into the glove
Of bark,
And graywood skin
Unmeant
For any brood of twig,
But set
A deathbed chore,
Emit
Droplets of bastard bud
Violet
Keen. Ejaculate
Leaf,
Flame out, crotch and fork,
Soar
It will, it will.

20. Burning Bush

Sprig,
Go up like prayer, primal
As breath
In winter's kill
Of mine,
Putting forth such tongues
At death.

CONFITEOR

21. And Began with Goodbye

With graduation I declined to wear my shoulder brace, I banished my mother from my bathtub, and I told my father that henceforth we would forgo all kissing and shake hands like men; he agreed, with his wry smile. Mortality was in his thoughts, for he observed that it was up to me to "carry on the name of Gibson", it would die out if I had no sons. I was not only ignorant as to which part of woman to begin them upon, my courting habits were odd: when intrigued by the bodice of a girl next door, I closed in on it by racing around the block to get ahead of her, so that in every walk she would pass me leaning casually against a lamppost on four successive corners. In any case, family seemed a tedium to break out of, not reproduce, and its bosom was no substitute.

Its symbol was any Sunday afternoon when, in my church-going suit like prison garb, I saw along all the baking pavements of the neighborhood under the sun nowhere to run, and trudged upstairs. My father after six days of work enjoyed his Sunday. He spent it with bare feet among the scatterings of the newspaper, fiddling at the radio—at first with earphones, coaxing voices out of a wire jiggled on a crystal, but later at the knobs of a "superheterodyne" with a curved speakerhorn for all—and cooling his palate with our private stock of root beer; my mother concocted it for us in the kitchen, of extract, water, yeast, capping some fifty bottles which were stored in a floor cupboard until tingly. In pants and undershirt my father, parked in the rocker with an iced glass of it in hand, his heels on the sill of the back window overlooking the heatwaves in the gulf of uptown Broadway while the radio emitted its crackle, would "tell the world" that he "wouldn't swap with Rockefeller". My mother with no such talent for leisure zigzagged all day about the flat, baking, sweeping, bedmaking, darning, but in the evening her pleasure was to sit on the rooftop with my father, in a ring of neighbors who bore their kitchen chairs up, and cushions for their elbows when they hunched along the parapet to spy on the silent open-air movie a block away upon a lower roof. On other Sundays my uncle Ben would turn up at noon in a new sedan, pack everyone in, and drive us via the ferry into a Jersey world as staid as a sewing circle to visit my father's mother, but these outings took me not an inch further on my road, which led somewhere back through the thickets of Ben's chuckling profanities to a bossier grandmother. It was out of family sentiment that summer, when I was practicing with my beebee gun against a dumbwaiter housing on the roof and my sunny sister skipped up to order me below, that somehow I shot her in the back.

I looked to highschool life in the fall for glamor, and in the interim manufactured what I could with a pencil. I had kept up a habit of writing in notebooks, false starts of narrative, done of a winter's evening at our kitchen table or on the rooftop in summer, imitative of whatever I was reading; begun in an enthusiasm of mood and aborted in a poverty of content, these entries were for the most part a solitary hobby, though a few times I talked one boy or another into collaborations doomed by the difficult ghost of Mary Dore. Since at each inspiration I ripped out the old failure in front, with a loss of new pages in back, I progressed through an ever flimsier notebook to a pageless cover as my collected works. The accrual was in me.

I was perfecting an interior escape, and was brother to all dumb animals in bondage. In late August when my father led us out of the city into his annual vacation—in poorer times to his folk in Jersey, but now to beach or lake in cabins so impure that my mother devoted the two weeks to housecleaning—I sat in a rowboat with men from dawn till noon, caught the only fish, and all afternoon pondered it in a zinc tub in our cabin, suspended, a captive soul, mute, dreaming no doubt of unseen reaches; and at last toting it a block back to the lake I spilt it free, to partake of its darting elation away. I struck out into the eddies of higher education the following week.

It took me out of the household, though I found myself more at sea than I had wished. For three weeks I travelled by subway to an annex far up in the Bronx, where I sat in a roomful of stalwarts who were relearning seventh-grade arithmetic; the highschool proper, a dozen blocks from our flat, enjoyed a city-wide fame for its football teams and pregnant coeds. I had chosen it to be with my young worldling, and to my misery now discovered he was miles away at another high, populated by the brightest boys in the city. It was too late to transfer, my school record might not even admit me, but my mother asked Ben to help; her brother was then in his prime of influentiality, a pillar of church and state, though on occasion wobbly, slipping a twenty to the priest when the parish house could not pay a plumbing bill and so heartily getting the Tammany vote out that everyone in his household cast a ballot for Al Smith, including the under-aged girls. Ben took my scholastic problem to the wardheelers. Ungrateful in equal measure to mother, uncle, politicians, all doing only their duty by me, I was invited downtown to the principal's office to have my intelligence looked at, and in a few days I was reunited with my friend in a classful of boys conversing in algebra. The highschool was housed in the city college whose Gothic spires I had seen in the sky a decade ago from Mary Dore's window, and, as its preparatory school, herded us through four years of work in three; throughout highschool I ran after my class three weeks late—I fought my way out of algebra to see them deep in geometry, as soon as I made sense out of French they were gabbling Spanish—and was in a cerebral fog until my expulsion from college.

Ingratitude to my mother was daily fare. At my freshman physical a doctor took a dislike to my foreskin, one of the few in school, and sent word home by me to have it circumcised. I was for several days unable to mention to my mother an item of my anatomy I thought taboo even when in faultless condition, but she was more realistic about me than I about her, and presently I was seated with her in a mobbed depot which was a hospital clinic. It was semicharitable; she had been coming to it with her own ailments for three years and would continue for another thirty-three; it cost her fifty cents a visit, an annual understatement of her husband's income at a time when on highschool forms I was putting down his occupation as "banker", and years of awaiting her turn on benches. Though we arrived early to be ahead of the crowd, so had everyone, and my mother sat with numbered tag in hand all day beside me in that muster of the sick and poor in their lumpy overcoats, bandaged heads, splinted arms, brown cheek and white and yellow, from infants at the breast to spectral old men visibly dying, who waited beastlike, not talking, not reading, waited in a sodden silence, the undead whom I would not be like. It was not until our return the second morning that my number was reached. I undressed in a back room and lay sheeted on an operating slab; offered by the surgeon a choice of anesthetic or no, as my mother's lad I of course said no, I was more worried about his nurse who would see my penis unless she closed her eyes while assisting, probably her custom in such cases, but the first touch of the knife overthrew that worry in an arching of my belly at the ceiling; I could stifle my outcry but not my heaves from the scalpel, and someone smothered my face in a bowl of darkness. I came to with my hand in my mother's, she sat to minister where I lay in a lower bunk with my groin a bloody calamity, her overlarge eyes upon me in a compassion I was not to take in until paternity a generation later widened my own pupil. Impervious to all the solicitude of her fingers, I was nauseated by the ether and cannot remember but know she supported my brow while I vomited into a basin, and when I was able to stand she helped me into my clothes, and I hobbled on her arm to a streetcorner where she found us a taxicab—a rare vehicle in our lives, the fare cost more than the operation—and in our apartment house she maneuvered my painstaking steps up the five flights to our door, and then helped me out of my clothes into my bed, and there her fatigueless hands brought me meals, and ungauzed, dressed with vaseline, regauzed my pursy member, and time and again emptied the milk bottle which was its urinal: ingrate, what I see most unforgettably is the afternoon of my aunt Milly's visit when my mother asked would I mind unveiling my penis, and I refused in a hatred of her.

So, when all winter long she pried into my mouth spoonfuls of whatever bottle of fish oil or tonic she was currently counting on to prolong her poor Billy's life, I judged her only hobby was poisoning me. My grain was forming after hers, assimilating each of her favors, but any deed against it was unforgivable. I lost with the foreskin a fourth week of algebra, the teacher tutored me in a deserted classroom, and at Christmas my mother in thanks bought him a thirty-cent necktie, which I bore to him in her tissuepaper and ribbon; it never left my hand, he said what's this, I said a present, he said oh he couldn't take presents from students, and I fled in mortification down the hall with the gift which, so customary in gradeschool, was here a bribe, a faux pas, a stigma of immaturity, foisted upon me by an ignoramus. And of such minutiae now, unseen by me in two smaller heads, my effigy as a parent is accretive.

To reproach me for ingratitude was not in my mother's book, she was too "independent", but at a price I too was to pay. Of a cramped intelligence—in the lifelong cascade of her talk I never heard her utter an abstract thought—she was in a fixed state of alarm at the complexities of the world, but of old, it was in her marrow, she paid it no mind, her true intelligence was of another nature and shrewd to her talents, for long ago she had drawn a household circle and within it expended her wealth of hyperthyroid energies to make of it a fortress; while she was on the roof, thrashing the dirt out of her rugs upon the clothesline, or at the sink, knuckling steel wool into her pots until all their bottoms bulged out—after her death I inherited a few and among our pots that bottom is unmistakable, her signature—or on her bony knees, scouring the linoleum to "get at the corners" that no mop could subdue, her fate was in her hands. It was a solitary power, but she had learned from Mary Dore not to share it, and was at nobody's mercy. Except of course her own, the price my mother thus exacted of her hands was infallibility, and she found her errors so nerve-racking that she never dropped a cup with me in the kitchen but she observed as a reflex, "Now see what you made me do." I in turn blamed her when my shoe skidded off every pedal. I had reason enough, for her knuckles were in me like steel wool in the pots until I gleamed inside and out, reflecting her face, but I too bulged. From the hour when I was held wobbling on the toilet at three months I had been to school with her in the rigors of control, and her rulebook of self-help bred me to exactions of myself as harsh as hers; all my life the notch below infallibility was humiliation, and my schoolyear ended in it.

I tried out for the freshman baseball team, rather to my young worldling's disgust, and cracked out a fly to the fence which

won me instant stardom; I was tentatively set for second baseman like my father's idol who slid headlong. It was the only ball
I hit all spring, rumor soon had me in a "slump" with another
boy a favorite to replace me, my glove rose to the challenge by
becoming too nervous to retain any ball hit at it, and when the
team was named I was not. I brought the miserable news home to
my father in sobs, insisting I was "better than the other guy",
lying and not lying, some weakling in me had undone my best;
like my mother I would discover my weaknesses were my iron
mine, but I had no forevision of it. I watched thereafter with
hungry eye my friend achieve an urbane popularity, busy with
school publications, dramatics, fencing, but I tried out for nothing, not again would I brave a failure in open ground. I too was
drawing a circle for my keep.

That spring took my parents into their fortieth year. My
mother was not hale, the hospital clinic to which she confided
her ills—the record speaks of her "epigastric pain, nausea and
vomiting"—had two years ago proposed surgery on the goiter in
her throat, but she was fearful of the knife. On his fifty dollars a
week my father, now an assistant foreman in charge of one of
the two shifts which alternated weeks of nightwork, decided she
needed a summer at the beach. He led us back to a hamlet on
Staten Island, like salmon: in his bachelor days my father and his
cronies had been wont to clambake there, something I did not
know, and in my own twenties I found my way to it again with
the girl who was to be the mother of his grandsons, innocent that
where our lovemaking was done the bare feet of his ancestors
had left their mark too in the sands, not yet trafficked by the
British massing to take New York. A mile from the church in
which his grandfather had been baptized, something he did not
know, my father rented for us a clapboard bungalow, of kitchen,
two bedrooms, living room, screened porch, a block and a half
inland on a dirt lane with hedges, trees, and grassy

yards. For him it meant three months in which he left or arrived in the small hours of the night, travelling by ferry away from the skyline lights of the city, by train into the dark of the Island, and by lonely bus or foot the last two miles to our hamlet, but by daylight he enjoyed the sight of his family at their happiest summer in years.

It was not evident to the camera that I was fading from view. Half an album of snapshots survives of that sunlight—though hardly any with our bungalow as background, everyone posed at the next house because it "looked nicer"—in which my face is a surprise, as outbubbling with glee as a parent could wish; my sister and I were much in swimsuits, tan, carefree, healthy, a sturdy girl of nine with blonde bangs whose stance is self-contained and assured of its center of gravity, and a thin boy with sleek pompadour whose limbs are now lengthening out, less certain, in a gangly bravado of hands on hips with legs apart, grinning. I learned to swim there, it "gave me confidence", which was unsettled by the playmate we swam with. She was a junoesque redhead not yet fourteen with breasts like beachballs, which, since she towered above me, were always in my eye; it was in their defense that her parents urged her upon us, fearful of their fate if she swam with older boys, but over the snapshots thirty years later someone remembered that my father too "could never get over that girl's figure", and I, using a doorway lintel in the bungalow, redoubled my chinning. It never occurred to me that my father's hunger might be identical with mine, or mine a renewal of something in my parents which in the dark backward had lifted me into human light, and their management of it after my sister's birth remains an enigma. From the age of thirty my mother was under a deadly prohibition of childbearing, but my sister thought they "would never" have used contraceptives, and my mother's only word to her was that my father and she had "lost interest" in such things "at the same time"; that shade is drawn. In a beach snapshot they lie with their bare limbs affectionate, my father relaxed on his side and one elbow, his free hand yoking my mother lightly by the nape, while she sits half upon his knee, awkward with fingers against him in that alertness to some peril which tenses her shoulders even in repose. The years together have improved them. My father has lost half his hair and a callow gawkiness, his face is more capable, fuller, contemplative with that goodwill which is becoming its beauty; my mother is no longer a timid stick, she has emerged at forty into a swimsuit declarative of her better-fed thighs and flatted chest, and she lolls on the beach with a smile not so carefully made. But when the sunlight catches her throat it molds in shadow the goiter there like a half-swallowed golfball.

It protruded more after that summer's retreat, for the snapshots record the procession of guests that prompted my father to observe we were "running a hotel"; they came to us out of every corner of our past, and from all of them I felt each year more estranged. Here is my father's lineage in the flesh of his white-haired mother on the beach, monumental in a shapeless black sack concealing her knees but not the false kneecaps that lard her limbs down to the ankles, and the handsome arrogance that tilted her chin when she sat with Pop Gibson is done, her face is diffident now, much aged; here is her daughter Milly stout in a summer dress on the sand and at her elbow the thin vestryman her husband, whom she first met in church, ten years younger and so severe a protector that after his death Milly "didn't know how to put a stamp on a letter"; and here is their boy who like our aunt Ada will be a missionary, taller alas than I but behind me in school, so since he cannot understand it I converse with him in French. Here in a rival lineage my aunt Minnie poses with my mother in twin housedresses that one sister has bought for both, their custom, wherewith the resemblance ends. Minnie's face is heavily powdered and lipsticked, her hair "bleached" against her years, not in vain, though they are cruelly seen when she stands in her bathing suit, a battered figure with doughy legs and "beer belly" and breasts long surrendered to time; the swart runt with arm around her neck is her husband and junior, not so severe a protector, who was obsessed by her refusal to tell him her age and in his cups inquired into it with clouts, so that at three in the morning our doorbell would ring and there always was Minnie, her facepowder undone by tears. And here is the girlhood unlived by my mother in the flesh of Ben's baby, seventeen, her face pert, displaying on her hip in a swimsuit a shapely torso that early next year will be heavy with child; she has been graduated from the nuns by fiat after Ben negotiated it with the priest and is keeping company with a ne'er-do-well, one night a winter past she dragged me through the Harlem streets to spy on him in a tennis court iceskating with another minx, but she will marry him in sufficient time and then a few others, my liveliest cousin; and while she pursues her self her two daughters with fathers vanished will be raised by their grandmother, as she was raised by hers, precisely as in time she will raise her daughters' children, three generations of almost motherless offspring faithful to the family ways Flo Dore would not perpetuate. The facts were plain, I saw my mother in a tryst of culinary decorum with Milly while my father went to the prizefights on ringside passes with his pal Ben, and taking in the traditions each of my parents had declined, but married in the other, I had my doubts about both.

And here on the shore is the throng of others, odd friends of relatives, and my mock aunts and uncles such as my mother's placid schoolmate, safe now in a tight bathing cap, and the bricklaying giant whose baritone roared at our piano in its travels from the honeymoon flat to the house my father died in, and our neighbors old and new, from the el gateman in his galluses out of my infancy on the tar road to the golfer in knickers with his clubs out of the next door in Washington Heights, and their assortment of wives, small children, grown children, swains, even their in-laws; of only those caught by the camera I count more than twenty for whom in that bungalow my mother kept house. My father would expostulate that she was "in the kitchen making big meals and everybody else swimming", but it gave her pleasure, housekeeping was her art and the guests her public, she discouraged none. She carried in so many bagloads of groceries that the tubby widow in the next house who was our landlady—and inhabits the album too, delighted to be included in the unexpected social swirl around her bungalow—was moved to toddle over and urge loans of food money upon my mother.

Its true cost appeared in the city, hand in hand with the choice I was to make between life and language. That fall my mother again consulted the clinic, which recorded her thyroid as "increased in size, with throbbing sensations, nervousness, tremor, tachycardia". My father did much of the housework, coming home from the bank to parade the carpetsweeper around, sit in windows with a wipecloth and basin, tie on an apron to wash the supper dishes, take a bar of cleanser to scour the oven, toilet-bowl, woodwork, and pump his arms in the lathery tubful of our soiled clothes; my sister and I with rag and lemon oil polished the furniture, and the fancy armchair of mahogany veneer with floral carvings that is so odd a personage in my planked work-room here, gray with the dust of two summers, was familiar with my dustrag twice a week when I crawled from chair leg to table leg to chair leg to rid us of every speck that threatened my mother's fortress; the wall telephone rang so often with friends about to "drop in" that my father, to spare her the bustle of further entertaining, had it extirpated. None of this help lessened my mother's labors, it simply freed her to scrub the ceilings, but in midwinter she disappeared from the household.

The scalpel that had left my glans so sensitive I could never sit into bathwater without a shudder had not likewise unskinned my wits. In the hospital where she had kept as intent a watch over me as over my sister in diphtheria, my mother lay in a ward, her throat to be opened for the surgeon to cut out the goiter; my sister and I, for children are poor in love, gave her little thought. The decision had been taken "in a hurry, her windpipe was closing," but my mother first insisted on two days at home—a need whenever she entered a hospital—to houseclean, she would not leave an imperfect house behind her. It was an operation she dreaded, not without reason, so uncommon when she underwent it at twenty-seven that her surgeon had been "the only doctor in the country who did that type of work", and he was now dead; then she had asked for extreme unction if needed, which the church denied because she "wouldn't give up her husband and child", and my father now went with her request again to a church near the hospital, and met another refusal, but brought back a priest to sit with her.

I never knew how close to death the knife cut. Ben's older girl, a nurse in training, visited her after surgery and said she was "very, very bad"; that night the hospital suggested my father phone her closest kin to come, so at ten o'clock Ben joined him at her bed. It occurred to no one to call her brother George in the "most expensive home in Larchmont", and Minnie was at two other beds, where my sister and I slept oblivious to the gathering in our flat of friends who awaited my father's homecoming with news. The crisis passed with that night. For eleven days then my mother mended in the ward while Minnie took her place with us; my father was at the hospital daily, and years later among my mother's mementoes I found a fat packet of convalescent cards all from him, a word to his "hon" once or twice every day in between visiting hours, and a few with the tonic signatures of her two youngsters, done under his eye.

And of all this I remember nothing. In with the snapshots I see a namecard my mother saved from a wallet, which in my lost handscript identifies me, and its backside testifies the wallet was awarded to her boy as first prize in a short-story contest of the highschool literary society; the date, soon after her discharge from the hospital, tells me where my love was.

I had by now solved my problem of content by borrowing that of famous authors. I retold their tales in my words, and submitted them as English compositions; no one advised me that imitation so enlarged was plagiarism, and when the literary club—I had sidled into its meetings to listen to talk about books—announced a story contest my entry was a rather conspicuous loan from the front page of the magazine in that Sunday's newspaper. Its hero was a doughboy who braced a bombed dugout on his back until his comrades could crawl out between his legs, then died in collapse, a sacrifice which, with its echoes of our legendary Jim, moved me to make it mine, the more so as I had no intention of ever putting myself in such a position, my soul was already that of a man of letters, and while my mother lay unworthy of my remembrance under the knife I was in tears over this never-to-be-forgotten whimsy of no greater love, which I reworked into one of an outlaw who saved his pursuers thus in an abandoned mine. Read aloud to the society meeting, like all the entries, it was promptly denounced by a senior as "stolen". Though I took the floor to deny this, my entrails were blushing with insight into the proprieties of self-delineation, and I withdrew the story; before the week was out I wrote another, something less personal about cowboys but "made up", with which I re-entered the contest. The faculty adviser adopted it as the prizewinner, possibly on moral grounds, and presented me with the wallet. Like the story it was not imperishable, and all that remains of both is the pasteboard treasured by my mother as a keepsake of her boy and his triumph; but I was identified more fatefully than by a namecard. The circulation among fellow students of my piece in the club's newspaper, mimeographed, with errata, was my first publication, and with it the gate of my keep clanged shut.

I and my parents heard never a creak; fifteen days after surgery my mother, in character, was in the midst of packing again, we were leaving the city, moving up in life to a pleasanter apartment where my father "thought the Long Island air would be better for her", and among the household belongings that went into the van that iron gate was invisible to all. I was now to inquire into my whereabouts from behind it. I was fourteen, in the dark, feeling with my feet for a plank across a bog of timidities, onto some rock of liking for myself, not imaginary, but set in other minds; in that gymnastic the task of my teens, though I conceived of it as escape, was to recreate in me a parental wedding of contrarieties, the impulsiveness of my father, which I saw in my mother's kin, to the orderliness of my mother, which I saw in my father's; and for that I wanted time and a hidingplace, my instinct was to be neither poor in myself nor exposed in society, it had a fancy for both the prodigal ore of mistakes and the steel wool of revisions. Plank, wedding, hidingplace, I found it all in wordplay. Behind its gate I was once more king of a block, albeit unpeopled, my only subjects were fragments of myself, and the coin of the realm was soliloquy. I had resigned from the trinity, and the namecard my mother saved for thirty-three years, unlike the convalescent cards of my father, was a promissory note; I could love no one until I had earned my self-love, and a rebuilt typewriter they bought me was the charger on which I would ride out again, but not to them.

22. Jingle

Heavy of heart and light of purse
    Makes this verse.

Yet loose of foot and tied of tongue
    More than I
In thicker hells and thinner skins
    Live and die

Twisted in means, and strait in end
    Have no lung
To air such cries: and what is sorrow
    Being sung?

Heavy of heart and light of purse
    Is no curse.

23. Cogitatione, Verbo, et Opere

In thought, word, and deed, I now floundered like sand through the fingers of my parents, so that my growing was another kind of death for them, yet I grew, through my fault, through my fault, through my most grievous fault, into that quantity I was to think of as myself until, some three years and two apartments later, on a wretched night in my midteens, I told my father we "simply had nothing in common".

My mother had cooked a dinner for my best, if sole, friend—the young worldling with whom we were all in love, I so much that his suave voice was a frequent visitor in my throat and my father, mildly vexed, advised me to "get my own style"—and as part of the after-dinner amenities I threw a half-eaten apple at my mother. It was my conception of aplomb, I said I would if she didn't keep quiet about something, she didn't, I felt I owed it to my friend to toss the apple nonchalantly across at her lap and my father felt he owed me a smack in the face, which struck the room dumb at once; I sat on the piano stool with my cheek and eyes stinging, then icily walked into my bedroom, shut the door, and lay on my studio couch in a rage, wishing my father was dead. Beyond the wall my friend bade everyone a poised if accelerated goodnight, my mother fled upstairs to the roof to cry, with my father at her heels to comfort her, my sister took refuge in her bed, and I bred murder in my head until my father, an hour later, having pulled out the couch in the living room and helped my mother to sheet and blanket it, knocked on my door to make peace. I said I didn't want to talk to him, he said but I wanted to live in his house didn't I, and outraged by his philistinism I said I would get out if he liked, certain of his dolesome smile and promise to "be right out in the street after" me, and with that surrender I counterattacked; much troubled, he sat in my room until midnight among the truths and falsities of a conversation neither of us more than half understood, a dark pit between us, and I would not help him cross it, when he offered to write my friend a note of apology I said it couldn't matter less to me, the issue was us, but it was talk between a father inarticulate with good and a boy gifted by ill will; the loss he feared in his future I wanted as my past, and the more patiently he listened the deeper I wounded him, saying I had more in common with my friend than with him, more in common with my teachers than with him, more in common with schoolmates I hardly knew than with him. Unforgiven when he left my room he could not sleep, and sat the hours out in a chair at his window with a pack of cigarettes, near my unhappy mother in their couchbed, to whom he said he would "cut off his hand" if he could take back the blow. And I lay in my own dark, in a room they had made my den with a secretary desk chosen by my mother for my studies and a windowsill radio for my highbrow music and a ponderous typewriter toted home by my father for my writing, all the instruments of alienation they had lovingly furnished, and lay befriended by those dear schoolmates I would see in the morning; whose faces, names, whereabouts, I never think of, but the husk of my father, which, granting every wish, in the earth for a quarter-century has forgotten me, I do not forget.

Yet our differences, minute, daily, mortal, were not an imagining. When my father taught me to press my first grown-up pants—in our kitchen every Sunday noon he pressed his twenty-two-fifty suit, laying it out on the ironing board for trouser leg, sleeve, lapel, draping over it a dampened clothstrip which usage had long discolored, testing the flatiron's heat by its hiss and riding the clothstrip smooth, peeling it back to scrutinize a steaming lapel, reheating the iron on the gas burner, redampening the clothstrip at the faucet, ironing until in the suit not a wrinkle survived and every crease was sharp as a knife, the while he advised me always to "make a good appearance"—he was teaching me his vision of the world. I had seen my parents for so many years be at pains to attain a middle-class decency that I lived most of my life under the misapprehension they were the children of immigrants; I thought their notions were parvenu. That the grandfather of Katherine Gibson's father was party to a Staten Island mortgage while Washington was farming in a crown colony, that Mary Dore's grandmother might have jostled redcoats in the old narrow streets downtown where my father now walked to work, that the precepts my parents were putting into my head had descended into theirs via parental heads from the habitat of the founding fathers, was unknown to me. The lives of my mother and father bespoke some constant in the lifespan of the country. Yet so did my floundering, it was my own declaration of life, liberty, and the pursuit of something more inward than making a good appearance; I felt at my throat the hand of love like a strangler, and I fought for that breath which was myself.

I was born for several reasons, none of them mine. My reason for being, though postpuerperal, was one I felt growing in my bones, I was alive to create me, and it was the continuance of that venture which brought me a generation later to my own reasons for fathering life. In my thirties the self I had been wearing since my teens, not my father's suit, was threadbare; I was a minor poet, and poetry is the speech of exile, uncommon usage of the common tongue that distills its maker's sense of his rareness, but selfhood has its limits beyond which it must root in common ground or become an attrition of self, and I was at them; for a decade and a half I had fed, if not fattened, upon a sense of my uniqueness which was a thinner gruel each year, and all my cloth of vainglory could not keep me from shivering, it only kept me from earning my daily bread. Prose to me was everyone's lot, the language of husbands, wage earners, fathers, and many a poet is buried young who has not made the crossing to it, but I had come from a long line of fathers, and when life huffed at me hard I was content to wrap myself in the streetwear of prose, I said goodbye to my literary man and became a family man, rejoining a trinity, and I no longer shivered in the cold wind of extinction that blew across my father's grave. That my pencil manifested a capacity to earn its living as soon as I had issue to support, and spread abroad the news of my uncommon soul when I was engrossed in diaper pins, was another issue, unplanned. It was in an expansion of self that I fathered our boys, and every word I say to them, from haranguing them about a toilet left unflushed to explaining at the keyboard the structure of a sonata, is wishing on them my vision of the world, the dogma of me, which unfolded in an earlier family and unfolds still in this; no fatherly act but is in the service of my own preservation, which now includes theirs, but the reason of their birth is not the reason of their being. And each of these boys, wresting out of me and his mother and himself that distinction in soul he will know is his most grievous fault and jewel, must separate our hand and his throat.

To find my breath of self I had to uproot it seemed the very ribs in me, all my bonework not mine, the calcareous deposits, word by word, of fourteen years of dogma; I was undoing the ribs of my begetters, but it was their bone and nerve which was extended in me, not mine in them, and of their hurt I felt nothing. I threw back at them each of their gifts, as in a love-match broken off, piece after piece of their selves and world, until in all matters obvious to the eye, school, hobbies, church, clothes, work, politics, friends, I was rid of every hope they had for me, and my father rightly saw my toss of the apple as contemptuous. I observed my parents with my young world-ling's cool glance—half a lifetime later he wrote me they "were always so kind" to him it bewildered him—and I was ashamed of them; I could hardly confess, to the boy or myself, my deeper prayer, I was not worthy that he should come under my roof, and I felt worthier when I despised the talk, taste, lives of my mother and father. In every deed they saw me choose to divest myself of semblance to them, until on his deathbed my father with his eyes on the son he had created to perpetuate him—young sloven in his twenties, who had quit church, quit college, quit jobs, quit his family for communists, quit communists for a bride, quit his bride for a mistress, and came from writing on a fraudulent stipend of public relief checks in a tenement such as my parents had put behind them a generation ago—in fact failed to recognize me. It was mutual, he was in me too deep for my recognition. Come full circle, my hand on boys I have fathered to perpetuate me, I see the floundering of my teens, like a jigsaw puzzle wherein by small cruelties I scattered the image of my parents only to recreate it, as wanting in frugality; yet a new piece is in.

It is the piece I was born to be, now so incidental a sliver in the old puzzle that I am hard put to rediscover the truth of my youthful despair when to become acquainted with that sliver's breadth was a matter of life and death. It is still my truth, though the immodesty of despair is gone, and the paradox of conscious-ness maturing is that, widening into others, it knows itself as less and feels itself as more, its diminution and its enlargement being inseparable, but it is born in one skull, prospers in one skull, dies in one skull, and in one skull the mansion and giant shackle of the

world is lived in, broken out of, built anew; I cannot dispraise
the sliver, breath, twig of selfhood, which, however fickle, is all.
I had no eye to see with but mine, born of my parents, and I
praise it, though in it they saw themselves mirrored as fools, and
no tongue to taste my name with but mine, born of my parents,
and I praise it, for all its betrayals of them, and no hand to do my
will but mine, born of my parents, and I praise it, even in its
undoings of theirs. For a lungful of self I was bidden to disown
kin, class, country, it was all of a piece, and involuntary as the
tickling when I hung like a foetus on my rope; and from that
docket of my sins, venial, but mortal enough, for all is mortal, I
could, and would, omit nothing.

I am my own man now, in truth not my father, and still I run
his gamut, fatherly largess, temper, the ancestral worm of his
remorse is in me, my "own style" is half him; the news is too late.
In the spring of my forty-seventh year I drove my family in a
station wagon six hundred miles off our route to satisfy my sons'
eyes with the hillock where Custer died. That dusk in the bad-
lands found us weary and the boys squabbling, we exiled the
elder into the front seat between me and his mother's reproaches,
and when he bitterly answered her, "Oh, keep quiet," my fist
jumped from the steering wheel to crack his thigh; he wailed,
and I drove on in the desolation of a twice-told tale, hearing my
youngster sob that he "hated" me and another boy thirty years
wrong impart to my father how unalike we were. I made my
amends—in a roadside eatery, the two of us secluded in a booth
over hamburgers, I resurrected for my eight-year-old that faded
grief, a boy impertinent with his mother, the blow of a father's
hand, a young head smouldering in malice, which for a generation had lurked in me to be lived afresh by him—but my father
lies beyond amends. And any hour the smite of him, in his
downward smile, or his vested back at the piano, or his jaunty
home-from-work walk with the newspaper slapping his calf, can
bring my eyes again to stinging, so bottomless in them is the

image of that man with whom I had nothing in common.

So I was long ago forgiven. I listened to my mother on her deathbed tell the doctor her son was "always a good boy", having forgiven me so deeply I thought it undercut her memory. It was more, it was profounder. Later that winter our boys, seven and four, having asked to sleep in one bed and been refused, barricaded themselves behind the elder's door in thirty seconds with a phalanx of furniture—bedstead, easy chair, table, secretary desk—solid to the opposite wall, and negotiated their terms through the keyhole while their mother and I, unable to budge the door an inch, collapsed to the floor outside it in a laughing fit of helplessness and admiration; and my eye, that thought it so outsaw the world my parents made, saw now its truth. My victories, even over them, were theirs.

Anger was my blindness. In the long enslavement of childhood I knelt on hard wood in cold churches, striking my breast at each mea culpa, and resolved to confess my sins, do penance, and amend my life; and so I do, I have forgiven my parents all their care in rearing me. What I pray for this year is not the remission of my sins, but the wit to remember them when they come back to me as my offspring's, and grace to see the luminescence of things lost in things present. The breath I want now is simpler, only to live, which is to be hurt, which is to love, while each of our boys creates himself by a thrust out of the ribs of begetters with whom he has in common nothing but congruence at long last; herewith, like my parents, I waive their penance, knowing that all in the past is kept, unforgotten, in each skull, where only by disobedience is bondage to it escaped. And if it seems to these boys that our outworn thoughts, words, deeds, which gave them life, will soon be the death of them, it seems to me that theirs, which give us renewal, are for us another kind of birth. In their eyes perhaps I will see what with mine I cannot; to see is a work of love.

24. Midwork

Irked
Washing my windows clean
    To see
So white a winter's green
    Lurked

    Glum
And hueless in a coat of
    Sloth
I think how I by rote
    Come

    Quitting
Household loves gone drab
    To do
My rag and fondling dab of
    Spit

    Whereby
Of each old half mistaken
    Dull
And gummy word I make
    An eye

CONFITEOR

In me
Imbued with ancient flowing
　　Dyes
Of sunset loss and so
　　See

　　Down
To where my hues and beauties
　　Kept
In glass forever mutely
　　Drown

　　Until
At dusk I houseward go
　　Among
Dark pine and haggard snow
　　Still

　　Red
Of eye so in its bruise a
　　Window
Swims and all the hues I
　　Said

　　Lurk
In a word around me lie
　　In wait
Of rag and spit and eye at
　　Work.

25. Between Sleep and Daylight

In the afternoons with my armful of books I came out under the graystone spires of the dungeon which was highschool, and alone in a tide of students from the clustered edifices of the city college was carried down the steep long street toward the river; across the glimpse of its waters I saw where the mainland rose in great cliffs to the spread of western sky, and somewhere in that direction lay farms, forests, freedom, but at the foot of the block I went under the pavement into the subway hole to begin my journey home.

The train emerged into daylight briefly over the valley athwart the city known as the Hollow Way when militiamen first made the British flee through its buckwheat and orchard, paradisiacal in the old watercolors with wooded hills and plain and river cove, but now a filthy crust of 125th Street warehouses, and I was then borne again into the earth for the undercity run. In artificial light I sat on the varnished straw seat with my books in my lap, addling my head with a variety of matter, sometimes my homework in solid geometry, misnamed, a bog wherein I was sinking as in a nightmare, and sometimes the solemn newspaper in which for "current history" I digested word of the stockmarket crash, not my affair, although as much as any teaching of my parents it would be the very air I grew in, and sometimes only the moron's entertainment of advertising cards above the heads of passengers opposite, which I faithfully read for the thousandth time; print drew my eye inescapably, and lacking other nourishment I would reread like Shakespeare the empanelled specifications of fine and imprisonment for spitting on the train. More punitive was the floating into the car of breathtaking naiads, a rare trip without ten or twelve, like mirages of water in a desert, and over my book I would furtively drink them in, young Tantalus among the fountains of breast and pools of knee, my modest dream being only to find one of them defunct and unclad in some abandoned lot where I might explore her mystery at leisure, and the sole problem in solid geometry I mastered in the subway was smuggling my erection out of it unobserved. It was no longer subway by then, but elevated over the eyesore jumble of Queens, grimy workshops, houses of tarpaper brick, gas stations, cemeteries, rooftops of moviehouses renovated for the talkies, and here, half an hour out of the city in a district known for no visible reason as Woodside, I took my books through the streets to the colony of multiple dwellings in which I lived as a hermit for the next several years.

Of twelve or fourteen buildings, back to back, this winebrick settlement was entered by an arched passage under every unit, and each of four corners of a neat court within admitted tenants to five stories of apartments; we lived again on the top floor. The file of buildings was lent an air of elegance by the "garden", lawn with a few clumps of privet, which was their interior yard. It was for my parents a happy change from the tenement disorder of clotheslines under which, among ashcans, broken cement paving, old board fences, I had raced in the years preceding, but the grass was wirefenced off; no tenant but the janitor had the pleasure of setting foot on it, mowing and clipping, and my instinct was dimly that in this as in other things we were achieving a good appearance at a deficit. Despite arches, garden, and rules against house pets, the apartments, owned by an insurance company, were inexpensive, and we now enjoyed the luxury of five rooms. They met compactly, a quartered square with small kitchen appended, bath squeezed in between the two bedrooms which my sister and I—"getting too big for one room"— were presented with, a reason for the move. I can call the apartment to mind, so tidy, cozy, decent, the cream walls panelled by strips of molding and the varnished floor still undimmed, the air of old times now escaping us with the honeymoon furniture of my parents which piece by piece was giving way to "modern things", a new rug, a dropleaf table along the wall, a console radio in the corner; each window takes its unforgotten place. Yet our piano and the couchbed my parents slept in persist in alternating rooms, my "den" jumps from one building corner to another, and my sister explains the apartment was in fact two, occupied in different years, on different floors, in different units.

I have lost one utterly, and more than an apartment, in the afterimage of life in that colony. Often enough on my subway trip to it the lights died out, the train hurtling on under city or river while I sat in its blackness unseen of myself, till light restored the carful and me again; in some such manner I traversed my mute adolescence in those five rooms, underground, borne through a tunnel from blackness into light into blackness, among images transient as in a delirium. I walked in the neighborhood like a somnambulist. Coming and going daily in the midst of half a thousand families gathered into two square blocks, four years by my memory, five by my sister's, I made not one acquaintance, could greet no boy or girl in the sidewalk groups, and never opened my mouth outside our door. Inside it the faces of my mother, father, sister, melted anonymously into the walls. It was the very interchangeableness in apartments and our daily lives—eventless, meagre, wirefenced off inwardly and out, embarrassed by our bowels, ventureless against the skyscraper city, as minute, obedient, and unremembered as ants—

which I saw as outrageous, and I was in truth gone underground, into myself, after a subterranean passage out.

The subway thus took me back and forth between two dungeons; but that of highschool was alive with new characters, rumors of far horizons, strange gods. Six years earlier I had sat in school with the same knot of children I knelt in church with, and in the summer evenings cavorted with them on the broad hillside where our parents perched on rocks gossiping, but the unity of that world was scattered. I had grown into another as modern as the console radio, complex, many-placed, contradictory. Hitherto my memory of significant event was entangled with my mother and father; now strangers—higher authorities, odd friends, riddles called girls—were to summon me out of the household circle, and each year my eye, at work on all that was me, grew more purblind to its makers. In the lives of my parents a parenthesis had opened, which was to be my life, and in this tale of theirs I go into it again.

In the new neighborhood I knelt at Sunday mass among a thousand unfriends of my faith; on Monday I was half at home in a student body so multitudinously semitic that on Jewish holidays the classrooms and corridors were as if plague-stricken, deserted even of teachers; between family and school my soul was stretched like a rubberband. The instant of severance was irrevocable. I see it like a photograph sharp in detail, a classroom in ancient history, myself among thirty students in battered chairs with desk arms, the young instructor on his feet before us, leaning with clasped hands over the back of his chair, handsome, quickminded as the glints on his eyeglasses, and behind me I hear a voice ask how, if the gods of the Babylonians were imaginary, we can be any surer of ours, and the instructor, always so fluent of tongue, answers with not a word, but, parting his clasped fingers no more than an inch, smiles. That delicate smile was in my life an earthquake. During it a chasm opened before my eyes, four thousand years of Judaeo-Christian dogma toppled into it, and when I sat at supper with my parents the chasm lay between us like revelation; on my side of it was hard fact, and across it I saw all their opinions as a vain imagining. I had lost faith in more than one divinity. My mother and father had withheld from me their sexual knowledge, and in its place stuffed my head with celestial truths which I now perceived to be such a confection of infantile wishwork that I could never again regard their judgment as adult in anything. Casting back for the hour I was exiled out of a family so cheerful I see that no other item set me so variously apart, or so delivered me beyond their sovereignty, or left me so mistrustful of the hearsay of the world; and more than twenty years later I named my firstborn after that apostle who would not believe except he put his finger into the print of the nails.

I had tried not to come to our difference. It was surely by premonition that, only a few months before, when a flock of itinerant priests descended in our parish to hold a two-week mission, I was in nightly attendance upon their sermons, and derived a sour pleasure from my devoutness. I think my mother's pleasure was not unmixed, she had never hinted any wish to see me serve as altarboy, a chance that Ben's older girl might become a nun instead of a nurse overhung us briefly like a raincloud, my missionary aunt Ada's three-year sojourns in Africa were viewed as noble but a bit cracked, and that I trotted ten blocks every night from our supper table to the church must have struck my parents as too saintly for comfort; but my own hopes were not altogether of heaven. It had been announced from the pulpit that the sexes were to be parted for frank discussion of the flesh, and secretly I expected something in the nature of a stag party, with instructions in the sexual act. I was in a misery which burned worse every month, fever of sperm, fever of brain, my chinning had metamorphosed into fifty-seven varieties of ruder masturbation, and afternoons when I was alone nothing in the apartment—mirrors, doorknobs, rugs, chairs, milkbottles—was immune to my amorous advances; perhaps I looked also to be unburdened of that perpetual blush, which was the thickening skin of my solitude. On both counts the priests were unhelpful. I heard from them only that my flesh was evil, but I loved it, surely my member erect was a thing of pride, the odor of my feces also was sweet, and when I heard my betters deny the bodily fabric of their existence it corroborated my suspicion that their lives were much more a hallucination than mine; I was never to be free of their prudery in me, but neither would I join them in that pact of semisuicide. The priests moved on to other pastures, leaving one lamb the blacker, and in a matter of months I was unburdened not by the church, but of it.

My piety was still a wonder on my mother's tongue when I came to tell her that the worshippers who in Sunday snowstorms converged on the parish portals would not now include me, I wanted to stay in bed like my father. Both parents were incensed that I had chosen such a faulty exemplar—his moral dicta were plain enough, "Practice what you preach" and "Don't do as I do, do as I say"—and informed me that since the children in their families had always gone to church my notions were untenable; the next Sunday I was handed my twenty-five cents for the collection and turned outdoors as though I had not opened my mouth. In a wrath at the injustice of the world I bought a chocolate marshmallow sundae, took inventory of storewindows for an hour, and at my usual time reappeared at home. No more was said, and for half a year at churchtime I continued my solitary survey of the neighborhood's merchandise. It was an inconvenience in bad weather, but to kill time with cold feet in a doorway was less a discomfiture than going to my knees for a mumblejumble of dotards, and my breach with parents in totemistic matters I made up for in sartorial. In emulation of their "good appearance" I became such a fop that on weekdays I stored a shoerag in my school locker and between classes hurried to it to keep my feet, however errant, spotless; on Sundays I inserted myself with care into my blue serge suit, freshly pressed by me, and adorned my black shoes, polished unto mirrors, with new gray spats acquired out of my allowance, and after half a morning's labor, brought to perfection from sole to head in herringbone topcoat, white silk scarf, and pearlgray Homburg hat at a precise tilt, set forth to eat my sundae. In this disguise of aplomb, drifting east along the storefronts under the el at the hour of mass one morn, I saw myself under curious scrutiny by a man ambling west along the storefronts opposite, coat collar up at naked throat, a trim of pajamas detectable under his trouser cuffs, feet in house slippers, a citizen out of bed for his Sunday newspaper, remarkable in nothing except that he was my father. Fascinated by each other's stare across the empty street, interrupted only by the el pillars between, we passed without a word of recognition on our opposite ways in life, I into my follies, and he home to tell my mother, "You think your son's in church, he's playing hooky in the streets." When I climbed our stairs to face the music I knew my ground; my mother was frosty with tears at my misdeeds, but I said I wasn't so sinful as sincere, to sit in church after I had stopped believing in it was insincere, and she said I had deceived them, and I said but I had first asked for their consent to be sincere, and my father said right and they had told me to go and I would do as I was told, and I said not unless he took me to it by the ear, which I didn't think would be very sincere, and after two hours of this debate they concluded that on Sunday mornings the only sincere course of action for me was to stay in bed like my father. Which I thereafter did, the apple and oddball of their eye.

It was not my first breakout from their hopes, but I grew like the twig on its bough, the more apart the more alike, and each difference was willy-nilly a mimicry. A year earlier, in the maiden skirmish of my secession, I had broken off my piano lessons. In our summer at the beach my father and I were often next door at the landlady's upright to "rattle the ivories", but it was by choice, and once out of the straitjacket of daily practicing I balked at putting it back on; though the buts flew for a month, the conservatory had opened its fall season without me. If no one saw in this misstep the prefiguring of my failures—I had music enough in me for a vocation, what I lacked was the modesty to obey a coercion external to my whim, and much of my later floundering was in search of a discipline as selfgrown as my skin—my parents had other reasons to be disconsolate. I see how lightened I am when my timid boy diminutive at our grand improvises like a broncobuster, I pray that steed to bear him through many humiliations, if he abandons it I too am frailer; my parents, more alive than I to my vulnerabilities, could not guess that the keyboard and I were married for life.

Undutiful brat, I wanted only to echo my father. In the song hits he brought home I saw his left hand ignore the sparse notation to swing its own bass while his right enriched the melody with turns, chords, tuneful fragments, and it was this "lot of style" that I longed to master; watching his fingers so instinctive among the black and white keys I despaired of ever learning what they did, but he showed me how he divided a bass chord for rhythm into root and triad, how he "filled in" the treble with melodic bits of the chord broken, how from a tune's shape he could infer enough of its chords to fake it by ear; in two years I was playing not unlike him. He promised me five dollars when I could perform without his mistakes a popular "piano novelty" he brought home, highly syncopated, and I practiced it for a week, played it to him once, pocketed the money, and, despite his wry complaints, never touched the piece again. Yet I was at the upright for hours now that it was bare of the alarm clock, sharing my years of estrangement with my eighty-eight friends of the keyboard. I invaded a hundred open windows around the decorous garden with torrents of pop songs; I sightread my ten volumes of salon gems, I blundered among chords by ear all afternoon, I toiled over the arpeggio embroidery of my "original arrangements" to charm my father; like the cockney clerk from the bank, who still came to him with songs in manuscript, I composed a few dreary gems of my own, and whenever guests came for an evening of chatter and music I was among those who took turns on the piano stool. On such an evening my father and I discovered that, if we played jazz with four hands at once, we could make the upright shudder. It was his pleasure thereafter to invite my hands to outdo his in keyboard duets, wherein we waxed so proficiently loud that my uncle Ben, who every few months furnished his brother-in-law to play at some "beefsteak breakfast" of a political or church group, took to furnishing the two of us; my rebellion against lessons had resulted in my being indistinguishable from my father.

I was a pride to him that year, when, not fifteen, I too won a medal. It was not for music, like his, though the piano was one rock amid my perplexities of math, muscles, and intersexual mingling, so necessary to me that when I broke my wrist a second time—I fell off a gym mat while recoiling from a classmate who invited me to wrestle with him—I persisted in playing daily with a hand encased in plaster, to universal cheers. Piano was all I felt I had to offer my worldling, who once or twice a month rode with his violin on the subway to our colony for an evening of my accompaniment, and I was at home in any strange apartment with a keyboard; if none met my eye I shrivelled, and the one occasion my friend took me visiting with him into a roomful of boys and girls dazzling each other all afternoon with badinage I sat as mute as wood, dredging my charmless head for a word to say, but it was drained of every trace of language. Yet it was with language that I won the medal, second prize in the story contest of the highschool magazine, for which I concocted so tedious a detective tale of murder by weights and pulleys in a locked room that, even in the magnificence of glossy print, I myself could not get through it. The medal joined the wallet namecard in my mother's collection, to reappear after her death.

I felt the sure weight of myself, writing or banging at the piano; it disappeared in my first job, wherewith I conceived a lifelong horror of employment. That I would go on to college was dubious—in the family only my aunt Ethel had attended highschool—and a summer job was negotiated by my mother's sister to introduce me to my future as a wage earner. Then in her fifties, Minnie was a saleswoman for a national insecticide company, supplementing the day wages of her laborer husband, who also disliked labor and had a variety of hypochondriacal reasons for staying home from it. Minnie was one of a squad of women soliciting orders both for the insecticide and its storewindow displays of pink and blue crepe paper, placards, and bottles, and I was of the squad of lads who put the displays in. To tack and stretch the crepe paper into a decor of tubular streamers was not a difficult art, even though a union of grown-ups devoted to it was outraged at children doing their work for twelve dollars a week, and after a tutorial day or two in storewindows I was on my own. Toting placards, crepe rolls, satchel with bottles, scissors, hammer, tacks, street guide, I made my way by el and by foot to all corners of Brooklyn into the windows assigned to me, little hothouses of faded groceries or hardware or drugs, where on my knees in the carnage of flies who had bitten the dust, my mouth full of tacks, nose sweating waterstains onto the crepe paper my fingers were worrying into gaiety, I saw I was there with as little reason or weight as the flies, blown on some parental wind; but worse, my windows done, I had to canvass miles of storekeepers in quest of a few orders for later displays, my only bait two free bottles of insecticide which I would rather have drunk. I was a pest to those middle-aged men, overworked, hot, grouchy, and after a day of their disfavor I reported back to an office loft to be hollered at for not bringing in more orders, I was unloved there too. I saw no one glad to work, all trapped in the flypaper which was the social fabric, while here and there in parks the shade trees were serene, the squirrels gallivanted, the pigeons rose uncaught, not one selling its time for money, and every afternoon I sat among them, my notion of a human life was one like theirs. I was learning to play hooky for dear life. I delivered my wages to my mother, and each week was given a couple of dollars for myself; but with this job, following in my father's footsteps, I was dour at where they led me, and, awakened deep in the night by the clink of his razor preparatory to work, I commenced to feel for his lot some contempt, some pity, some anger.

Six weeks after I went back to my last year in highschool the stockmarket crashed, and tolled in modern times. It was this climate in which my head reared itself, beanlike on a pole, for suddenly, on my fifteenth birthday, I was the tallest of my schoolmates. I breathed in the world's ills, not saw them, my eye was enmeshed in the interstices of my own body and displeased with most of its cells, arranged now too vertically; my height was more foolish than my lack of it, and Minnie's calling me "a long drink of water" echoed too aptly my own sense that I was chronically in danger of collapse due to structural weakness. The elastic exerciser I bought to convert myself into a mass of muscles I could barely stretch out, and it dangled on my doorknob unused, I thought it better to die of thinness than of boredom. I inspected my face in the mirror three or four times a day, and was dismayed by its absurdities. My ears stuck out, my mouth, though large enough to admit food, was too small, and my nose seemed sufficient for air for three; I wormed forth the blackheads that speckled it, and dabbed depilatories on its fuzz, convinced I would be the only man at class reunions with a bearded nose. I saw from the subway ads that I was a victim of "coarse pores", and twice a week my mother urged me to pluck my eyebrows where they joined because I looked "like a monkey, dear". Taught to shave by my father, I used his razor whenever I found a hair, so intent on improvements that I continued with it down both forearms to my wrists; I could not understand why he so darkly forbade me to do it again. I shaved my pubic hair to encourage its growth, or so I thought, and at every step was gored by its stubble. My chin commenced to blossom out in pimples, the blight of my teens, throughout which I lived in heartsick dread of accumulating the fiery lumps that uglified the cheeks of two classmates; and I took my complexion to my room in a sullen confusion the afternoon my father said in some pain, "What are you doing to yourself?"

I knew, but had not been caught at it; how he knew baffled me, I thought masturbation a recent discovery, probably mine. In my young worldling's circle it was said to breed not only pimples but hair in one's palms, and I watched mine like Jekyll in fear of Hyde, the chemistry of my loins too sweet to deny. Twenty sights a week set it to simmer—a schoolmate's booklet of a comic-strip flapper delighting in the fellatio she did not permit herself in the Sunday paper, or the young wife who daily with loose neckline bent over a baby carriage in our courtyard and her creamy breasts clanged like bells in my wits, or the multigraphed excerpt from a treatise on coitus which was limp from its travels among furtive hands in the art class, or the daughter of the local hardware store whose eruptive gray sweater so confounded my eye that week after week I bought thumbtacks from her until I owned more thumbtacks than her father, or the photograph my friend had which depicted an upright lady unclad except for stockings and a modest hand on her pubes while being climbed upon by two naked gentlemen spiky with erections in a laocoon-like group—and from that misery of body I was released by autoerotism only into a misery of spirit; I saw my will was as contemptible as my physique. From the peekaboo nudes on the newsstands to the giantesses in swimsuits on the billboards, I could not escape the titillations of an entire society saturated in sexual discontent for lack of more creative business, nor ever wished to.

Late one night my father, who had forbidden me a reading lamp after bedtime, heard from his couchbed the eerie sound of pages turning in the dark of my room, and groped his way in to discover me tented under blankets with book and flashlight; he said if I was that crazy about reading I should for God's sake use the lamp and save my eyes, but he was unfamiliar with the book, the complete short stories of a French author whose heroines were all in a baffling condition unknown to English, *enceinte*. I was indeed a feverish reader and spent much of my allowance on the rental library of a candystore two blocks away, gulping down several mysteries-of-the-month each week, and from its shelves once dared to take home a medico-thriller on the mystery of the century, how to copulate with my wife, keeping it nervously out of my mother's sight until memorized. I was less successful with a few magazines I bought which kept me au courant on events in Parisian nights, stories and cartoons I thought insufficiently risqué, but when my mother's hands encountered them tucked away on a shelf my father was called into the case, and I was confronted by my parents much troubled at my closet, where it was borne in upon me that such reading would somehow lead to my ruin and that family talks led nowhere; the magazines went down in the dumbwaiter with our other garbage, and I went further underground.

I collided with learning other than sexual in highschool, but it was in the course of my somnambulism, drifting through a cloud of classrooms which only at term's end took on the terror of reality; for half my subsequent life I was to have nightmares of reporting for exams I had inexplicably forgotten were to occur. I flunked nothing, understood little, loved less, and of it all remember best a locker room where I went for the sandwiches packed by my mother in a brownpaper bag now sticky with honey, and a hurlyburly of boys in the cafeteria where I munched away at the edge of the merriment around my young worldling. The life of his humor, which in truth was uncommon, was disdain, and the highschool faculty—epitomized for us by a crotchety old physics teacher who was wont to hurl a hammer at boys who irked him—was available as the immediate target of his wit, but it played derisively upon everything in our ken, democracy, religion, business, creating a vision of world civilization as a longstanding morass of stupidities in which we were the first shoots of hope; it seemed reasonable. In his conversation I felt my soul opening to humor as the salt of life. I was a flavorless boy, but to bring a smile to his lips was such a reward that I set my brain to four years of acrobatics which stretched it more than my geometry theorems; leaping after farfetched jokes for a twitch of his love I learned the ropes of his sardonic humor and outlook. I could never learn his charm, so seductive, and it peeved me when my mother without fail after his visits said he "sure had personality plus". I was in any case scornful of her and my father for being so ignorant of the higher matter that had crept into my ear in the classrooms, great names, historic events, tidal thoughts they had never heard of, when to me and my suave friend the word intelligent was synonymous with deserving of life. In that cafeteria I chortled at his mockery of our elders through mouthfuls of my mother's sandwiches, fondly made of wholewheat bread to guarantee my health, and thus fortified went home in the afternoons to bestow on her more of my polysyllabic disdain; when I once said to her coldly, "Do you doubt the veracity of my statement?" it was hooted back at me for six months by everyone in the family, but neither of my parents ever imagined how much of my disrespect was emulative of the boy they so admired. Yet one day that love too opened a crack. I was with him and a crony of his, idling out the lunch period in an empty room whose blackboards were dizzy with equations; at one blackboard the three of us were convulsed, and there were joined by a happy math teacher whose smile died when after two words it became clear that, while his amusement was at the slovenliness of the work, ours was only at the student's interminable Polish name, and I stood suffused with a shame I was never to forget; I saw my idol's values were shallow by a worklight out of the depths of my mother's. I was drifting away from him too into a solitude, and wandered in those halls to the library, a modest chamber but quiet, the only room in the high-school where I sat to any table of contentment.

Yet the book I see most vividly was a tome brought in by a schoolmate to the cafeteria. It was all photographs, of male faces mutilated into monstrosities past believing, their flesh bleared like wax, sockets void of eyeballs, cheeks agape with holes in lieu of noses, satanic profiles with jaws vanished, page after page of faces which were silent screams, the veterans still alive in hospitals a dozen years after the war wherein my young uncle had disappeared. In a corner of the noisy cafeteria, with schoolbooks under our arms, we stood in a dumb knot to gaze at those faces; no contempt that my friend or I felt for the custodians of our world was savage enough to cope with that glimpse of the horror that lay in wait for us.

The army had another face, more jovial, and it turned up now in the person of my uncle Frank, the warrior of my mother's family, who materialized out of his legend to nourish my life for one unforgettable day. I had long heard from my mother and

Minnie about their cavalryman, his good looks, his irresistible
gallantry to ladies, his ramrod figure, and though his heroism in
my mind was minutely tainted by his enlistment in the service as
a hidingplace from an irate husband, he was nonetheless a personage of much glamor; throughout my time he had lived on
army posts in Mexico, the Philippines, Panama, and now was
transferred home to a fort in Brooklyn, where to my surprise I
saw he was the cook. Fleshy of nose and midriff, whiskey-
voiced, pushing fifty and due for retirement, my uncle was not
the handsome rascal who had run away, albeit that ghost reappeared when he stood for snapshots with his belly sucked up into
his chest, natty in the army uniforms which he always had
"tailor-made". Frank's homecoming was celebrated by a family
dinner at my aunt Minnie's, who with her husband and a mongrel and a goldfish now lived in a flat in a neighborhood of
trolley tracks and bars two miles from our winebrick colony,
and there all the surviving Dores—down to my mother's
pal Nelie from schooldays—came to greet their prodigal except for his brother George, whose preparations in Larchmont
for a sojourn in California kept him busy. For the next few
months Frank lived in Minnie's flat, and on visits with my
mother and sister I would glimpse him stretched on a couch in
his room necking with my "aunt" the spinster pal; in the sever-
ity of youth I could not fathom what attracted either to the
other, but Frank said with a wink he "needed a little lovin' ". My
uncle's military saga of stays in the guardhouse had been one of
women, whiskey, and song, and his off-duty hours were spent in
the bars of the neighborhood, where he was "very entertaining",
always the core of a group listening to tales of his advice to Black
Jack Pershing on how to nab Pancho Villa, unfortunately overlooked. Too often Minnie's husband was at his elbow drinking
with him, and next morning would be prostrate in bed—Frank
was up at four to report to the fort, still "rugged"—and a day's

pay lost. To forestall this Ben's girl, killing afternoons at Minnie's with her little daughter, would be dispatched on a tour of the bars to bring the husband home; in one she was introduced by her new uncle to an Italian gangster whose attentions to her so worried Ben that he asked Frank to beg him off. It was thus not a total loss when our soldier moved out of Minnie's, and around the corner into the flat of a woman in her forties whom he met in a bar. Neither my aunt nor my mother would offend this beefy inamorata, but they thought her "too crude" when "loaded", and drew a nice line short of acceptance: they received her with Frank in their flats, but declined to set foot in hers.

I was at this time described by a neighbor as "stern, kept mostly to himself, always so studious," and it seemed unlikely that my uncle's deplorable career could be nutritive to mine, but at the fort Frank had quarters to himself, and in them our lives truly intersected. Master sergeant by rank, he invited all his relatives for a grand Thanksgiving dinner in the mess hall where we sat like a royal family among the deserted long tables, overwhelmed by the quantities of turkey and trimmings brought to us by the soldiers; in his room afterwards I came upon the first typewriter I had ever seen in person. It was the aged machine on which my uncle "typed all his menus", and while he escorted his guests on a tour of the fort's wonders I sat alone in his room exploring the keys with one finger. No item in the surrounding arsenal could seem to me more potent than a machine whose genius was the miraculous transformation of my thought into the public fact of type, and although my thought as it became visible was attended by a startling number of dollar signs and question marks, I one-fingered it forth all afternoon; the room grew dark, someone put on a light, people came, went, came, and around me at last were struggling into overcoats, but I pecked on to the moment when my parents led me from my uncle's typewriter, my head drunk with glory.

A few weeks later Frank Dore was dead. In the wholesale butcher's where he picked out the meat for the fort he was felled by a heart attack, and died in the sawdust among the hanging carcasses; his was taken to a hospital morgue, then to the fort, then back to my aunt Minnie's parlor, where for three days it lay in a flag-draped coffin with a change of soldiers on guard; the family's ne'er-do-well was given the most honorable funeral in its history, and, borne at snail's pace to a soldiers' cemetery in a horse-drawn caisson with six guards marching alongside, was committed to the earth under a heroic salute of their rifles. His brother in Larchmont stuck to his own guns, and did not attend.

I grieved less for my lost uncle than for his typewriter in the final months of highschool. For three years in it I had felt incompetent at every task, and so was coming to see my future self as perhaps a writer; my ambitions were not so modest as my vocabulary, I said "journalist" when asked, but only I knew how fearful I was of the hectic life around the school newspaper, which I never went near because to meet a deadline without a catastrophic blunder seemed a human impossibility, and instead I sat evenings in the quiet of my desk lamp, writing my stories. I was still abandoning them—the passionate lava I wrote out of at night was in the morning a lard of lies—but as the class author I was expected to complete one for the annual contest of the school magazine, which I did, featuring an ex-champ unable to abjure the ring or his hope of victory. That I was writing of my masturbation was not divined by the faculty judge who awarded it first prize, the gold medal. It was now rumored that the class dinner, hitherto stag, would be a dance to which we must come with girls; our school was for boys only, and although I nonchalantly told my young worldling of how I had "picked up" the houri of the hardware store and was squiring her to the movies, it was merely a sad wish, I went to the movies in a Sunday loneliness, and since our change of neighborhood I had not addressed a syllable to a girl of my own age; suicide seemed my only recourse. In the last hour it was decided to continue stag, and I lived to see the magazine appear with my story, no joy by now, although in the captions under our gallery of budding faces the class prophet foresaw me writing in Hollywood for $50,000 a year. The evening I was graduated in the great hall of the city college my family sat leading the applause when I mounted to the rostrum to receive my gold medal, which turned out to be gilded iron. The sensation of the day was a love gift awaiting me at home: my mother and father had stored it with a neighbor, and I was dumbfounded to see it in my room, my own typewriter, a reconditioned and massive genie who was to serve me for ten years.

Yet history too was coming between my elders and me; I had graduated into a country in which there were no jobs. My father's was not in jeopardy—the depression came to us next winter only in the bank's termination of its annual bonus, whereupon my father, not one to stint because of a worldwide bankruptcy, "took out a Christmas loan" to buy his gifts as usual, and each December, having repaid it with interest in fifty weekly installments, borrowed it back at once—but the evidence of bad times grew. Investors stepped out of windows and veterans peddled apples in Wall Street, newsreels became monotonous with factories bereft of chimney smoke, broken-paned, their gates haunted by knots of hangdog workers, and housewives we knew went every few days to the police station for handouts of canned beans; families were destitute because there was too much, and such idiocies of the time invited a state of mind different from anything in my father's forty-two-year-old head. It was a world with no use for me or my classmates, who not for ten years would be wanted, and then only to kill our contemporaries, that future was not illegible, and I can remember no year thereafter in which I did not feel endangered by my country. I lived in its mouth like Jonah. I grew as suspicious of its public tongue as my mother of the grocer's scales, but with more reason, shortweight meaning an early demise, and when I heard the politicians, their hearts full, their minds blank, adjure all to patriotism I felt quite as I had when kneeling in a church whose deity was not there; I sensed that to statesmen I was only their raw material, to be used in execution of their vision much as I used words in execution of mine, and while not yet did I smell something evil in men that led them into places where they could do good, I had in mind a more voluntary choice of fate. And when my father had a kind eye even for our thieves—of the dapper mayor, soon to flee office and country, he said indulgently, "Well, more power to him"—I concluded he was indeed of a generation of fools.

It seemed now I was to take the path of least resistance across the campus into the city college, still at the heels of my friend; for the summer my father pulled strings, and I spent it working in the Wall Street bank whose loyal servant he was. In its personnel office I filled out an application requesting me to specify why I thought my services would be of unique value to the largest bank in the world, and I wrote because I had learned in highschool a mathematical formula for computing compound interest, which I divulged to them in some shaky detail, and without delay I was assigned to work as a runner who took telegrams to remote desks. I sat with others on a bench outside a roomful of telegraphers, where thirty times a day I was handed a cablegram from abroad with a number scribbled on it, and I trotted with it to the desk indicated by the number. Somewhat brainless, this chore took me by foot everywhere among the bank's departments, scattered throughout an entire skyscraper, I was in a lair of world power, roving in a sea of desks, people, and office machines clamorous with the moil of global commerce, and I wandered through it like a sleepwalker; I saw only the stenographers in their summery dresses and high heels, and for me the double center of finance capitalism was a creature on the tenth floor who specialized in diaphanous blouses with nothing underneath except her bra.

Since the cableroom was operated in some proximity to the mailroom, I also saw my father, though his eccentric hours overlapped my workday briefly. Working in the dishabille which for him meant jacket off and sleeves rolled up—he always retained his vest, with its pocketful of pencils, his tie impeccably knotted to a shirtcollar so tight it cut into his neck flesh—he was constantly among the thirty clerks of his shift, sorting this, signing that, checking a stamp window here and turning to a "Hey, Gib!" there, never off his feet even at his desk phone, and if I had been less brainy I would have understood why at home he sat with bare heels up on our windowsill, airing the "corns" on his malformed toes. I saw he was the most generous of bosses, and when the personnel department asked him to grade his crew for pay raises he listed each man as "the best", and defended it by saying if he didn't think so he wouldn't want them under him; "his boys" were fond of his balding head on the move among them, and the climate in the mailroom was one of tomfoolery and hard work.

I was developing the "nervous stomach" my mother owned, and one day I vomited in the men's room before I could reach a toiletbowl; I fled in a panic, but the outraged porter sought out my father, who left his work to clean it up, and told me gently enough I was no longer in a child's world. But the world I was in, if adult, seemed to me so prisonlike I could see little profit in manhood. The truth was I could not understand the cheeriness of my father and his boys at their chores; I apperceived him, them, the thousands of employes around me, as sleepwalkers more insensible than I, who morning after morning rose in elevators to well-lighted limboes where all day they marched about like robots on errands not theirs, and each night signed the timesheet out, unblessed by any revulsion that it was the death warrant of their souls. The bank was for me a vision of hell by daytime, and I wanted no part of that death in life which I saw as my father's daily plight.

In the fall I was back under the graystone spires as a "college man"; I was to make two ill-fated assaults upon a degree, interrupted by an effort to educate myself, for my choice of degree could not have been more witless. With my father out of his depth, I had gone for counsel in the last weeks of highschool to my English teacher's desk, he asked what I wanted to be and I said maybe a writer and he said I shouldn't make that decision too soon but why didn't I "sign up for a B.S., it's a very popular degree nowadays." I thanked him and followed his two minutes of advice into two years of higher learning which taught me never to take advice again. I at once lost my head in a whirl of physics, biology, chemistry, and at a time when my main interest was to ascertain the internal shape of my sentience I was kept busy day and night examining, via test tubes, calculus, pulleys, textbooks, microscopes, lectures, bunsen burners, the properties of a universe in which I saw not a grain of me, and in whose reality or significance I could not believe; for four semesters I flailed to keep my nostrils above a desert of knowledge. I never quite sank below a passing grade, but I went from bewilderment to boredom to despair to rage, and typed out a poem to inform posterity that I "would rather hear a violin than learn the secret of the universe", a datum which in any case was not included in the baccalaureate.

My typewriter was in daily use, clacking out verse, fiction, my mother's recipes, letters to anyone, and a digest of early human history which I personally vended at my locker. The rejection slips from slick magazines which in my twelfth year had come in response to a story I mailed off in illegible handscript now came in response to a few I mailed off in faultless typescript; I commenced to haunt the mailbox, and at each glimpse of my plump envelope within its slotted panel I sagged, but I was being habituated to write in spite of rejections. No other act so resurrected the inner stir which bank and college presided over the burial of. It was only in literature classes that some pipeline, half clogged, fed my buried self with hints of what I might be for, and though my recall of the chem and physics labs in which I spent hours on end is blank of instructors, I can summon up the faces of all who taught my minimal hours in fiction and poetry; sitting in his cubicle off the main corridor, still unknown to me, was the teacher who would confirm my life.

I never consulted those instructors about my private writings, but history was a public matter, and my digest was written for sale to students in a stroke of shrewd practicality. The mimeographed syllabus issued to us in history was an outline of a thousand items to be learned about by library readings in fifty books; after a semester of such reading I had a plump notebook of responses paralleling the items, and the inspired thought that with my notes any student could survive the course without opening a book. In my void between semesters I put the notes into a coherent text matching the syllabus, a sentence for every item, and hunched for a week with two fingers over my typewriter cutting stencils. My father took the stencils to a mimeograph machine in the bank, an obliging clerk ran off the copies, and when my father staggered home with the bundled poundage it overflowed my bedroom; I sorted out thirty piles of pages on chairs, desk, couch, floor, until I had more than a hundred copies neatly assembled. When college resumed I tacked up on the bulletin boards three posters announcing my invention of bookless history, a dollar a copy, on sale every lunch hour at my locker. In the stench and hollering around it I sold twenty a week, my young worldling lifted his eyebrow, and the history teachers encountered a new breed of freshman strangely gifted for passing exams while remaining ignorant. In time my digest was in too many hands to escape notice, and with their syllabus as inalterable as man's history the faculty perceived I at least was not; I was called in by the head of the department and ordered to desist. I had not foreseen this finis, but it was half a relief, I had cut the price when sales dropped off and I myself felt that tarrying at my locker every noon for no customers at seventy-five cents lacked dignity.

The eyebrow of my friend was still potent for me, it seemed to lift higher as his family's income sank lower, but so did their standard of living. In the continuing depression his parents escaped rent by returning to service as caretakers of a town house off Fifth Avenue at what my friend, with a smile of contempt over pride, said was "a very good address to give people"; in this graystone mansion they occupied the basement rooms by day and attic rooms by night. I was sometimes privileged to sleep over, and we played duets for his mother at a grand piano in a parlor full of shrouded furniture. Its bookshelves included in open view a three-volume set of case histories in sexual psychopathology, contraband in my world, which I peeked into whenever I could without loss of nonchalance, and via a back window my friend one summer morn beheld in a mansion opposite a naked fellow dive into a naked wench; nothing like that ever happened in my neighborhood.

The violin I "would rather hear" was I suppose his, since I heard no other, and had no social life whatsoever apart from him. I would sometimes walk two miles from our colony to visit another forlorn classmate in a well-to-do apartment, but without love, though we played chess and talked of painters. One week at college it seemed my isolation was to take a happy turn when, in the lunchtime mob, an upperclassman who was a stranger selected me for conversation, asked me to join his fraternity, and said he would expect me two days hence at a given hour; when on the day I ran through the streets to the brownstone and poked its bell, no one opened the silent door, and after half an hour of worrying over some irremediable mistake in place or time, wandering off and back, ringing a final time and then waiting to ring once more, I saw I had been misled into thinking I was desirable, and went home wiser to the street where I knew nobody. Weekends and holidays I took myself on long wanderings by foot to the shore of Flushing Bay, or on my second-hand bike I pedalled across the bridge through the city to the 125th Street ferry and ten miles into Jersey, said hello to my aunt Milly and cousin, and pedalled home.

I was always eager when my friend dined with us—he brought candy for my sister, who was so in love with his savoir faire that she followed him around to light his every cigarette, until my father told her to "stop falling all over him"—yet I had come to trust my ore of loneliness more than his glamor. It stuck in my mind when, walking together down Fifth Avenue, he informed me he much preferred to be in a fine suit without a dime in his pocket than to jingle money in cheap trousers; my experience was less poetic. I had long been enamored of a pair of white basketweave shoes in a storewindow and often travelled blocks out of my way to gaze upon them, like sculpture, but while my shoes cost three-something these were priced at fourteen, and when after much saving I bought them, hurried them home in a box, and eagerly laced them on, I was at once desolated by a sense of folly so total it became archetypical of all possessing. I saw that material things to my young worldling were, on another level of taste, only the nice appearance my parents talked of; matter went up in smoke, I was after something more real. I was now to hear its voice in serious music, which lured me deep into my parenthesis, where I was lost to him, my family, and college.

In my pursuit of muscles I had joined a Y in midtown at which one friendless evening a week I swam, envied some penises, shot some pool, played some pop piano, and revelled in a library delicious with fiction; here I commenced and exhausted my career as a journalist, and met the angelic messenger who led me to other music. The branch had a bimonthly publication, and I invited myself to contribute to it a "column" of my adventures as a bookworm, but then I inherited the editorship. It was in the hands of two outside experts, a radio writer with scant hair and his tawny young friend with too much, whom I came to assist, but I squirmed at the falsity of their "house organ" style, all backslapping and illiteracies in quotes, and a profile of the branch director for an issue I was to take to the printshop was so callow that I ventured to reconduct the interview, wrote a fresh story, and threw the editor's out. When the issue appeared so did the editor in a wrath, demanding to know what authorized an ignoramus of sixteen to sit in judgment on a professional writer, I said it was his style, and he forthwith marched himself and his friend out of the publication, which became mine. I took pleasure in it until I was seventeen, but it left much of me unsaid, and I abandoned it and the notion of journalism together. Meanwhile it domesticated me in the Y, and once while killing time over pop tunes at the piano I saw an elf with a curly head materialize at my left hand to listen; he asked could I not play better music, and when I launched with tremolo octaves into one of the "semiclassics" from operettas which cost my father fifteen cents extra a copy the elf said no, he meant real music, named it, and seeing my face blank invited me to meet his records in Brooklyn.

I went by subway one evening, an hour-and-a-half journey out of the house of my parents into another country of masterworks, radicals, and girls; I never found my way back. Three years my senior, the elf lived in the downstairs half of a redbrick two-family house with a father and elder sister, but he was the sad beauty, the sister was a beefy nurse with a cynical tongue and bohemian friends. I went time and again for the records on a portable in his room, where I lay on a twin bed under a ceiling bulb drowning in the tidal voices of nineteenth-century giants, and he said if I had a player he would give me an odd record or two. From my aunt Minnie's parlor I repossessed our cabinet phonograph left over from old times, extracted its turntable and subtended horn, screwed it onto my windowsill, and cranked it by hand for my own concerts at home, consisting of one record with half-a-movement by a different composer on each face; my father disliked this music, which he said was "all scales", but it was the onset of a deluge. When I accompanied my elfin mentor to a library which maintained a listening booth I walked between tall stacks replete with volumes of music, and so discovered the undreamed-of literature for piano. I now took home music to sightread at our upright, trying out everything from moments musicaux to rhapsodies until I was deep in sonatas; the more drunk I got on them the more deafeningly I banged them out, while in his rocker my father sought oblivion behind the sports page. I began to pre-empt the radio for the symphony broadcasts on Sundays, flooding the apartment with its roar at top volume, and with the old sabbatical peace gone forever my father one afternoon shouted at me in wrath, "For God's sake, will you turn those scales off!" My feelings outraged, I withdrew to sulk in my room; holed up in that den with my supplies of manna in the wilderness—my typewriter, my art gallery of clippings from the Sunday paper, my turntable and six records, my score of books borrowed simultaneously from three libraries and the candystore, plus the "classics" in simulated leather bindings which I collected at a dollar apiece—I sat immured from my family, my heart heavy with chemistry formulas. At every such contretemps my head burned with heroic thoughts of fleeing into freedom as a countryside tramp, except that it seemed so uncomfortable. Instead I took a subway back to Brooklyn, where with my melancholy elf I listened to music unhollered at, and in the kitchen over a Jewish glass of tea was embarrassedly half at home among the obscenities of his sister's friends, as though I had stumbled upon a lost tribe of the Dores turned intellectual.

I was present to my family now only in the flesh; the night my father lost his temper—it happened still, as when in the midst of helping my sister over a difficulty in her piano practicing he tore all her music into shreds—and struck me in the face, it was in a reach across several gulfs to the flesh. The resolve of his young fatherhood that we would always be "pals" was trickling away in the conversational deserts between us. Two short years before, rendezvousing with me and my sole friend downtown after school, he was spending his pocket money on our dinner in the automat and seats for that most worldly of pleasures, "a Broadway stage play", one of our choice with corpses overhung by vampires or vaudeville magicians; and out of affection I saved up to repay the treat, taking my father to a melodrama of jailbreak in the death house, a double delight. I had listened to his talk then, when on the subway he spoke of the "heavy dramas", actors, playwrights of his own youth, and there was much, too much, to ask him, but now I was alone on the subway to Brooklyn. In any event, whenever I heard my father say something like "Well, is it hot enough for you?" I knew the relationship between us was over. I had my questions, but so anatomical—how is orgasm possible, the penis in the vagina, no hands?—they were unputtable, and my beliefs were a family scandal, I could talk of little that was significant to me without insulting everyone, and even on that wretched night when I wanted most to harrow my father, telling him I had more in common with anyone I might name than with him, I could not say the worst, that I thought he was a failure. Wrong on both counts, I knew what I knew, that in the last three years my interests, body, ambition, had led me into a country whose language was not his. I said it wasn't my fault if I had outgrown him, and my father said it was "all these books", but he would try, he would read them too, would I explain them to him? and ten years behind us lay a happier day when in the grandstand hours before a World Series ballgame my young father bought every New York newspaper to read and explain all the colored funnies to me. Yet that treat I could only repay, like the blow itself, to an unborn generation; and fumbling with talk until midnight we could not grasp that what was unforgivable and what was unrepayable was one, the knothood of father and son, and nothing less than an unravelling of the flesh between us, backward to the day of my birth, would have spared us our grief. In my studio couch, his property, I lay with my flesh his prisoner, thinking it would be free if his died.

My visions of making my escape as a hobo were obsessive. I was haunted by a book I had from the school library, the autobiography of a poet who "tramped through life" from coast to coast, studying at colleges here or there when the mood was on him; I thought this an ideal method of education, complete with air. I was so faint for air it disrupted my appearance, I helped my flesh struggle out of its bonds by leaving my shirtcuffs unbuttoned, my shoelaces tied halfway, my collar open and necktie loose, small liberties, which dismayed my mother, and daily I ran the gauntlet of her fingers which tugged at me, brushed me, buttoned me, knotted me, and reeling out of her clutches I was pursued on the staircase by her cries from above to smooth down my eyebrows with spit. I could breathe no better in the classrooms of the city college, and played hooky again among the rocks and trees which had been a comfort to me since childhood in the lost garden. I cut hours to sit on a ledge above the ten thousand rooftops of Harlem, a sink of grimy lives, in the midst of which my mother too at my age had eluded her family in her own parenthesis, to make her stubborn conscience; now in the jumble of streets below me I could almost see her brother Ben, letting his ice company founder in the depression as he staggered chuckling from speakeasy to speakeasy on a months-long drunk that nobody could beg him out of, and I took to the other direction. I cut half-days to ride the ferry over and hike along the great wooded cliffs of the Palisades, a few miles beyond which my father's kin in sight of a steeple led the seemly lives, even their saturnalias being church suppers, from which he had hidden in his parenthesis; among them now I could almost hear the exalted voice of my aunt Ada, home from godless Africa to raise at Pentecostal revivals the funds to send her back, but in neither direction could I fill my lungs. To enter the college each day was like crawling inside a padlock, and outside it all the sounds of life—typified in music, that containment of impulse in order, my need was to devour every note that had ever been written—were flowing away from me, unheard. As the semester drew me toward the precipice of final exams I prepared for them by more protracted hikes, and in the Christmas vacation I made my family a gift of the news that my college studies left me no time for learning; I was abandoning them.

The consternation in the household flourished and died. My parents, seeing all their hopes for me in ruins, argued the lamentable case of my father's flight from school into drudgery, shuddered at my bleak prospects of happiness in a decade when even men with college degrees were jumping out of windows, pestered me with promises that they "wouldn't always be here to look after" me, and, about the time I was reduced to a clammy-brained terror of things to come, recovered the fond trust in my judgment which left me wondering how I had pulled the wool over their eyes. My father suggested I might be interested in getting a job? but I said I had no leisure for that. My proposal was to busy myself with a curriculum of studies I could "really use", and after hearing me out my father said all right, he wasn't rich enough to give me "money, but I'll give you all the time you need."

Under their roof of lenity I undertook my deepest retreat into my skin, and opened a one-man college in my bedroom. With myself as faculty, student body, proctor, all of us skipping off to the 42nd Street library whenever possible to bring home an armful of books, I launched into readings in a field of everyday practicality neglected by the other college, criminology, and pursuing the relation between homicides and head types was taken aback to find myself on every page; soon depressed in this branch of learning by the prevalence of statistics over gore, I turned to the nation's history via biographies of our presidents in sequence; I made little headway through the first granite figures, but my intention to continue with math, however unpleasant, was constantly in mind. My only study was in truth music, and it was live, passionate, addictive.

I was at the radio now for every sixteenth-note it contained, the morning hour of masterwork records, gypsy strings at luncheon, a lone pianist with fifteen minutes of an afternoon; I was in an ecstatic sweat myself at the keyboard, triple fortissimo no matter what the composer said. I exchanged volumes once a week when I rode the el in to the library for an hour with records in its listening booth. Inside it I was either host or guest, rarely alone, the booth was in such citywide demand it was signed up for seven days in advance, and there I sat in company with the elf or with the hangers-about who begged in— willy-nilly I was finding myself part of a hungry underground, music lovers, in league against the other society, and my politics began in music—or with a new crony who had drifted my way from among the moths around my worldling's light. Destined for fame in the musical theater, this companion in idleness was an amiable shuffler, so dreamy his necktie was always label upper-most and days after rain had ceased he was still in rubbers, but most worshipful of music, and I went to his apartment too to hear the twenty records he had annexed somehow in the midst of family bankruptcy; like me, he had neither school nor work to interrupt his devotions, and month after month now we wandered around the city together in quest of the god. The two of us colluded to reserve the library booth for consecutive hours, politely alternating as host and guest; for no charge but tax we picked up "student" tickets to recitals by unwanted pianists and violinists making their debuts to a handful of their relatives and us; we discovered a small gym in which three mornings a week a symphony orchestra rehearsed and three mornings a week we came to sit against the wall within two yards of the conductor in his sweaty undershirt, our heads like happy kettledrums under the breakers of brass, strings, percussion. The depression worsened, but not for us, we made treks by subway and foot to museums throughout the city for free concerts by the out-of-work musicians gathered into orchestras on the federal pay-roll, and all else failing, we dawdled along park paths while my friend in nose and chest tones improvised eighteenth-century symphonies.

I bore some resemblance to a bum, for whom I was conceiving a respect. In our winebrick settlement meanwhile the normal life of my parents went on with their "chick" my sister, a happier child, more indigenous to the family than I; she was now in highschool, prompt to acquire friends there or in the neighbor-hood, all Irish Catholics, and they were much in the apartment with the giggly high spirits which my parents loved to hear and I thought of as the sounds of the enemy. When my sister's first dance was imminent to benefit the Young Republicans—my father was a Republican by birth, but so tepid that more often than not he voted only to "help out" some Tammany grafter recommended by my uncle Ben—her pals were in the living room every evening with the furniture pushed back, the rug rolled up, my father at the piano, and my mother brightly teaching them all to foxtrot and waltz. It was a rite I could not learn, from my mother or from Ben's girl in Harlem to whom I made several journeys for help, the rhythms so instant in my hands on the keyboard would not move down into my feet, so that from my pimply chin to my toes I was a sociosexual failure; in my room I hid in a book and contempt. My sister's beau was a giant who pitched for a baseball team, all the youth of the neighborhood in a nearby lot, and afternoons on a rock there my father sat for hours to watch those boys leap, shout, throw, catch, hit, run, but looked in vain for a son among them.

I was elsewhere for a headful of reasons, one of which was that my public firing from the team in highschool was fresh in mind, only five years in the past, another was that my lamentable prejudice against the conversation of such healthy-minded youngsters as imbecilic was accurate, and a third was that whenever in my boyhood I was taken by my father to lots where his fellow clerks convened to play baseball I saw the others in battered sweaters leap, shout, throw, catch, hit, run, while my father leaned forward at the pitcher's mound, in his trim suit and straw hat, umpiring. I was only his son, however he may have wished me to reincarnate his brother Jim, and soon I had another glimpse of what we lacked in common.

My own cowardices I was on intimate terms with. If I accompanied my parents to the semipro ballgames in Long Island City to which they rode by el most Sunday afternoons—my mother was long indifferent to the game, but taking it as her wifely duty to share my father's interests she set herself in her forties to learn its rules and enjoy it—we would pass along a strip under the bridge where a knot of baseball lovers with foul tongues squatted around dice and loose change, and once the obscenities exploded into a fist fight, two men swinging at each other until one was reeling, his face horrible with blood, bawling curses, while my mother half-screamed and my father steered us across the street; the sick fear in my mother's bowels at blood, violence, instinct, was in mine too, and I was one with the loser, the hurt bloody face would always be mine. I think much of my adoration of intelligence was a lifelong flinching from man as brute animal, throttling bananas in a rage, but that my father lost his temper mostly with women and children escaped my notice until I heard him exchange a few words with two gentlemen in blue who got out of a police car for the conversation. With the country in the depths of its bad times—mobs had stormed the banks to demand their savings back, and thousands of banks said no—my father took counsel of his own get-it-and-you-got-it fiscal policy and bought on time a new Ford sedan; the family's first car, it cost six hundred dollars, and was kept for two dollars a week in one of the garages behind a row of houses down the street. My father was taught to drive by a couple of his "boys" from the bank, and I sat in on the lessons. It was during one of them, while the Ford was struggling without luck to turn itself about in a street of empty lots, that the police car drew up to inquire what we had in mind; we showed our documents and all was amiable, but my father with a nervous laugh then asked one cop "where the hell" the muffler on the car was, and in that unaccustomed curseword I looked through a crack into his soul, seeing suddenly how something frail in him too was intimidated by the everyday world of rough men, machines, authorities; it was a perception I rather disliked, but with it there stirred in me for the first time a wish to protect my father. How little margin he had at the edge of male humiliation I never guessed, but my whitehaired grandmother knew him better: master of the steering wheel at forty-five, he drove the new car to Trenton, and his mother peering out the window as it arrived blanched and exclaimed, "That nervous boy, driving a car!"

I was not in it, nor with them thereafter on the Sunday drives they took to visit friends and relatives, nor when my father transported his chick's beau and half the baseball team to neighboring communities for their games; I was with my strangers. I had commenced with my elf to attend middle-class parties in redbrick houses throughout Brooklyn. I was a glum spectator of my agemates dancing to the radio, but when I showed off with my father's jazz at a piano it drew flesh-and-blood girls to sit beside me; I immediately fell in love with several. I discovered that in my young worldling's tone of insouciance I could manage a strangulated bit of conversation, and that if I invited a girl to the movies she would not claw my eyes out but accept. That fall when I had pocket money my Saturdays were full: all afternoon I worried over three new pimples, bathed, shaved, dressed up, was out of the apartment by six, paid two nickels to ride two subways for two hours to a girl's house, was polite to her suspicious parents, paid two nickels to ride her on the subway an hour to a moviehouse, stood an hour in line with what I saw was a numbskull, paid a dollar-thirty for two tickets, paid two nickels for candy, sat stiffly through the movie with her overcoat, my overcoat, and for all I knew our neighbors' overcoats in my lap, afterwards paid thirty cents for two sodas, paid two nickels to ride her back on the subway an hour to her house, was polite to her yawning parents, said goodnight, I would call her again when my rich uncle died, and paid my last two nickels to wait in the drafts of subway platforms for the now infrequent trains on which I rode homeward for another two hours, until at three in the morning I awoke my mother and father tiptoeing in the living-room dark past their bed to collapse into my own: the day was full, but of nothing. I was blind to the household because I now had only two objects in view, one bestial, one spiritual, both hopeless. My bestial aim was to kiss a girl, and throughout the week I planned many a suave and circumfluous approach to the deed, all unfailing, until I was with a real girl in her vestibule, when, no matter how long I detained her, both of us depleted of conversation, bored, sullen, and immobilized there in our overcoats by my sense of grim duty, I found that to broach it was impossible. Yet when the elf said he heard I "almost kissed Hilda" I was mortified that I was so transparent and she such a gossip; next time we took girls home in his father's car, I marched to her door one whom I barely knew and thrust somewhere betwixt her nose and chin a do-or-die smack, whereupon she murmured in some amazement, "Oh, how nice," and I got back in the car feeling silly, but a man to be reckoned with. My spiritual aim was to locate a girl who understood books and jokes, a mythical type, referred to by me and my worldling with wistful sarcasm as a "soulmate". In this quest I conceived, as a shortcut, a touchstone inquiry to be used at all parties, and approaching those young ladies, fulfilled at last in their high heels and lipstick, with "Do you read *Alice in Wonderland*?" was regarded as some kind of backward nut; I never found her.

Yet my four years as a mole were at an end, I was coming up into my daylight, and it was among acquaintances who were—logically enough, if baffling to my parents—all Jews. I felt dimly that with them I had come home, outcasts together, but the sentiment was not mutual. My first beloved was a petite bourgeoise with a slavic face and posterior, for whom I gallantly spread out a handkerchief much dirtier than the step she was to sit on, and too small by half, but I yearned upon her as a comrade, escorted her to the movies, played the piano in her apartment for her smiling parents, and was stunned when she wrote me I could come no more; I phoned her, she said her mother didn't approve of me, I said why, why, and learned I was a goy. It was a bruise from which I could not quickly recover, and two or three mournful afternoons I took the subway trip into her neighborhood to haunt the lots along her street, until I waylaid her coming from school with an armful of books against her breast, and explained to her that what she lacked in courage her mother made up for in stupidity, but the girl went home to her anyway. The next lass who chose me to choose her was a rabbi's daughter, not quite kosher, she had an Irish nickname and humor. I spent a New Year's Eve necking with her in the dark on a bed in the sad elf's house, though my bestiality turned out to be all spiritual; many a night afterwards we necked in the back-seat of the car while the elf, for his own inscrutable reasons, chauffeured us on his errands around Brooklyn, but of that girl's parents I was not allowed even a glimpse, or vice versa, she waited for us on streetcorners in the crowded neighborhood of the poor where she lived. I saw poverty too as a homecoming, and was equating it, not foolishly, with liberty. When I followed the elf to a nest of sisters in the slums of lower Manhattan I found myself climbing the staircase of a coldwater tenement I knew by heart, but not to Mary Dore, it led us into a family of working-class Jews and three daughters in Russian blouses with their lovely heads full of a coming revolution to reaffirm the equality of man, pending which it was thought imperative next time for my equal face to stay out of sight in the car downstairs; the most literary of the trio was the skinniest, my spirituality turned out to be all bestial, and soon I was parked nights at the river with her sister the young beauty in my father's car, pursuing my inquiry into the nature of the female thigh and breast. So long awaited, that feast of eye and hand was as much as I was after, but she took me to the beggarly garret of a painter no older than I where I squatted to examine pictures by the light of a held candle, and at a streetcorner I listened in some perplexity to another boy of her acquaintance on a stepladder with a flag demanding the overthrow of communism because it was not radical enough, and saw I was in a ghetto where poverty, atheism, art, sex, revolution, were one lungful of breath. To these girls, freshfaced without lipstick, in their leather jackets and low heels, my unbuttoned collar was de rigueur; I was at the edge of a society in whose air I sniffed a promise of more, I could take other liberties, unbutton my self.

I had first to find my way out of college again, for I was back in, dumped by a wave of contrary feelings. I was frightened too by poverty, it was what my parents had worked all our lives to deliver us from, and the winter I quit school to drift through the city—so many men on the park benches in a boneless slump, still there two hours later, and the clusters of women at narrow doorways under the Sixth Avenue el where employment agencies tacked up the job-cards, pay upstairs for each address, and the stores that after a fire stood black and gutted for months, worth nothing if rebuilt, and far below the Queensboro Bridge the squatters in a hodge-podge of linoleum-and-cardboard huts that sprang up over the dumpland, lonely with cookfires at night and little figures flapping their arms—not a week passed without my heart going so cold it half failed; in the winebrick colony my father bought his chick's girlfriend a winter coat, her own father was jobless. The infection was in the family now. In Jersey, my aunt Milly's husband became one of the fifteen million unemployed when the great tire company in whose offices he was so diligent a clerk melted away, and, dressed in his stiff collar, spent his days in quest of any odd job for half a dollar, he cut grass, he did housework, nightly he prayed, and at last, though he "hated it", they went on home relief; in Harlem, my uncle Ben after being drunk for two years came to what was left of his senses to learn his ice company likewise had melted away, and, unshaven and in his undershirt, spent his days cheerfully at a table of pinochle and mugs of coffee with other unshaven characters in the flat, his houseful too on home relief; the rain fell on the just and the unjust alike. I never told my parents how often I sat with my eyes unseeing on a book, chilled in my marrow as idler, debating how to undo my mistake, resume school, learn a trade.

I was earning a dollar or three weekly that winter by playing piano in a danceband. My elf had introduced me to a club of "cellar rats", elderly fellows in their twenties who rented a basement in a Brooklyn redbrick for use as a nightly copulation center while upstairs some needy landlady not unlike my mother chose to be deaf; their club boasted a band, but lacked a piano man, and I worked dates with them in a few overheated meeting halls until spring. It was my least unhappy employment, sporadic and brief, but my bandmates had brains like pigs, the rudimentary talk between sets was more unvaried than the scraping fiddle, thump of drums, sax tooting in my ears, and I made no plans to boost my earnings by any assiduity in this field.

I hoped rather to become rich overnight by selling a short story. Whenever I concocted one I took it to the postoffice in a plump envelope to be weighed unsealed, an embarrassment like an unbuttoned fly, bought double postage, and with all the clerks and customers sneering at me stuck half the stamps on a return envelope within, and thrust it out of my life into the mail slot, only to see, upon my return home, that it was in our letterbox awaiting me with a "printed" rejection slip; paradise would be that day when the rejection was uniquely of me. It came at last, from a new literary magazine whose beginnings were announced in a books column: my wits reeled at a letter saying the editor would like to discuss with me how to make my story publishable. I wrote yes at once to his invitation and hour, and after the necessary asperities with my mother, who believed more shoe polish would tip the balance, I took the subway in to Greenwich Village. The editorial offices were located to my surprise in the rear of a tenement with toilets in the hall, but I was let in by the editor himself, a blond charmer with a literate mustache, pipe, drawl, and studio cozy with books and hassocks, and I was in a cloud of his compliments and intelligent pipesmoke over my manuscript when a leggy brunette in sandals appeared from the bedroom putting up her hair, whom he introduced as his secretary, and after a muttered business conversation in re how many eggs should be bought she took her purse out the door, the editor picked up my manuscript anew, suggested a change or two which should make it publishable, tucked it under my arm, and showed me out to the sidewalk, along which I floated to the subway dazzled by his friendship, gay life, and praise; after a few days I received a bill from him, consultation, seven dollars and a half. When I could type without tears I wrote him it was not my usual experience to be billed for invitations accepted, and though he wrote blithely back the bill was an error of his secretary's, I concluded I would be wise not to omit meals until his magazine made its appearance.

In every dirtybearded old vagrant in rags now I saw my future, an outcast and cipher; late that spring I had a seizure of rationality. I visited in his cubicle a professor who remembered my sophomore themes—"nonsense, but done with verve"—to ask his help, I wanted to come back into college to be an English teacher myself. In five minutes he escorted me in to talk with the registrar and I was forgiven my defection. Because I was a year behind my class I enrolled for two summer courses, in music and literature, relished them, earned the instructors' fondest grades, and in the fall was again a fulltime college man, back on the tracks, and once more prostrate under the locomotives of natural science which roared down upon me; no one, including me, had thought of changing my degree. It was not the sciences alone to which I was inattentive, for when a class I began zestfully in the history of fiction opened with the Greek idylls my eye physically refused to read about those unlikely shepherds, book reports were due in sequence, and months later my classmates were in the middle of eighteenth-century London with me still bogged down in Arcadia. Yet the true crux of my difficulty this year was in a classroom around the corner, where in a course in writing I had met a teacher who laid his finger on my soul, a lock sprang open, and after eleven years of education I was at last educed; found to myself, I was lost to everything else.

This professor, not yet forty, was legendary in the college even then. Five feet tall, pasty brown of face and black of flat hair, self-termed a "butterball", a vain, thoughtful, delectable man, cold in reason, fervid in a lifelong amour with literature, he won our ears with verbal surprises: when the bell rang the end of the hour he pursed his mouth, kept twenty students frozen while he searched the ceiling until his bespectacled eyes widened with a glee of words, and said dryly, "Everyone but Cohen may leave. Cohen, get out." It was not with pyrotechnics, but with truth, that he won our hearts. In the first hour he assigned us to bring in an anecdote out of our lives, and promised to flay anyone who dared a "short story"; next session a smug youth read aloud to the class a memoir wherein a safebreaking at midnight in a skyscraper culminated in an affiancing of rapturous lovers over a cadaver, and our teacher kept his promise, peeling skin after skin of dishonesty off that author with such a pitiless wit that never again was a word written in class not rooted in our own knowledge.

My anecdote was of the obscure journey with my father the night my sister was born, and all semester I wrote of that same boy, older, mute on a bus with brash schoolmates, or lost at a party without a brainy girl, or melancholy on a streetcorner with a daughter of Zion whose mother had forbidden him the house, or judgelike in a flat garrulous with kinfolk at the wake of a widower father. With this sally out of the literal I stepped into my teacher's mind, who of old was in mine. Benign to my pieces from the first, he said of one that it "lacks eminence, the only work of art that can exist without eminence is a pancake," but when a student was critical of an unexplained woman who entered amid the kin at the wake, the sole mourner, our professor said curtly, "It's a mistress, that woman is a stroke of genius," and I lived for days on his word. I looked forward to each conference in his cubicle as to an assignation; there, knee to knee in a roomette jammed with small desk, two chairs, and noonday lamp, he dissected my manuscripts with respect, my first teacher, a childless Jew whose buttony eye on me achieved what the bishop's slap on my cheek had not, welcomed me to an act of communion.

So was conjugated a discipleship I would hang onto for eight years, and break off, to escape his vision too of me, and after nine years of silence come back to, we were friends again when his wife found his body in the shower, its heart stopped; and I never told him he was my lifeline. Dead to all else in college, I came to life in the electric crackle of his classroom, twice a week, and at home worked over my stories as offerings to him. I grew for him, for when I put down a long narrative of a father who struck his teen-age son—the last I wrote in the class, and the first I published—I saw and told the experience not as the aggrieved boy, but as the father; in this piece too the mother was dead, out of the way, it was the umbilical cord to my father I was gnawing at. With my teacher's dictum that my growth was "extraordinary for a semester" I was on a path out of college again, not into the sleepwalking of my father, but into a daylight of many suns, the authors that man loved. I had glimpsed another coastline of man, and that I could aspire to it without folly was a faith born of his. I was stunned when one day he put me out of the class because I was snickering to someone while he spoke, but, too stupid to see the compliment in it, I was too clever to let him know I bled; an older student told me I moved through my tale of the wake like a "wraith", untouched. Yet our professor would allude to me teasingly as "iron man McGinty", I carried more weight than I knew. In his cubicle once he divulged to me the plot of a story he hoped he might be "lucky enough" to write, scanned my eyes, gave a mirthless cackle, and said it was "not very good, was it"; I simply had not followed its unfolding of symbol. And closeted there, deep in the semester, he asked me abruptly, "Do you scorn me?" and I stammered no, why, and he said sometimes my face in the back row wore a scornful expression, and I said no, it wasn't so, and left unsaid, then or later, that I venerated him. I left unsaid how much I learned from him, the least of it in craft, learned that however meagre my reality I was an authority on it, he taught authority, and learned that by writing I could gain more than his esteem, he weaned me to self-esteem, and, most profoundly, learned I could use my unhappiness, shape it into words, wring joy of it; he confirmed me in what I was and must be, and I left forever unsaid that in him I had come upon my true father, with whom I had all in common. Except, of course, that he did not love me.

To the father who did I said I had it on higher authority that I was a writer. My father argued that I had returned to college to become an English teacher, and I argued that I must again quit college to avoid becoming an English teacher, and my father said in vexation, "It'll be ten years before you make a living at writing!" and I serenely said I was sure he was mistaken, and so he was, it was twenty. For the remaining month I travelled to the campus twice a week to sit in my deity's classroom, but in no other, and ignored all final examinations save his; my solitary grade that semester was a perfect one, and I received in the mail the registrar's notice of my expulsion from the college. I put it in a frame, like a diploma, and hung it on my bedroom wall, where my mother disconsolately included it in her dusting.

It overlooked my secretary desk for a few weeks only, because in the spring we moved our furniture, cartons, barrels, piano, out of the five rooms in the winebrick settlement of five hundred families whose conformist air was suffocating me; my parents, reconnoitering on Sundays in the car, had located a one-family house for rent in a Queens suburb at the city's limits where in all directions, fifty dwellings to the square block, mile after mile after mile, the immaculate homes and lives were identical; I was horrified. It was the dream of their betrothment come true, a middle-class paradise, to which my parents, up from their childhood forty years ago in the tenements of Harlem, had made their victorious way, and in it the climactic act of the marriage was to be suffered. But my election of a stranger as father marked the end of my long forsaking of parents, and of my parenthetical life with them; I was out of their house within six months, headed back to the tenements, in search of the ancestral dirt which would feed my twig and new leaf, authorship.

epistle

26. A Gift of Suns

Grace be unto you and peace, children, gentle readers, myself or whomever it concerns, for it is not altogether clear to me which of us I am addressing in this long meditation of that which was from the beginning, nor does it matter.

That I address others who will not read I know by recalling the week in which I pledged it. In a tiny bedroom of my sister's house, where my mother lay dying and I sat with the gates of my soul so strangely open, I was leafing through a book of common prayer when a line stopped my eye—"I heard a voice from heaven saying unto me, Write, From henceforth blessed are the dead, for they rest from their labours"—and I thought indeed I would write, but no such lie; her labors were the fiber and sustenance of my mother's life, and she took a dim view of rest. Some weeks later, in my workroom with her mementoes and missal, I saw this verse was in fact the epistle in the mass for the dead, and certainly it is to the dead also that I write, whom it no longer concerns.

Born, labored, died, and interred now in a perpetual rest of which they know nothing, why on earth should I write blessed are the dead? That the extinction we must come to is the bitterest fact of our existence is no news; after the first espial of death some terror of it is in every brain like a fretful grain of sand, and around it man has created many pearls of wisdom, mostly false;

one is that consciousness is an affliction. I have been lucky as my kin were, average citizens in a plentiful land, and in my remembering of that which was from the beginning, which I have heard, which I have seen with my eyes, I cannot put down that any of them begged to be delivered out of this vale of tears. I think our history is worth the telling because it is so ordinary, and it contains no suicide; none of us but, like most men, took in every breath possible. Hemorrhaging and in pain for weeks, my father on his deathbed still wanted to live, and banged on a wall with his bleeding fist that he could not. My mother in her last hours, impatient to quit a life wherein she could labor no more, murmured not a word to disaffirm her love of this world; I overheard her thanks for it the day after I read of the voice from heaven, and it was her phrase, so much wholer in acceptance, that impelled me to write. Seeing my parents dead in coffins, I could have thought them blessed only in that their flesh was incapable of my grief, which is no pearl except of pity for self.

The truth is our wisdom sets my teeth on edge. By everything I know, the death of the animal is fortuitous, meaningless, and total; insofar as man, a maker of meanings, is at the utmost stretch of his talent to bestow upon his dying a purpose, I wish him luck in it; but when each meaning he arrives at is used by him to multiply the deaths it consoles him for, I think I am living among lunatics. Is the decomposition of the flesh hideous? it is a door to the light beyond, said the priests of infinite love, let us kill all who think otherwise. Is our life brief as the grass? we are immortal in the glory of the empire, said the bearers of every flag, let us die to plant it in another place. Saints, patriots, bards, which of them in the name of a greater life has not counselled us to kill and die? From the day I was born I was taught, against the yearning in my bowels for the sun, that I should consent to my death for the illusions believed of my elders; and in all the battlecries of the world, honor, order, liberty, valor, justice, duty, faith, I heard a baaing of sheep, as ignorant as I of what the sounds in their throats meant.

Children, I write this epistle to a punctuation of incendiary bombs my neighbors vote to let fall, as seeds of freedom, upon the heads of children no older than you. I am by trade a maker of fictions, but no word of mine is so counterfeit as the myths by which men who kill and die will ask you to live; the world is a windbag of pieties, that in each age blows multitudes like you into its graves, and weeps over them as blessed. Its touchstone of greatness is bloodletting, Saul hath slain his thousands and David his ten thousands, and no king or president is venerable in our thoughts but like the Judas goat has marched a people under the slaughtering hammer. And beneath the baaing of trumpets and dreams, faint, the only sound I hear as fact is the death rattle of each man.

That sound is my premise. I am the elder now, I tell you my wisdom, not one of the dead is blessed; consciousness is all. I am of course less epochal of mind than the statesman, who in eulogy of the corpses that have served their purpose, his, is confident none has died in vain, well done, thou good and faithful servants: a dish I think fit for the devil is the tongue of every man who asks the power of life and death over others. I speak as that ignoble, small-minded, disaffected citizen, servant and master only of his trade, I mean the artist, joyous and haunted by time, who, making of his spittle a shape, a soul, a voice to survive, wants no interruptions by history or its heroes. Selfish and harmless, in love with my life, I tell you no more than what everyone knows, and is ashamed to live by. Consciousness is all, the sun is born in and ends in your skull; the struck match of self in your skull is all.

So much is simple. It may be pinched out in an hour, therefore, burn in this hour; it may persist a half-century, therefore, burn wisely in this hour; but burn. Yet to make of each day an end and a beginning is not simple, and what is self? I have other selves of me, flesh of my flesh, whatever I believe in is of me, and much of a man is outside his skin; men not fools will die for a fool's light as their own. Then burn, believe, die, but, children, I beg you, not for the lies of statesmen, and I think it better to hide and live.

I learned these things at the deathbed of my father, between two wars; on the wall hung a poem with a pasted snapshot of his young brother's head, blown apart in the war that began in the year of my birth, and upon the night table sat a clock ticking, ticking the irrecoverable seconds away, and at his shrunken hand a portable radio bleated its news of a worldful of sheep who predictably would soon march under the hammer of another war; I did not intend to be in their ranks. It is a most beautiful earth we inhabit, but not in the eyeholes of the dead. So a savior knew who two thousand years ago said, A new commandment I give unto you, that ye love one another, and that night was betrayed. Are we less than lunatics who, aware we go into the grave at sundown, even in the failing light cannot love, but wrestle each other in? And when I remember what pains I took to hone this grievous and only jewel, my consciousness, I will not surrender it to any leader half in love with death, neither do I wear it in shame; nothing in his head is worth my life.

Daily I hear a whisper in me of the first and holiest commandment, Thou shalt not die.

Not in our time, but one day when there is silence in heaven about the space of half an hour, all the people will voice their right to live in a joyous shout, and the pillars come tumbling down. States, churches, armies, banks, schools, edifice upon edifice cemented in the blood of our bowing to the hammer, will lie in a rubble; the world will be born again as a comedy whose text is blessed are the living. In that day, great men who invite us to die for causes will charm the children as clowns in the parks, and cowardice will be in style, the ancientest virtue which preserves us, all manner of weakness be revered, and over every kindergarten door will be carved, I shall not die, but live, and declare the works of the Lord. Not in our time, when that primal commandment is only a whisper, served, yet deviously, and in dishonor.

Well, I too shall break it, in the end, and you. Till then, little children, keep yourselves from idols, greet ye one another with an holy kiss, and let us be neither goat nor sheep, but lovers of the sun, which is no fool's light.

OFFERTORY

27. Fifty

Today the sun
  Is chill.

The leaves that fall
  This year
Will never rise:

What do I care
  If eyes
As knowing fill

To see the green
  Is back
In light to spare?

I told that lie.
  Today
The sun is low

Set in the trees
  And fact
Is in the air:

OFFERTORY

It is this leaf
    This eye
This light between

Is me and mine
    To know
I love or lack.

And all the wood
    Is bare.

28. Blood in the Leaf

It was our autumn, though spring, when we took up life in the suburb someone had christened Bellerose, where the seven windows of our sun porch looked out upon a paved street and in either direction a gauntlet of two-story houses indistinguishable from each other, all with spindly saplings, little rugs of lawn, privet hedges, and wooden stoops to sun porches with seven windows. Elysian with an abundance not hitherto ours, it was the last dwelling we would occupy as a family, for in it my father died, and my sister, I, my mother, the knot unravelling, simply came apart.

Death had paid us another call prior to the move. The benign grump of a walrus who a decade ago had slipped me the dollar I hid on a dark sill, where my mother first discovered I had a secret life, was my only greatuncle, most of whose name my father bore. In his late seventies, George Irving Jennings was the patriarchal occupant of a tall clapboard house in Mt. Vernon with his daughter, her husband, their daughters, their husbands, and their children, an old-fashioned tribal lair so commodious that the middle room of the second floor was devoted to a billiard table around whose green felt, on our annual visit in my childhood, all the men gathered with cuesticks, chalk, and jokes; meanwhile I was agog in a looting of the bookcases throughout the house, for my greatuncle had been until late years what his womenfolk called "a terrible reader". It was a delight he had indulged during a lifetime in that literary institution, the customs house, from which he was retired. Of a lively mind, he never lacked for occupation; he took himself on bus trips to see regions he had read about, he researched the Jennings history back two hundred years to the bastardy of a duchess, and having come of age after the Civil War into a "very black Republican family"—my father's mother said that "if the devil ran on the Republican ticket against the Lord they'd all vote for the devil"—he busied himself as captain of his political district; but now he was deaf, his voice a chronic shout, and although he was still handmaking the ornaments which exhilarated the many Christmas trees of his kin, including ours, his watery blue eyes were failing him. I remember him picking out this book and that for me, cowboy sagas, scowling at the titlepages with a magnifying glass. I rarely saw my greatuncle nowadays, but his existence in some dim way put a blessing on me, unknown to him, since with my own namesake Will dead—it was to the old man's house that Will stumbled on his last day before the straitjacket—that patriarch and I were the only bookreaders left in the clan, and across the sixty years between us I felt less of a freak. My regard for him was not exceptional; my father captioned his snapshot as "a lucky guy everybody loves him". Inveterately an early riser, who made his own breakfast while the household was still asleep, he was discovered on the bathroom floor one morning, dead of a heart attack.

I was not at his funeral, because in the presence of no other of the blood relations by whom my nature was shaped in the dark did I find any light cast upon it; I thought they cast opacity. I had to argue my way out of it, and the argument was so illtempered on my part and illogical on theirs that I took to absenting myself from funerals, baptisms, holiday meals, all gatherings of a family who, when I judged them with the incorruptible eye of late adolescence, I decided had not much right to live. I suffered the existence of my parents and sister, but other kinfolk on both my father's side and my mother's I banished to limbo with impartial injustice. I was however often cornered by them in our own living room, and if I found our new house a durance vile it was partly because I saw its canon and theirs as now one.

I was out of the family long before I was out of the house. My grandmother would come to visit her only son for a week each year, and I hardly made her acquaintance. She was an old lady of seventy-five with a sad kindly face, the ancient pride in it gone, her white hair nebulous, pink with scalp, and under its roots another world of stalactitic memories of her dead, her parents, her brothers, her husbands, her sons, amongst which she sat in our rocker embroidering day after day a tablecloth or napkins for her daughters, of whom she considered my mother to be one; mater dolorosa, when of my ungodly opinions she said with a tolerant smirk, "Oh, Billy's just going over Fool's Hill," I was repelled by the falsity of her teeth, and the tonnage of her flesh which could no longer climb out of bathtubs was noisome in my nostrils, and the rocker's creak, creak, creak with her in it would shatter my eardrums. It was not personal, I was just as indignant when my mother's schoolmate and her wig spent their annual silence with us, another unbearable week, and I shrank from every kiss sprayed upon me by my aunt Minnie. Starved on the scant pickings of affection from her mate, and childless since the deathfall of her boy into that cellar so long ago, our goodhearted slob Minnie had bribed her way into the disaffection of my sister and me by smothering us with sweets, toys, dimes, and kisses so salivating we promptly got rid of them with our palms; once my mother had rebuked me for it, and I said cleverly, "I'm not wiping it off, I'm wiping it in," a phrase which Minnie requoted with contentment after every expunged kiss for years. I was long past such idle appeasement. Deep in a life-and-death inquiry into the lineaments of the shifty teen-ager within my skin, I knew the unpardonable sin was a polite word, it surrendered the brain, and I would not forgive my mother for volunteering it was "nice to meet you" to strangers; the criminal indictment on which I found my elders guilty was not that they were fat, skinny, teetotallers, obtuse, malodorous, prudes, adulterers, or even un-musical, but fundamentally, Christians all, such liars.

Yet it was a particular strain of mendacity I was in revolt against, in the new house and old relatives. It angered me less in my mother's tribe, whose sentimentality so often delivered them into a state of crisis where truth was an embarrassment that they abstained from it on principle: their lies were more like vaude-ville. When Frank Dore had materialized to live with his sister Minnie he announced he was worth thousands in army insurance and pension money and was "making it over" to her because, after years of obliviousness to her in the tropics, he "idolized" her; with a soldierly hug he would say gruffly, "When I die, sis, you get everything." The week of his funeral was a busy one, for Ben's older girl—the nurse who modelled herself after my mother—was in a Yonkers hospital in labor, a childbirth which continued for three days. On the first day her husband phoned word to my father at the bank, the family's only telephone, and my parents that night made a courier's trip to Minnie's, my mother cautioning her, "Now don't go to the hospital in black, it will only upset her," but my aunt was incensed that she was the last to hear of the confinement though everyone knew she was the oldest. Next morning she sat down to write her niece a letter of fuming abuse, an echo of her mother Mary Dore, which she mailed off to the maternity ward. In the girl's seventieth hour of labor my parents found her hysterical with the letter, and when Minnie turned up—"all in black, with the jet beads"—my father bawled her out for writing it; Minnie, in a panic at her niece's danger, denied writing a letter. My father then procured it to put under her nose, Minnie read it judiciously and said no, it wasn't her handwriting. My father expostulated that it was signed by her and poked his forefinger at her signature, and Minnie, injured to the point of tears, said, "Would I write a letter like that to my favorite niece?" My father tore the letter to pieces, and the niece produced a boy, and my godmother Minnie in her jet beads trudged home to await word from the army about Frank's legacy. It now appeared that my uncle had also somewhat misstated the facts, the insurance and pension were assigned not quite to Minnie but to a wife he had divorced in Texas, who had remarried and died, and the posthumous thousands went to a widower nobody in the family had ever heard of. Poor Minnie implored Ben's lawyers to check into the army's veracity, which stood up, and her facepowder was flawed by many a tear; she was "heartbroken" that her brother would lie to her.

Prevarication of this transparency never occurred in Jersey, a difference in altitude, my father's kin were more highminded. The sinners in the family were harmless to me, it was the saints whom I had to exorcise, and as fast as I could I plummeted from those placid fields; his womenfolk in their raiment of starched housedresses, artless of cosmetics and perfume, jolly with pieties, such good cooks, who told no lies, loomed in my malign eye as living a whopper; they were as undissonant as hymns. It was the untruth of that wholesome doze that I smelled in our suburb. I glowered upon them as incarnations of a figurine of three simians then popular in households who with their own paws incapacitated their ears, mouths, and eyes, allowing themselves to hear no evil, speak no evil, and see no evil, a virtue which appealed to me somewhat less than castration. I myself saw no good in my cousin's lapel dripping with a medal and its sequential bars, one for each year in Sunday school, and I heard no good in so much chitchat of heaven as though it immediately overhung Englewood; I spoke no good when at mealtime graces I debased their text—"God bless the food we are going to take, and make it good for Jesus' sake"—ascribing it to the book of Asparagus. Gentle and decent as my father's sisters were, I was in an alliance with the backside of those monkeys, saw only how much in my bowels such women would deny me, and viewed as the archfiend of sainthood the most extraordinary of them, my aunt in the pith helmet, Ada.

I was also missing from the dock when the family waved Ada off on the fourth of her five safaris, each of several years, among the heathen of Africa; most of my life she was dwelling with the blacks to whom she turned soon after her family moved out of Harlem. I knew her as a portly spinster, staid and aloof, rather imperious. In an oldtime snapshot the austerity of her palms at thighs evoked my father's caption of "forward march", and even then in her grave face the bespectacled eyes were lifted, otherworldly. Devout and sickly, she was for forty years her mother's helper, and not until she could bring herself to "give up" the baby Ethel she had reared, who was rearing a baby herself, was the call to Africa audible; she resolved to go in her worst attack of the asthma which had choked her for decades, but vanished when she reached her dark continent. Because of it the church had thought her unfit, and would not sponsor her. She said, "I'll go on faith," and sailed off "independently" to Cape Palmas with no means of support; friends sent her money for food, the church saw the error of its ways, and her labors the rest of her life were official.

In part her aloofness was from my impertinences—my sister recalls that when Ada said her houseboy "knew the Bible backwards" I suggested he give it more thought forwards—for she was earthier than I suspected: her antidote to nervousness before speaking in Jersey churches was to remind herself that the parishioners were "all cabbageheads". So they were, measured by the experience in hers. In Africa her work commenced with a five-day journey into the interior, and included classes in the Bible and sewing, converting females for converted males who could not wed unbelievers, administering a compound of a hundred girls, landscaping, delivering babies, founding and conducting a school up to the sixth grade, medicating its pupils for syphilitic and other sores out of which she "saw the maggots run", supervising the construction of roads, and travelling ten days into the jungle to bring "Godword" to headhunter tribes; she sold Bibles to their chiefs for cups of rice, to forestall a child wedding she bought the bride, and, lost on a wrong trail, she sat out the night teaching her bearers how to ward off the carnivores by singing hymns. She wrote home, "Sometimes I feel I am just a machine, you wind me up in the morning and I don't run down until a long time after I am in bed," and apologized for a tardy letter, "This is Saturday so we are free to do something personal." She enclosed snapshots of her mud house, shared on occasion with serpents, and of the "heathen natives" lined up in a naked aplomb of penises and breasts, and of their nuptials as Christians in white duck suits, and of black children with monstrous growths on their cheeks, sarcomas, ballooning out as big as their heads, and of herself, riding a native piggyback across a stream, or travelling by hammock, its roof borne on the pates of four converts, or standing stout in her housedress and pith helmet over dead apes and leopards.

I cannot explain by what act of perception I saw my aunt's life in the jungle as the height of conformity. So intent on my own difference that I thought no other differences existed, I equated my relatives with the duplicate houses along our street; I was as right as wrong, what I did not understand was that individuals like water seek their own levels of conformity, and I had not yet settled to mine. Meanwhile I believed less in Ada's self-denial than in Minnie's self-indulgence, felt hemmed in by false females, and lived in such a haughty avoidance of them that I was taken to task by both my parents for "snubbing" their good folk. It was easier to avoid aunts than my mother, the original female, until I managed it by fleeing the house she had at last created in the image of my father's kin; I could not but believe that "real life" was elsewhere.

This house, which cost thirty-five dollars a month, consisted of six rooms, sun porch, and cellar, and I only fled it, I never escaped it. If I think simply of the front door, which we seldom used, I see us in a dream of habitual moments—my mother each morning at its brass knob with rag and polish to outshine every knob on the block, or my father in his slippers seated on the stoop with neighbors each evening—but unblurred after a quarter-century is the summer noon I supported my shuffling father up the steps to it, homecoming from his operation; and no dream is the winter dusk I came down the street to see our door so different finally from all the others, flowers nailed upon it, when I would have given both eyes to have it identical again. Wherever real life was, I first met real death here, and not a square foot in the house but would be in me to my last day.

Upstairs, three bedrooms opened off a short hall. In the twentieth year of their marriage my parents once more had a bedroom to themselves, ample, with two windows fronting on the street, furnished with a five-piece suite—twin beds, lady's vanity with bench, man's chifforobe, and bureau—of walnut veneer, night table and lamp, cottonlace curtains, and the mahogany rocker which was a survivor of the honeymoon days; this was the room into which my father's life would shrink down in his last months. I took the middle bedroom, smaller, whose window above the driveway afforded a splendid view of another house ten feet away, and my sister had a frilly bedroom at back, with a window on the driveway and another on a green yard as deep as our single garage. The bathroom at her end of the hall was not a dozen steps from our parents' sill, a distance which was to lengthen into a fearful pilgrimage.

Downstairs, the back door by which we entered let us in on a tiny landing; from it an open staircase led down to the cellar, and two steps led up to the kitchen. The cellar below was white-washed, clean, crude. Its corner was a coalbin to hold in two heaps, the larger of chunks for the elephantine furnace which in winter sent up steam to the radiators throughout the house, the smaller of pea coal for the petite stove which in summer kept hot water in the faucets upstairs and in the slate washtubs of the cellar. In these tubs, with yellow soap on a washboard, my father still scrubbed the dirty clothes of the household, from handker-chiefs to sheets, then departed for a day's work at the bank, and my mother would hang them to dry, sometimes in the cellar, but in good weather on a clothesline in the backyard. The cellar was merely tidy; the kitchen, up from the landing, was my mother's soul and delight. Glossy white, large, with windows on three sides, which she decked every other week in crisp white curtains with red dots or trim, and one wall of white cupboard whose glass panes she veiled with curtains to match, and a white refrig-erator, her first, which we could not unlearn to call "the ice-box", and a white porcelain sink in which she never let even a dirty teacup sit, and a white gas range whose burners were kept as impeccable as by a dentist's drill, the entire kitchen, down to our white table in its center, was aseptic as a hospital; and in it my mother and I for six months took turns in boiling sterile the glass and metal parts of a hypodermic needle. Snug in one corner was a "breakfast nook", a built-in table with opposed benches where we ate all our meals, and between it and the refrigerator a swingdoor led to the dining room.

Used only when we had company, the dining room was som-bre with an oak-veneer set—china closet, oblong table, padded chairs, sideboard—weighty and elegant, newly bought for the house, but secondhand, from acquaintances of friends. Not too light, with its two windows curtaining out the driveway, the room was dignified by a chandelier with an opulent lampshade which overhung the table, and under it, on a full tablecloth of lace string, a glass platter offered an assortment of wax fruits, apples, grapes, oranges, which to me typified the inedibility of bourgeois life; at this table night after night I sat up late to study Marx in the belief, not quite baseless, that the citizenry too was starving to death. At my back the sidewall was given to a banistered stairway that led up to the bedrooms, and from its top step, seated, with a houseful of people below her, my mother would emit the involuntary scream that pierces my ear to this hour. Divided from the dining room by the jambs of no wall and paired strips of chintz drapes, the living room was cozy and airier, two curtained windows again but also a glass door, curtained, to the sun porch; the upholstered sofa and its coffee table, the twin circular tables with doilies and twin lamps, the upholstered easy chair and footstool, the console radio, all faced the upright piano like a fireplace, and atop it was stacked as always the sheet music, next to which in its green felt cover was the slumbrous mandolin. It was in this room that the body of my father would lie in its coffin for three days. The sun porch beyond was narrow, all windows, with odd chairs on a fiber rug, two or three stands with potted plants, and my studio couch.

Such was the house which millions of my compatriots then would have gladly moved into, and I moved out of. My studio couch was on the sun porch because I was now too longlegged for comfort in it and had inherited a double bed, the dismemberment of which was my first act of revolt; the beauteous bedstead turned my den into a boudoir, and I stripped off headboard, footboard, siderails, and to my mother's dismay worked them all up through a hatch in my sister's closet into the crawl space above, where for all I know they still are. With bedspring and

mattress supine on my floor I could inhale and exhale again—
though my mother, unable to vacuum under it, was frantic—and
I occupied my bohemian room like a beachhead in a war. To me
the house was a crystallization not only of the family, but of a
class, and one so prevalent that in any of our rooms I was in a
heartland of the country, enemy territory, whose name was my
parents' happiness; I saw it all as a colossal lie, and effected my
escape by a sequence of disasters which only in retrospect seem
to have been brilliant.

Apart from me, our sole worry was my mother's health. She
was in periodic touch with her fifty-cent clinic, now in a throng
of medical buildings uptown, where every few months among
the crowded benches she sat with a numbered card and awaited
her turn for check-ups, of her thyroid, of her ulcer, of her
varicose veins; a legacy from Mary Dore, the varicosity took her
into surgery again. It consisted of slitting open her legs to tie the
bulbous veins, not a major operation, but so painful—anesthetics
left my mother nauseated for days, she would "rather die than
have a sick stomach", and whenever doctors permitted she
elected the pain instead—that she told Milly "never to have it".
In three days she was out of the hospital, but the search for
contributory causes had discovered a tumor in her uterus the size
of an egg, which also explained the clots of blood she was
noticing in her urine. She travelled again to the clinic for radium
treatments that "dried up the uterus", inducing an artificial men-
opause; and thereafter she often experienced "hot flashes", so
that my sister seated with her in the movies could feel her
forearm startle with sweat, but my mother said it was nothing.
She rarely complained of her ills, though the stomach upsets and
sick headaches persisted throughout her life, and I found her
more than once on her bed with the shades drawn and an iced
cloth over her eyes, a little apologetic at "giving in to herself".

Her usual therapy was housework, a triumph of conscience

over the flesh. My father had known the house would tempt her to "overdo"; prior to renting it he had convened us in a family talk on how each must help her, but it was feeding crumbs to a maelstrom. Housecleaning that I thought was exhaustive my mother called "a lick and a promise", I was no sooner out of my room after bringing it to the pitch of perfection than she was in to clean up after me, and I saw no profit in my dusting the under-parts of furniture indoors only to glimpse her outdoors sweeping the sidewalk whenever anyone walked on it. I viewed her round of daily housework as bizarre enough, but in the spring and fall the house underwent a convulsion to its bones. Down from every window and doorway and cupboard came the drapes and curtains, to be scrubbed in the cellar tubs, ironed, and folded away in the linen closet upstairs, and not a pane in the house escaped her scrubbing, and on the windows she hung her change of curtains, full ones in winter, tie-backs in summer; the furni-ture lifted, from each floor in spring we uprolled the wool rugs, freshly vacuumed, and my father and I wrestled them down to store in the cellar while my mother on her knees scrubbed and waxed the floorboards anew, and out of storage in the cellar my father and I wrestled up the fiber rugs to be unrolled on each floor, the furniture lifted; the upholstered sofa and easy chair and footstool, grave in their original wine-hued damask with lace antimacassars, were now encased by my mother in a chirrup of cretonne slipcovers, which at summer's end she whisked off again to the cellar tubs; out of the china closet came the good dishes, speckless, and out of the kitchen cupboard came the bad dishes, speckless, to be washed in the sink to the last saucer, and she scrubbed the shelves, laid strips of doily in the china closet and of pretty oilcloth in the cupboard, and replaced all her dishes in geometric stacks, now speckless; up on tables and bureaus in her stockinged feet she wiped the ceilings clean, and scrubbed down the walls and woodwork, and took the bedsteads apart, to dust them, and stitched fresh covers on the mattresses whose obscene ticking was never seen of mortal eye, save hers, and kneeling at the bathtub she washed all the blankets; out of the closets she carried the family's clothes, suits, dresses, overcoats, to be brushed and aired on the clothesline, their pockets pulled out and the cuffs of my father's trousers everted, while she scrubbed the closets themselves and laid fresh papers on their shelves; with soap and water she visited all the furniture in the house, upstairs and down, washing its oil off so she could oil it, and she emptied every drawer, to line each with virgin paper and restore its contents to the strictest order; the kitchen cabinet was evacuated of its groceries, the broom closet of its miscellany, and my mother scrubbed not only the shelves but each can of peas, dusted the cornflakes, cleaned the cleanser, and, pulling the stove apart, soaked its burners and knobs and pipelengths in ammonia water; the ceiling fixtures from every room were in the sink, and in the dining room she even dismantled the chandelier. Spring and fall, the harder my mother worked the more cheerful she became, it replenished her life, and I saw it only as done for the neighbors' opinion.

The three precepts my father gave his daughter for ensuring a happy marriage—keep the house clean, keep yourself clean, and have supper ready when the husband comes home—summed up most of my mother's day. Her diversions were simple, chats in the backyard with her two neighbors, outings along the avenue for the groceries, and a movie matinee now and then with her old friend, the wife of the singing bricklayer turned jeweller, domiciled in a similar house a few blocks away; and two or three afternoons a month my mother would undertake a grim expedition with the car, five miles to the big stores in Jamaica or ten to her sister Minnie's. I had taught her to drive. Though her tendency in crisis was to freeze to the steering wheel until we were safely stopped by an el pillar, she had persevered through all my shouts and passed her test without bribing the inspector; on the day of her first solo trip my father—who had passed with a five-dollar bill, and for weeks would not drive alone—left her a note praising her as "some gal", with the perennial "I.L.Y." Two scraps of paper commandeered by his large handscript, this twenty-six-year-old note was among my mother's mementoes.

The kitchen was bright, my mother was in a fresh housedress, and supper was ready when the husband came home to their unfailing kiss, washed his hands at the sink, put on the leather slippers my sister ran upstairs to fetch, and sidled into the nook to his peculiar diet. The food was plentiful, bland, wholesome—meat loaf, broiled lamb or pork chops, filet of sole on Fridays, sirloin steak twice a month, potatoes mashed or baked, boiled carrots, stringbeans, beets, lettuce-and-tomato salad, wholewheat bread, milk—but my father ate no vegetables, salad, or fruit; he ate meat and potatoes, buried in a black snow-storm of pepper, dessert and coffee. He used bread only termi-nally, slice after slice drowned in gravy, which he said made "the best dessert", and then would take a hefty wedge of cake, gener-ously butter it, wipe the gravy platter with it, lay a few knifefuls of mustard onto it, and have it as his real dessert. It was home-baked, I was twenty before I laid eyes on a store cake, for my mother was a superlative baker. Out of the oven came a parade of golden and white cookies, crescent, globular, fit to set in a crown, and shortbread cut into diamonds and hearts, butter-soaked, dissolute on the tongue, and her lemon-meringue pies, tangy yellow and frothy white, and great ovals of coffee ring two feet long with raisins and citron and nuts imprisoned in a milky glaze, and her deep-dish apple pies, hot, appeased with melting gobs of pale hardsauce chill as virtue and twice as un-bearable, and massive rings of pound cake so laden with eggs and butter it was not yellow but orange, impregnated with raisins in one half and the other half plain to satisfy ascetic tastes, and her eclairs in their lava of chocolate, corpulent with whipped cream, of which my father would eat seven at a sitting, and the glazed brioche rolls my mother kneaded and raised for three days to such a lightness they became almost spiritual, flavor without substance, so of them my father at Sunday breakfast ate fifteen, seventeen, nineteen.

And forking into all her variety of other layer cakes, crumb, peach, date-and-nut, cream cakes, my father somehow kept thin and never suffered a twinge of indigestion. Decline of the flesh had appeared only in his teeth, which loosened with pyorrhea until he could no longer chew; one afternoon the dentist yanked them all and cut away the bone underneath, and for two days my father lay on the sofa with a basin alongside, spitting blood. However shaken he may have been by this reminder of mortality, or gloomy in his toothless weeks, his subsequent plates of false teeth, yellowed and made irregular by the dentist's cunning, simply mellowed his looks, the protrusion of upper teeth was gone. It was his sole ailment through the years, he was not once in a hospital, other than to visit my mother.

So we felt no chill and shed no tear when death now pinched out another George in the family, her rich brother in Larchmont. I had not seen him ten times in my life, and knew him only by the stories current among the Dores, all uncomplimentary; his costly home was a "museum" in which his wife was said to keep even the bedsheets overlaid with protective newspapers, and when on our first visit years ago she restricted my sister and me to the kitchen floor—lest we urinate on her rugs—my mother decided it was our last. I knew my uncle well in another way, for of all our family George Dore was the only one in whom I could see the luck-and-pluck newsboys of my early reading come to life, and the recognition was perplexing. My mother spoke often of his beginnings, how as a lad he had saved a dime a day by walking to and from work across the Brooklyn Bridge, and how his bride banked something each week out of his wage of twelve dollars; less familiar was the ending, that such thrift should win him everyone's dislike, and the loyal wife be supplemented by a lady friend whom she tracked down to their rendezvous in the ice-company office. It was not such peccadilloes, nor George's retirement from the partnership because he "was fed up with Ben's drinking", that my mother thought so unnatural in him, it was coldness of heart. George never set foot in any flat of ours, although the month my mother lay ill with diphtheria he had come to the door—the Bronx office of the ice company was in the neighborhood—to ask after her and declined to risk infection by entering to greet her, which "made everyone mad"; it was of a piece with the other stories, as when he let Ben out of his Cadillac at the stoop and begged off climbing the five flights to see their mother Mary Dore, dead two days later, because he "had the dogs at home". In the funeral procession George drove his own car in preference to sharing the familial limousine, and drove in it out of our lives. I remembered him as handsome, senatorial, and dressed too circumspectly with his overcoat forever buttoned, so that my father would observe wryly, "There goes Buttons with all his money," and since it was said he "was never happy with it" that prosperous figure on the horizon of my boyhood came to personify the moral that success, like crime, did not pay; something had gone amiss with the national dream. Yet the clan was proud of the mansion and money they derided, and always took interest in the trickle of iridescent news about George—his stockmarket coups, his winter home in California, his daughter's fling as an actress—until the day his heart failed even him.

The news came from his wife, with a message to "tell Flo and Minnie not to create a scene" among the pillars of society at the funeral; my indignant mother sent word back that if she did she "would feel like a hypocrite". Minnie and Ben were another matter, one with a weakness for tears, the other for drink, and my mother forbade both to them, they were "going first class, we'll show them we're as good as they are," and with Ben in his decline my father took his suit to be pressed, bought him a black tie and new shirt, and escorted him to the barbershop for a haircut. The funeral was a success too, the three kept inconspicuous while they saw their brother buried by his peers of the Larchmont Yacht Club, and wished the widow well, and came home; my mother said, "That's a closed book." Of the nineteen children, she and her pair of aging charges were the last three.

Autumn was in the tree, and I could not see it, in that suburb it seemed it must always be summer; my parents' lives were at their ripest. They enjoyed being in each other's presence, and invariably on Saturdays my father skipped his free "hot lunch" in the bank cafeteria in favor of a sandwich in the kitchen with my mother. It was she who most often picked him up at the depot, and in the two summers left to them after my departure she would pack a picnic supper into the car on evenings when my sister had a dinner date; my father and she would divide it on one of the public beaches, and watch the sun down. Other nights they visited with neighbors—my mother said we "always had good neighbors"—on the stoop. Or they listened to their radio programs, crooners, black-voiced comedians, "true stories" of sin and heartbreak, and if my mother mused that she "felt like something nice" my father would drive down to a busier suburb and bring her back a box of favorite chocolates, on which she nibbled while studying the newspaper's page after page of sales in the city which she had no intention of going to; she liked to read the prices. My father as always played some piano, and now and then would cajole my mother into unsheathing the mandolin, and she would pluck away tremolo at the old songs to his accompaniment, singing. Every Saturday evening they walked the two blocks to the avenue movie, and usually came home saying it was "not so good", still unsure of its title. It was never the title that enticed them; after five years of depression the exhibitors were luring customers with dishes, turkeys, money, and of a hundred "bank nights" the only one my parents missed was on a weekend they visited my sister in the country, returning to hear from all the neighbors that good luck had smiled upon them, they had won and forfeited two hundred and fifty dollars. My parents were rueful but laughed about it, they foresaw no shortage of bank nights, nor of each other's presence.

In this house even my father's workday, which for eighteen years had every Monday turned itself upside down, became normal. Downtown in the mailroom a mysterious hand was dipping into the stamps and money drawers at irregular intervals, and after much sleuthing the thief was arrested; he was the head of the department, a family man like my father, but in his locker the detectives—I learned this twenty-five years later from a co-worker, not from my father—found a few packets of condoms; his life broken on a hidden reef of sexuality at fifty, that grayhaired man went to prison, and my father was elevated to his job. It was a post he was loth to shoulder. My mother could speak of him with pride as an "officer" of the bank, but a title was his only profit, the promotion was accompanied by no boost in salary, only in work and worries, and to them my mother always attributed his illness, perhaps not foolishly. Though she kept it a secret from us, my father was making sixty-five dollars a week, riches enough in the depression, and for it now was answerable for all the traffic of the bank's correspondence with the world, in and out, by day shift and night shift, with more than sixty men to keep track of in the flow of cash and millions of pieces of mail; even in convalescence after his first hemorrhage he received a communiqué from a higher-up—influential, for not one letter of his signature is legible—advising him the insurance companies would settle the "registered mail matter", some loss which they concluded had "happened across the water". My father with the promotion had homework again, he sat evenings under the lampshade at the dining room table with his records spread forth, personnel, mail volume, fiscal, and over them he calculated, sweated, wrote, erased, sweated, and berated himself for his skimpy schooling. Sleep came to him fragilely, and it was thus I inherited the double bed; if my mother moved a leg at night my father would awaken and be up for an hour in his rocker at the window with a glowing cigarette and a headful of duties to rehearse, his old habit which did not cease with the twin beds. Yet his workhours at last were regular, forenoons with the shift going out and afternoons with the shift coming in, and commuting to the city by railroad now, one in the whitecollar tide of thousands of clerks in by morning and back by evening, he was home for every supper in the family nook at six o'clock.

The depot was seven blocks from our street, and I often met him with the car when my mother was hovering at the oven. I waited at the mouth of an underpass until he appeared in its flow of nameless men, still unique, trim and natty in his gray suit with vest, small-knotted tie, gray felt hat at a modest angle, and his face so benign and candid, alive in a smile at seeing me; it was a moment he had lived before, my first memory of him, oldtime straw hat emerging out of a crowd of obscure folk on a high el platform to stoop and loft me onto a shoulder, to me a lifetime ago, and, as I could not know, to him only yesterday; now I was two inches taller than he, and surely grown much too complicated for him to understand, but my heart still like a child skipped a little at the sight of his rare figure, sauntering among the others, easily slapping with the newspaper at his calf, so contented to be home. We always shook hands. I would drive, with my father seated quiet beside me, newspaper in lap, his elbow out the window, his eyes taking in the pleasure of the leafy trees and children on tricycles and men sprinkling lawns, neat dwelling after dwelling, five blocks of them on the richer side of the shopping avenue and two blocks on the other, until I headed in at our driveway and inched into the tight garage; and there we squeezed ourselves out of the car among the garden tools, hose, lawn mower, rake, over which after supper he would relax in the tiny backyard. In his old pants, a relic from the two-pair gray suit of three years ago, cutting the grass, cultivating his five tomato plants, standing with the hose to spray his row of zinnias while he chatted about baseball with the nextdoor clerk spraying his, my father, one in a million, was utterly at home in and not unproud of the tidy suburban house into which his lifework had succeeded in bringing us.

Viewing it as more jail than offertorium, even I once saw that in it was something precious, and doomed. I remember us at a foursome supper in the nook, very quiet, because in the next house the mother had thought to help her son's bellyache with an enema and now the boy, seventeen years old, lay dead of a burst appendix; a neighborhood conspiracy of silence was keeping from the mother what she had done. Seated in that nook, for once in my life I looked at my mother, father, sister, and saw them—my sister's face, chubby and blonde and pretty, and my father's face, tan, youthful even with his bald brow, the blue eyes friendly, the nose well-fleshed but shapely, his mouth so prompt in its downward smile, and my darkhaired mother's face, pale under light make-up, plain, straightnosed, her thin lips and hazel eyes worried, thinking of her neighbor—and I in that moment knew how lucky we were, to sit there, alive, together, with our heads over the platefuls of supper, four and a shadow stalking.

Of that autumnal glimpse I said nothing; when fall in fact came I was not there, and it is only by a poor act of imagination that I can guess anything now of what my father's eye, looking at my empty place, saw.

29. In the Eye of My Father

It is not yet dawn when my father, having sat in his pajamas for a few minutes on the bed over a first cigarette, finds his slippers with his feet and shuffles on his way to the toilet past the door of my room. In the next bedroom his chick is asleep, who in two hours will be off to highschool, so my father is quiet in the bathroom, washes, shaves, leaves it deodorized with cigarette smoke, and returns to his night table for his teeth in their glass of water.

Dressing at his chifforobe by the light of the pink ceiling fixture—narrow body in long underwear, black socks with garters, starched white shirt, blue polka-dot tie, gray suit with vest, black shoes, all nattily conservative—he sees the twin bed from which my mother has arisen to make his breakfast, and it flushes up a memory of his son. In its sheets last summer the boy spent a sweaty afternoon with a girl and was betrayed by his bedmaking afterwards, no match for that of his mother, who in outrage stripped the bed; next day her white face, telling him it was never to happen again, was offered no denial and no explanation. Little in the house is not evocative of the boy, and my father on his way to the stairhead glances in at my open door. It was wont to be closed in the days when there was news within, and now is ajar on a room unchanged; only the little radio is gone, and the typewriter, and the occupant. If the memories are unsatisfactory enough, the room withal is an emptiness in him as my father goes down the stairs to his breakfast.

My mother serves him in the bench nook, and peering out a frosty window observes worriedly it's been a cold night and she hopes poor Billy is all right; my father says of course he's all right. Curled up at the radiator a beefy mongrel, deserted by his master, lifts a a bloodshot eye and thumps a tail. My mother says why can't he write a penny postcard, and my father remembers an auto trip with the pup to see their son in his first absence, a job as a waiter-pianist at a lake resort where if he was homesick it was only for the dog, forgetting his parents to cavort with him all afternoon, and a week later was ambling down the street with his suitcase, fired, for indifference to labor, he had not lasted long enough to see the first guest; the following month, on a job my father wangled for him as messenger in a skyscraper, the boy wandered off at lunch and his employers next had a letter saying he had been called to California, mail his paycheck to Queens. Finishing his coffee, my father says there's nothing to worry about, and sidles out of the nook for the closet in the dining room.

In his rayon scarf and gray overcoat, he returns with hat and gloves; my mother is at a quick cup of tea. Letting himself down the cellar stairs, my father under the lightbulb shakes the furnace down, shovels in some coal, and sees the corner with card table his son chose as a writing place, grim and odd. Careful of his overcoat, he bears the ashcan in both hands up the stairs, the boy's chore, out the back door, and down the driveway to leave it at the curb under the leafless tree; it is graying light, and he opens the garage doors to back the Ford out.

With my mother bundled up beside him, he heads for the depot. The car too is not without its memories—in quest of a job on a newspaper the boy drove to a state office so remote he spent ten dollars in gas on a list of weeklies he could have had for a postage stamp but never wrote to one, and three nights a week drove into the city to a tradeschool for auto mechanics which after a month he quit too, and another evening stammered out a tale to his father who said wryly well let's have a look at it and walked with him to a garage to okay repairs on a smashed front end—until the depot is at hand, busy with cars letting out their menfolk. One snowflake falls, my mother says it's snowing and she hopes poor Billy is all right. My father says for God's sake what could happen to him but he'll stop off after work; and her face is brighter when he kisses it.

Seated in the train among all the heads my father watches out the window. The neat houses pick up speed past him—miles of them, in and out of whose driveways his boy rang every doorbell to peddle mops and pails last autumn, a rare burst of enterprise, and quit the day he'd saved up money enough to qualify for home relief—then the streets grow huddly; and my father's window creeps in past warehouses to stop at the platform where he must change trains. At its newsstand he buys a tabloid. With it tucked under his arm, he gazes out over the niggertown rooftops. It was into these the boy first disappeared, the same story, when they wanted to see him they stood with a streetcorner crowd in which on a stepladder their son was calling for the overthrow of the government, and my mother said why can't he wear a necktie, and they worried about the police but months later sat in a packed hall to hear him debate capitalism with of all things a minister and a rabbi, and when he was so respected a leader he walked out on it all, and was once more expelled in disgrace. The incoming train blocks my father's view, and he steps in; no seats, he stands to read in his tabloid of the fuehrer marching into the wherever it is but folds it under to the sports page, and the train enters the river tunnel.

It is almost the last of the day's light my father sees. In midtown he is out of the terminal, then down into the subway, and out in the financial district in the slits of street between skyscrapers that seem to meet overhead, even the gutters jammed with clerks streaming to their jobs; my father finds the door that whisks him in to his. Under electric lights for the next nine hours with his sixty boys among the deluge of mail, he has little time for his own worries, and is off his feet only at lunch upstairs in the clamor of the bank's cafeteria. With three of his clerks he lingers over coffee, shop talk, sayings of their kids, thinking it was with his own he sat here a few summers ago advising him on the cableroom but they hardly met now—once when he was back from the revolution with his dirty laundry my father said did he think his mother was his washwoman, and another time ignored his stay, and once with communists all over the porch where a blackhaired girl lay between his knees my father flared to my mother he lives here or doesn't let him turn in his key it's not a hotel for bums—and something he ate has given him a heartburn. It is with him all afternoon while the dividends are running heavy in the check department. At six o'clock in his overcoat and hat my father rides the elevator down; when he is again out on the sidewalk the night is gathering, another day gone, he is ten dollars richer and his corns hurt. The wind is icy off the water that surrounds the tip of the city, and huddling against it he walks east to the el.

The uneasiness in him is more than indigestion. The drafty train rattles into the slums of midtown, where, in a lighted delicatessen under the el, spending three of the ten dollars on milk, roastbeef, rye bread, whatever his eye falls on, my father is nagged by a sense of worry, error, something undone. Outside it is a dying neighborhood, dim saloons, doorways of tenements, pawnshops, stores boarded up and stuck over with old circus posters under which a drunk with a bloody face lies in collapse, not unfamiliar, the el thundering over my father's head is out of his past and all the years he labored to get out of this decay seem to unravel behind him; and when he turns the corner to enter a hallway, it is into the odor of old times rotted into the wood. Up past the toilets at each landing, in a climb not unlike that he so often made to the old lady's in Harlem, my father at the fourth floor rear knocks on a battered door.

Unbolting, the lanky boy is in the doorway with hand on the knob, says hey, and with a smile makes way for him to walk in. It is the kitchen of a railroad flat, and out of the parlor comes the blackhaired girl, shy, but lifts from her low heels to kiss my father's cheek; she acquires the bagful of food, and his son removes his overcoat and hat to the parlor, where a radio is tinny with the music my father dislikes. It clicks silent. To the boy emerging my father says he didn't mean to interrupt a concert, the boy says no that's all right what's in the bag, and the groceries take over as a topic of conversation.

Cigarettes in reach, my father sits on a kitchen chair while the youngsters, boy in corduroys and girl in peasant blouse, set the table with mismated plates; her hands are uncertain, his take charge. My father sees an afternoon when alone with him in the car the boy suddenly said I'm married and at the wheel my father said oh you damned fool then smiled but his son's profile was mute with you understand nothing, and my father says these kerosene heaters give a lot of heat. Throwback to other days, it sits with a sizzly pot of water, and the kitchen around him is dingy, bathtub with lid, coalstove, broken walls with roaches meandering, the mops and pails have paid for it all; it was for this coldwater flat and bride and furniture from a junkshop that the boy walking out on his comrades was expelled, and my father thinks he'll walk out on this too.

The supper is eaten over idle chatting, how are things, fine, nothing said, and is not too awkward; it is vaguely wrong. At its end my father fingers into his vest pocket to lift out his watch, a train to catch. In the parlor he puts on his scarf with a glance at an old upright piano; the music upon it is open to black chords and runs. When he turns to the overcoat in his son's hands he sees his eyes are unremembering—the last time they sat to a keyboard together it was with a four-hand volume the eager boy brought from a library and they never got past the first page, my father's fingers stumbling so, he said vexed it's just scales where's the music, and his boy left him at the piano, next day the music disappeared, and later in the week my father said listen listen you didn't give me a chance—and buttoning up his overcoat says well, takes out his gloves, and the girl is offering his hat. At the kitchen door she kisses him on the cheek, the boy says and thanks for the feast, my father smiles, shakes his hand, says drop your mother a card for God's sake she worries, and at the stairhead hears the door close behind him.

Going down the staircase in the smell of the toilets again he is tired, dissatisfied, bleak with something, and with hat pulled down, collar up, bends against the night in his walk crosstown, something he left unsaid, and in the haven of the terminal with its lights, benches, pedestrians, buys his newspaper and boards his train to sit with it unread, but is without words to know what it is, and through his ghost in the window hardly sees the tunnel lamps tick by as ungraspable as the years which have gone too fast to get it said, and the train bears him up into the night past factories, streetlights, neighborhoods growing less disreputable, the city far behind him with the son who has condemned his life, and ahead the six-room fortress of his loves: under whose roof I in ignorance have submitted for all time the offering of myself, that it might arise before him with a pleasing fragrance.

30. Pod

What gnarl of idiom roots my tongue awry
(I think my limbs, deformed,
Hang out of hand my sweets, to dry
Unpicked, and wormed)
I would

Unplait,
Oh, would be plain
(Bow garden low, and let my phrase
Hang single as a bean)
To feed my folk in a summer's common place,

For I perceive
The season ends (its frosty lip
Of night lends no reprieve
To all their blackened ears) in winter's lop;
What good

So late
To find, gnarled, on my hands, my leather pods
(Impervious, not seen
Of sun or worm) in private sod
Intact, and green?

31. Ne Cadant in Obscurum

That they fall not into darkness is the last offertory plea in my mother's missal, this battered little tome in black, which travelled to church with her a thousand times in her widowhood and, neat on the doily of her night table, kept her eye company at bedtime. I leaf over its pages, worn dogeared and soft by her lean fingers, also fallen, and in the wake of her eyeglasses I read fragment after fragment of the poetry that was her solace: out of an alien tongue, the psalmist in his wolfskin on a rock in the hills, three thousand years dead, spoke to her like the comforting of a neighbor intimate with her loss.

And I looked for one that would grieve together with me, and there was none.

It is twenty-six years since my father was buried, and with every death in the family another witness to his life goes out like a light; my boys never saw his face. They are silent when three years after my mother's death I ask them what they recall of her, and for the elder then she stands again in our kitchen making French toast for him, for the younger she kneels on the floor playing milkman with his truck and miniature bottles, and the edge of darkness moves in on her too. And I sit in a workroom filled with ghosts, the recording angel over my book of the dead, intent on letting no fact go unwritten that can for a moment like a matchhead illuminate a face.

Behold, how good and how pleasant it is for brethren to dwell together in unity.

It was here for a blink and is gone, born, lived, died, and the houses survive, I have stood before each and known that if I climbed the stairs I would find myself in a layout of rooms familiar as my hand, but dreamlike, staring at the walls into which my mother and my father melted so anonymously, and pulled at by strangers, for every room which was uniquely our home is now overrun by them. Who are these interlopers, so unwitting, living in our footsteps? Sleepwalkers, enacting the same ritual of mistakes, born and the darkness lifts, and I know these children who serve their impatient time under parents too foolish to inquire into, and escape into marriages of sullen back to back in bed with grievances too rancid to inquire into, and age into parents with their hungry eyes forsaken of children too fleetly gone to inquire into, and the darkness falls like a guillotine. Surely life is an imagining, was I ever here?

Lighten mine eyes, that I sleep not the sleep of death!

Under the lamplight my mother sits on the couch in our living room, newspaper outspread in lap, her weekend with us come to a close; I invite these visits, work, read, courteously avoid her, moving in and out of the boredom of her chatter in sham contact, and for two days she busies herself with kitchen tasks, grandchildren's play, letter writing, gossip with her in-laws; in the last hours, when I think she is content over her newspaper ads, I find the glint of her eyeglasses on me, and venturing a smile she says we "never talk, we're like strangers." Seventy, still in hopes of making the acquaintance of her son, she hears me reply there "wasn't time", people, chores, next visit, but we know it is a lie. Now the couch is empty of her, and at the upright desk that the boys and I have gutted out of a piano the elder over his Latin is disappearing into a tongue I am untaught in or the younger is lost in gadget kits of wiring I am unable to follow, and it chills me to think their departure too is begun, I cannot know them better than yesterday. Why do I sit in this workroom of my life, alone, with ghosts, rearranging words like an idiot with pebbles?

My little children, let us not love in word, neither with the tongue, but in deed and in truth.

I hear them hollering under their hill, the snowflakes floating past the windows I scrubbed a winter ago when I saw out into what, a poem, so I stand to spy out at them over their sleds. It is their world, inviting, every branch reborn with its lode of snow, every slope untracked, and watching them in it, bellywhopping down as I bellywhopped down another hill forty years behind me, I know I cannot change now, the studio is my keep, and each year between that lost hill and this my love, my deed, my truth has been, and is, in the word. Mother tongue, it is milk breast, eye, mistress, medicine, children, crutch, school, wife, it is roof and fire and bed, and in its bowels my griefs and joys make love, all colors and contradictions of feeling tumble, copulate, sparkle, and alive from intestines to fingertips as no citizen is, artist, with whose half-life would I exchange? For my father, clerk, as for his father, cratemaker, life like a broken vessel was owed in pieces here and there, and the importunate piece was job, their days indentured to a stranger's purposes, and what they drudged over was nothing of what they loved, suffered, enjoyed; for me, their lives were a mirage. Their obstinate child, refusing a manhood which parted work and play, I took my experiencing of myself as my proper lifework, and language as the medium in which I would market it. And by this difference something in me was separated from them forever; my eyes were lightened by self and the word, and the faces around me fell into a darkness not that of the grave but of my glittery sleep, until the day I awoke, and none was there.

The groans of death surrounded me; the snares of death prevented me.

And I was prevented by the snares of life, the impediment of flesh, for the truth is our hunger is for the confluence of souls in an act of cellular interpenetration, which lovers in orgasm have a momentary dream of, and out of that dream I was born in my skin. Where is the key out? So, to my father, where he lay in what I knew would be his deathbed, I brought dumbly a piece of paper, with love, my poem and parting; so, to my boys, asleep to me and the dark wind that shakes the house, I leave a piece of paper, with love, my poem and parting. Let it be vainglory, I can say the language is not of my making, ancient as the cambium in the tree of man, and every writer in the twig of himself is working back into branch, trunk, heartwood, into a confluence of souls in the word, and what I write tonight is what my brother three thousand years dead sang on his rock in the Judaean hills.

My tongue is the pen of a ready writer: instead of thy fathers shall be thy children, I will make thy name to be remembered in all generations.

Yet I am bonesick of it all, ghosts, the groans of death, the tally of my opacities, and now that I come again to my father's deathbed I must outsit how many days while the words are dried up in my mouth? In this picking over the rags of my dead, week after month after year, I have turned fifty; it is the age at which he died, and for six months I have put off the task in this eerie year when I am him of reliving the events of his dying, I am bored, my lips are gummed with these deaths, I have much else to do, I am afraid. It is also natural to heal. I am weary of lifting open with my thumbnail the old scabs, one after another, and peering under them for the purulence of love; the instinct of the skin is to forget, of the eye to ignore, and my own rind of cheery hope, so like my mother's, turns as easily to the sun as any fruit; I am sick of my unhealth. I have sat with the dead so long here I almost think death is a state of being, I have made friends with it, lain with it, out of its labia drawn forth by the heels these twisted and stillborn infants, with love, poems and pieces of paper. Is it not sufficient?

For ye were sometimes darkness, but now are ye light: walk as the children of light.

Outside my wall of windows in a rare dusk the blue snow coats the earth too in a forgetting of rocks, woodchuck holes, dead leaves, frozen pond, half veiling the wooded hills round-about, and the beauty of dying light calls me out, and out of the house below calls my wife, boys, sister-in-law, niece, and for an hour with a lantern to mark a ledgerock lost in the snowfall of night the six of us are sledding, hollering, scrambling, and our house with its bright eyes is an answer to death, and the delicate snowflakes that descend in the evening everywhere, to our tongues, in the hills dark and unknowing, on the stilled rivers, fall upon the healed scar of earth where a remnant of my father lies.

I will smite the shepherd, and the sheep of the flock will be scattered.

It is not yet sufficient. In the proper of my mother's missal with its introits, epistles, graduals, I come at last among the losses and comfortings to the offertory plea in the mass for the dead, that they fall not into darkness, the deep pit, that darkness not swallow them up, and it will, the earth turns, the tide of night washes it clean of men, almost of memory, and by day again the children run like foam upon a beach; a poem one finger left in the sand says I will not forget. Gone, the dead do not hear, and the unborn are none of mine yet, and if now I undo a scab that in no man ever heals, the death of a father, it is for me and mine, here, now. My little children, I love how I can, and this book is a running sore which I keep open, with reason enough, making my offertory to parents a second time, making their names to be remembered in one generation, making you a history, but mostly because I am a maker of pieces of paper, which comfort me; of this death too I will make something of use, shapeliness, joy.

DIES IRAE

32. December 28th

Christmastide
Is on my tongue: I taste its salt.
This is the week

Carol and gift
Bring back the magi to all our mangers,
Telling us bide
Time when a word will exalt
The sick to lift
His bed, the dead walk forth:

Christmastide
Is on my tongue. Now looking back
I taste its salt
But not for history speak,
Cities, strangers,
The dumb, the blind, the halt.

This is the week
By numberless moons and ebbs worn dim
A child was born
To hang. But not for him
Christmastide
Makes of my tongue a mourner:

DIES IRAE

Here is a dawn
When once in a gift of kindling suns
My father died
And darkened every corner
In the world
To come. This is a week

Christmastide
Is in my throat: I taste its salt
Upon my cheek.

33. Lacrimosa Dies Illa

Of weeping, yes, on that day when the man rises again from the ashes, but to be as honest as the earth, or half, is a desideratum too, and I am lectured to it daily by a mammoth white oak; it fills the square of nine windows I gaze out of, houseward, from my workplace. Dominant on the hillside, it soars a hundred feet or more, and around it the boys and I linking hands would enclose not much more than half its gray and lichened girth which, a dozen feet above, divides into five trunks. It is a fantastic tree, and never more so than in the winter sky when, bare of the leathery leaves, its thirty boughs are a writhing, each in itself an oak, so vast a sinuosity of arms and elbows and wriggling infinitude of fingers that the eye is made giddy. Lightning struck it one summer, plunging along a bough to the huge torso and forking in a blazed channel down either side into the ground; it lived, and for several years put forth proudflesh to heal, but still bears the passage of that fiery tongue. Examining it with my boys I thought of what an emptiness in their sky such a sire, fallen, would leave.

Of weeping, yes, that day when the man rises from the ashes to be judged, but here in any direction from the oak our feet walk ten, twenty, thirty paces on earth which is in contention. Giant, its annual windfall of acorns has raised up a hundred sons, from striplings taller than I down to sprouts with two leaves, and when I cut the field clear of autumnal brush I let this generation come; I see in aftertime a hill of oaks for the boys. I note how slowly they increase, and not because they are oak. Underfoot is an unseen tree immense as the giant's shadow, of rootwork, which in no less fantastic a sinuosity of fingers is everywhere in this soil, feeding, sacking the hillside of each raindrop and crumb of nutriment, whereof it must make overhead a hundred thousand leaves to lap at the sunlight. In its actual shadow these sprouts for a time perhaps are sheltered, but, needier each summer of sun and the affluence of topsoil, struggle to create themselves in terrain which is a silent battleground; and if their extravagant avid leaves were tongues to cry out, would it not be that an emptiness in the sky is their desire?

Of weeping, yes, whatever day the dead rise again from the ashes, but this field preacher lets me not forget that the burial of every father is an hour of darkness and a liberation into light, not innocent of triumph; and half the weeping on the day he rises in us is not that he comes to be judged, but judges.

34. Sunset I Saw By

It was in the spring of his forty-ninth year that one morning my
father left for work in the heat of a fight without kissing my
mother goodbye, a most rare omission, and a few hours later was
brought back to the house in a taxi by two of his clerks, too
weak to walk unaided, his face ashen, his eyes frightened; in the
men's room he had vomited up a basinful of blood. My mother
put him to bed, and there he stayed, the hemorrhage past, while a
neighborhood doctor examined his heart, blood, stool, and spoke
of a bleeding ulcer. After a week on liquids my father could
manage the stairs, and mended in the living room, the kitchen,
the sun porch, watching the twigs of our tree at the curb warm
to life and the backyard stir; and in three weeks he was again at
his duties in the bank, the diagnosis confirmed by x-ray, a gastric
ulcer had eaten into a blood vessel.

Not the first betrayal of his flesh—my father was wont to
boast every six months that the medical exam at the bank showed
"nothing wrong with me", but that winter he had fallen down
the cellar stairs, his back ached thereafter, a plague of hemor-
rhoids then led him to a doctor, and the constipation that kept
him in the bathroom an unhappy half-hour over a cigarette was
becoming chronic—the ulcer was the gravest. Who is to tell the
little history of the year when he fattened in a false health, now
that all memory of my mother's ministrations to him is in the

273

grave with her? That the minute breach in his stomach wall was the thumbprint of death not even she suspected; and the furniture in the household was as worried about my father as were his children.

My sister, graduated from a secretarial course in highschool, was working in the city at a job in excess of her skills; with her shorthand forever in arrears of her boss's dictation, she spent lunch hours at her desk typing up his letters from memory, agitated over each mistake because he was stingy with stationery, and she discarded the spoiled pages into her purse instead of the wastebasket, smuggling them out at night. My father could rescue his chick from this—a vice-president of the bank spoke to a vice-president of a corporation which then hired her as a less noticeable clerk—but not from the turbulent wooing of a hothead who for three years arrived and departed in a roadster at sixty miles an hour, always in crisis. So unlike me, my sister too was discovering her body and soul, and my father's hemorrhage made as little imprint on her eye as on mine.

I was in a quicksand of other remorse, that spring. If I set foot in the house because of the hemorrhage I have no recollection of it, and little enough of my parents in the score of months before and after. Certainly they visited me and my bride more than once in the coldwater flat, but all I see is my father in his business suit, his face kindly, the evening he came after work; the other images of the flat that haunt me are empty of parents. I was almost the orphan I pretended I was, in a generation of young artists of the left who lived on relief as a form of governmental grant, peered in upon by investigators to make sure no one was out working. I became a true if unpaid artist by publishing in a little magazine my story of the father who struck his teen-age son; I then insinuated myself onto a works project for writers which, designed as a survey of historical records, turned into an inventory of garbage and gas permits issued in bygone days. Its weekly paycheck of twenty-one dollars moved us out of the honeymoon flat, and into troubled waters.

Contemplating my marriage my father had told my mother he would "give it six months", but was a hundred per cent wrong; it lasted a year. Inside the family reach again—by summer my bride and I were in a fourth of a frame dwellingbox in my aunt Minnie's neighborhood, and by fall in a Jamaica basement five miles from my parents—the exchange of visits that endeared the girl to my relatives, prior to the hemorrhage, took place in a decline of ardor between us. I wrote at night, and from spring to fall was butting my head through the obdurate wordage of a long tale of tenement miseries in a race against the close of my twenty-first year; the evening of my birthday my father came with my mother to the basement apartment to suffer a reading of it aloud, my gift to them. It was better than my next work of misery, the news that I had banished my wife from the basement, back to her parents. Though I said it was for solitude to write, I thought it was to philander, and the sundering within each of us was as real as the hemorrhage which soon after put my father in bed; that ours might have contributed to his was hardly in my addled mind, nor was he.

Yet I brought a happier piece of news in this month of con-valescence. My tale was bought for a hundred and fifty dollars by a shiny magazine, which he said was "the best medicine"; it was on the newsstands that summer, my father exhibited a copy to every clerk in the bank, and in afteryears I was to hear too often from my mother his prophecy that "we may not live to see it but that boy will be famous". I had melted into the city once more, footloose, four addresses in six months, my workdays a time-killing in the cellars of old municipal buildings, my nights a grieving for the innocence of first love. It was winter before I was settled in a Village room-and-a-half with furniture of my own, and another piano, and the image of my father emerges again.

Obedient to an ulcer diet that year—six meals a day of starchy items my mother of old was familiar with, and took pains to make tasty—my father "missed most" the daily black-and-white soda he was used to at work, and instead lined his stomach with milk which was half cream; he was twenty pounds heavier, much of it in a plump belly which seemed unnatural on his narrow body. I was with him the evening he bought the last of his twenty-two-fifty suits, and when the salesman was measuring his girth my father said, "It's temporary, I'm taking it off," and the salesman said, "That's what they all say," insignificant joking that stuck in my ear. And his penultimate Christmas is seared into me less by the final gift I was to receive from his hands—a wristwatch engraved with my initials—than by my night in the household. I saw my wife often, always like a ghost of someone I had killed, and when my parents invited the two of us for Christmas and put us up in one bed it was in a climate of holiday heartbreak; earlier than breakfast my father, sauntering back from the avenue with a newspaper, met me fleeing the house in such a dishevelment that he cried out in distress, "What in God's name is wrong?" I could not tell him, but left him on the sidewalk staring, and ran for the bus which carried me out of my ruins. In this period my mother wrote me a heartsore letter, taking me severely to task for my callousness; it did not extend to my stomach, which was digesting itself so persistently that I went to the quiet doctor in the city who had my father in treatment, and that spring both of us were on the ulcer diet.

In the Village flat too he came to visit, already dying, though none knew; my own future was in the flat with me in the flesh of an illicit love. So long divided, I needed to anchor this half of me in a familial recognition, and my mother's code kept her from crossing the doorsill. It was the streak of the maternal in my father—Ben's daughters remember how often in the old days he was up the five stairflights after work to look in and amid the whiskey and fighting say, "Come on, kids, pack your things," and lead them by trolley home to my mother—that I turned to; I asked him to a Saturday lunch. In our nest of sin he was so gracious to the girl that to this day it brings tears to her eyes, and he played a tune upon my upright piano, amused that it so crowded the room-and-a-half we had to stand on our double bed to cook at the stove, and sat with us at a card table to the meal of unharmful foods I had bought. Not till a generation later would I know that the hunger in him was of a father for his son, for which there is at last no food. It was seven lean years since the winter afternoon he had kept a rendezvous with me at the great 42nd Street library and signed for a card in his name with the bank as a city address, so his boy could borrow the books that were to come between us; only now, that I was out from under his hand and roof, the truth that we had nothing in common was become a lie, and I was meeting him again as a friend.

The attacks of indigestion which soured his stomach, even on the diet, were for months not mentioned by him to the doctor; my father thought them too passing. Yet the pain grew insistent, and when he could not eat he submitted to questioning in the midtown office whose carpeted hush was now familiar to me, and listened to the doctor arrange by telephone for his admission to a hospital for observation. In the household that weekend I could not think it serious, my father being immortal, but he sat long on the cretonned sofa in the living room; I see his candid face puckered with hurt, and worried. It was a sunny morning in early July when my mother packed a suitcase with all he would need, and rode with it and him on a train into the city.

Downtown, in a neighborhood grimy with warehouses and bridges, the old hospital was our gathering place for fifteen days. My father was in a room with two beds, and whoever lay in the other I hardly saw; at his bedside near the window my mother and I met—my sister was away on her vacation—for idle chats, making light of his stay, until the period of tests was done. I was there when our doctor in a careful choice of words explained to my father, propped up in a bedgown, that the nature of his ulcer made surgery a wise procedure, and my father said with a twitch of fear in his downward smile, "All kinds of ulcers, I have to have the worst kind." I knew the fear was unnecessary, but my mother called my sister home from the country, and the three of us were in the hospital corridor the morning my father was wheeled out. The surgeon had informed us the chances were fifty-fifty it was an ulcer he could cut out, in which case the operation would take several hours, else my father would soon be back; we sat it out in a small corner room, all restive, but I with a book was counting on a long wait, and my sister talked with my mother, stiff on the edge of a chair. It was not an hour when my mother, now in and out of the corridor, reappeared with her face stricken and said, "Daddy's back." I walked in a confusion to his doorway and saw a nurse busy at his bed, with a substance of legs beneath the white spread, but half guessed the surgery was simpler than predicted, and after I returned to our corner room the three of us stood in uncertainty, five minutes, ten minutes, until the surgeon came to find my mother. Courteous and prompt, he said he could do nothing for her husband, it was a stomach cancer and inoperable. Yet only when she stammered, "Doctor, how long does he have?" and the surgeon said, "Six months," did I comprehend the truth: the earth that opened at my feet in that minute was never to close. In the unreal hour that followed my tremulous mother instructed us my father was not to know, and that afternoon it was she who through his fog of anesthesia delivered the good news to him, the ulcer was cured and he would soon be getting better at home.

For out of my sickly mother now came a rigor, not unpredictable, which was to cope with whatever befell. Old neighbors, relatives, fellows from the bank, came to congratulate my father in the week he was recovering from the knife, and one took a snapshot of my mother in a rattan chair on the hospital roof; with her children standing beside her—a healthy blonde miss in a summerprint frock, dangling a white purse, and a lank youth in unpressed wool slacks and jacket, shirt wide open—she sits in a neat polka-dot dress, a lean lady of fifty with legs crossed, looking forty in her pearl earrings, and a white chrysanthemum at her bodice; all the feet are sporty in white shoes on the roof tiles, underneath which my father convalesces in his bed, unseen and doomed. It is the faces that baffle me, the youth's in a surly grin, the girl's prettily beaming, my mother's eager with a lip-sticked smile to please the camera, all caught in the family lie from which I had fled to my suffering minorities. Only, my mother's hands are knotted against her stomach, and I was to watch how her bright denial of the underworld was armor to carry her through it; back of the brittle smile, which for half a year she wore for my father, was the durable will of an older mother who had buried a husband and fourteen sons.

I was at the hospital with the Ford the morning my father was discharged, and the four of us rode home together; I drove in the slow lane of traffic, not to jar his abdominal wound. Still in some pain, but out again in the air of life, my father at a back window gazed contentedly at whatever we passed, and with her gay chatter my mother beside him shared his view of the towering city in which he had been born, of the midtown streets they had strolled in the horsecar days of their courtship, of the bridge over the islanded river and the green ballpark where Sundays in the benchstands they would not again sit with orange pop and franks, of the boulevard they had often crossed from the prosperity in their winebrick colony to the poverty in her sister Minnie's flat, and at last the parkway, pleasant with grass and woodland and the vision they first had together from it of rooftops in a suburban multitude below, and among these, in a street still young with saplings, the little house in which he was to die. I parked at the curb, my mother hurried up the driveway to unlock the front door from within, my sister stood by with his suitcase, and I helped my father out of the back seat; with him bent on my forearm we advanced up the steps, past my mother, and through the sun porch into the comfort of the living room, where my father, welcomed home by us as he looked around at his easy chair, the sofa and twin lamptables, his piano and stool, startled us with a half-sob and, still upon my arm, cried tears. Seated with him on the sofa, my mother was all cheery banter, promising his strength back. I then supported him up the staircase, along the hallway to the front room, and onto the twin bed that waited with coverlet turned down, where I left him to be undressed by my mother and put to bed.

So began the six months of an old sorrow, but new to us. I took a step so natural that only now it seems a choice, I broke up my flat and came back to live in my room. My sister turned to the faith that moved mountains, was unfailingly at mass on Sunday, in the city prayed in a church before work each morning, and, making novena after novena at night with other petitioners on their knees, read from her prayerbook that "all you ask the Father in My name He will give you"; literal believer, she asked that hers not die. I was to make the same prayer, but only in my dreams. My mother's lips, whatever the hope of holy miracle in her head, were tight; she told the truth to almost nobody, not even to my father's mother and sisters in Jersey, lest someone in a slip let it out in his hearing, and month after month the air in the house was heavier with our secret.

For all, the first month was the easiest. My father was incapacitated most by the wound, which knitted, and aided at the outset by whoever arm was handy, but soon unhelped, he was back and forth the dozen steps to the toilet, dressed himself, shaved, and was of good cheer; a higher official from the bank, visiting, bade him not to hurry his return to work. Downstairs,

my mother and the official sat on the sun porch in a low-voiced
conversation, in which he told her of the bank's decision to
continue my father on salary until his death. Though weekdays
my sister and I left for work, neighbors and other visitors came
in and my mother was not always alone, except in her thoughts;
half the time the housework was shared by her "oldest and dearest friend" Nelie, who at night slept on the sofa in a dusting
cap, and Minnie arriving by subway and bus for the day would
fill the house with her "for Gawd's sake" joshing of her brother-in-law. Only these two women, the one monosyllabic, the
other our generous bungler, knew what my mother knew. My
father grew strong enough to make his way downstairs, a gala
day; now the household was almost normal, he tuned the radio to
baseball, tried the piano, and in the flowering backyard sat on the
springy chair my mother bought him, head back and eyes closed,
renewing himself in the sun. The boys from the bank who
visited in threes and fours found him there, all smiles to see them,
and hale enough for a cigarette—forbidden on the ulcer diet,
cigarettes were again permitted by the merciful doctor—which
my father explained as a success of the surgery. For such guests
my mother was blithe, and for the first time kept liquor in the
house to serve, instead of pineapple juice; new to bartending, she
made highballs with ginger ale in her tallest tumblers, half whiskey, and the visits were gay indeed. On the weekend I chauffeured my parents on gentle rides of a few miles out of one
community into another, replicas, but a change of scene for my
father.

A quarter-mile from our house was a two-block string of
stores, built in the twenties and fallen into disuse with the depression; here for ten dollars a month I rented a store long uninhabited, whose windows I curtained with newspapers, and putting in my card table, chair, typewriter, cot, had a workroom and
trysting place. I took August off—my practice was to save up

seventy-five dollars, give notice I had a job "in private industry", and devote a month's leave from the writers' project to writing—and daily I sat there, as in an oven, at work in my underwear shorts. Unaired except by the door, which I kept shut, and festive with flies on their backs in a death buzz, the store was odious and a refuge. I never entered it but furtively, my writing in it seemed as illicit a pursuit as the sweaty conjugations with my girl at night, and the only word I exchanged with the tailor in the next store was one afternoon when his radio was shrill with an alien voice, the fuehrer against Czechoslovakia, and I stood to listen; the tailor observed, "He's esking for it, he'll ged it." I said ahuh, and shut myself up in my store with the flies. I had long believed the war was coming, to me as to my dead uncle, it was one of the monstrosities that for a year had driven me onto a stepladder to harangue the streetcorner crowds, but, much nearer now, the dying of millions buzzed no louder than that of one man; and the yellowing newspapers on my windows were meant to exclude even him. I was eighteen months into a verse play, and I intended to finish it.

That month my father had the first of the hemorrhages which bled the kindly confidence out of his face. Unexpected nausea and a bloody spewing into the toilet, it put him back in the twin bed, white and shaken, and my mother running into a neighbor's telephoned the doctor in the city, who told her to pack ice on my father's stomach until he came. It was not his sole journey to our house—I would pick him up at the end of the subway, to drive him the five miles out and back—and the later visits were only to reassure a patient whom he called "a real friend" in a letter my mother received after the funeral, and kept; on this visit he injected morphine into my father's arm, watched him into sleep, and downstairs in the kitchen instructed my pale mother and me in the use of a small hypodermic syringe. He left it with us, it sat thereafter in a corner of the cupboard recess, together with an inch bottle of morphine pellets and a spare needle. To my father, as she arranged his pillows and refilled the ice-bag, my mother said the bleeding meant merely that the surgical incision had not yet healed, and he was relieved.

Without appetite, he was growing thin, and the strength was reluctant to come into his legs, but it came. It would have been less difficult to see him worsen; what was grievous was to watch his gratitude in the abortive recoveries. Once again on my mother's arm, setting himself distances, he left the bedpan behind, and for a week sat at open windows in his pants, shirt, slippers, and then worked his way down the banister to the living room, to the sun porch, to the backyard, and the color of pleasure returned to his face, each day was a restoral, each destination a further reach: the next shock of hemorrhage erased it all. My mother settled him in the bed, her hands quick with the ice-bag, and quick in the kitchen to boil and assemble the parts of the hypodermic, but upstairs she was timid to pierce his arm with it, and I took over the task. In bed my father lay with eyes closed, the rubber ice-bag on his belly, a blanket keeping him warm in the heat of the summer day, and slept; and I walked the five blocks to my store, where I put aside the play and undertook to write him my parting word, or loveletter, which was a poem.

I was three weeks over it; he was bedridden still, or again, the morning I took the typed page in, said I had written something for him, and left it in his hands. Back now on the job, I could not linger but in any case was embarrassed to, the forty lines were too frank an avowal of how much of him I hoped was in me, named his goodness as the bonework of my knowledge of man, and, muted by what I could not mention except as the fate all must share, said neither of us was to enter the silence with my debt unspoken. Home at five-thirty, I went upstairs to his room to say hello, as always, and saw my page on the night table between the twin beds; his eyes following mine, my father said,

"Bill, it's beautiful," and I said I was glad, there was a pause, and he said, "What does it mean?" So, in some despair at the isolateness even of my art, I sat upon the other bed, and with the poem in hand explained it word by word in prose.

Summer went under, the year was ebbing and so too the outer edge of my father's world; the last time he took to his chair in the backyard he grew uneasy, and shuffled indoors, not to emerge again. I was not in the house the evening he forewent the downstairs half, and with it the brotherly companion of his life, the Horace Waters piano. Up or down the ten steps to the bedroom, he would now sit upon them midway, for breath; on a visit to my sister the giant youth who was once her beau saw my father at the stairfoot pause, hand on newel, awaiting the will to climb, and simply carried him in his arms up the stairs.

At the bedside there stood henceforth an enamelled white bucket, containing a few inches of water, for the next spewing of blood. It was not yet frequent, but my father was enfeebled by loss of hunger and abdominal pain, glum that the incision was so slow to heal, and critical of the city doctor who he said was "not doing me any good"; at the doctor's advice we called in a local "consultant", and on the sun porch my mother confided the facts to his suave face. For a month my father's hopes were up as the new doctor wrote out a variety of prescriptions, my mother observed to my sister only that the pharmacist was his brother, and the bottles of expensive medicine accumulated on the night table, to no effect. Exhausted by a third and fourth vomiting my father said, "He doesn't understand my case," and my mother called in another doctor to add encouragement; this man said bluntly he "hated like hell" to have such a patient, sat at my father's bedside with his bagful of useless instruments, scribbled a prescription for sugar pills, and that autumn lent his burly comfort more to us than to my father, who, emptier of faith, said indifferently, "He's a fake."

Nothing in the weariness of his day upstairs could distract him from the gnawing ache in his stomach. Off for work, my sister and I were in the bedroom each morning to say goodbye—I was old enough to kiss him again, the sweet odor of his brow at my lips recalling the Sunday mornings when as children we climbed into bed with him to giggle over his nonsensical stories, all forgotten, but not how we loved the odor of his pillow dent—and until evening my mother, in the midst of housecleaning, tried to lighten his pain with a diversity of moves. She would plump up two bed-pillows for the mahogany rocker so my father, sitting at the window, could have a view of the red-tinned roof of our sun porch with the bit of tranquil street beyond, and in my sister's room she plumped up pillows for another chair at the rear window to which he came to see his backyard garden, kept trim by her for his eye; back and forth between the two chairs, in one soon restless for the other, my father travelled on her arm, and in them an hour of the long· morning, an hour of the longer afternoon, would pass. The pillows were needed because the flesh was leaving him, his buttocks were bony, and more often he was at rest upon one of the twin beds. On good days, with my mother's support he would get into the old pants and shirt that now hung loose on him, and feel more optimistic for being dressed; other days he kept to his bed, in pajamas, where my mother would bathe him with alcohol, and twice daily unmake and remake the bed to freshen it for his back. Left alone, my father would read for an hour—a newspaper, a cheap novel his chick or I brought him from the drugstore library—or dial around my little radio for some daytime music, find only the soap operas, and click it off. Visitors came, to pass another hour. My mother would use it for downstairs work, but whatever chores she could bring up to the bedroom she saved for their departure, peeling vegetables then in the rocker, brightly gossiping, and misquoting the doctor in prediction of an upturn tomorrow to perk up his spirits. It was all in vain, the heel of his hand pressing was futile to ease the bellyache always under his ribs, and worsening; his one desire was for the morphine.

My father disrespected himself for asking it of us, and my mother and I were uncertain when to grant it. In the kitchen the doctor had counselled us to be sparing, how insufferable the cancer might grow was not known, and if we habituated his body to morphine in the beginning we could give him no help at the end; concerned thus, my mother and I would conspire to talk him out of it. My father at first was with us, still expecting nature to mend what the surgeon had somehow botched, and to be a "hophead" when on his feet again was a worry to him. All day he bit down the words, until I was home to boil the needle; but the interludes of numbness to the pain grew briefer. It was less often we heard him say he "wouldn't want to get to depend on it", and what in August was a contest of my father with himself had by September turned into one between him and us. I was acceding to his wish for the morphine before I left in the morning, and my mother withstood his pleas throughout the afternoon as best she could, then yielded too, overcoming her finickiness about the needle. To see my father relax after it— going limp, murmuring "how good that felt", letting his eyebrows unknit at last—eased us too, but we bargained with him to put it off, for two hours, one hour, half an hour, and would agree to a time by the clock upon his night table; he would lie with eyes sidelong to it, and be unable not to plead with us again, too early. I injected his arm a few times with sterile water or a solution of half a pellet, but he was not deceived, accused me of it, and distrusted my denials; our needs had parted company, and the candor in his blue eyes was clouded with a new doubt of us.

It was only when he hemorrhaged that we used the needle without misgiving. The upheavals which came now were dismaying, my father half out of the bed while my mother cradled his forehead in her fingers, and his retchings and disgorgings into the white bucket of fresh and caked blood—scarlet, black, mingling in palpable clots and layers in the water, not without their obscene beauty—were so convulsive that the wall was bespattered. Never predictable, it happened by day or night, and in the bedroom my mother kept a basinful of ice cubes ready, with towels; her fear was that my father would die in a night hemorrhage while she slept. She always awoke, of course, and from my own sleep I would waken to her hand on my naked shoulder and a whisper in the dark, "Daddy's sick, fix a needle, dear." Downstairs I would put up a potful of water to boil, and in it sterilize the glass cylinder, its plunger, the metal needle, and a soup spoon; I let a morphine pellet dissolve in a spoonful of the water while I sat in my shorts, in a kitchen still bright and gay with the red cushions on white chairs and my mother's red-and-white tablecloth arranged in a dangle of four triangles and on it a vase with a few flowers from the yard; when the parts of the syringe were cool I fitted it together, touching only its externals, and drew up into it the spoonful of potent water, and took it upstairs. In the lamplight on the pillow my father, his face like death, would lie with eyelids and mouth half open, ice-bag on his belly and a pajama sleeve up, my mother cleansing the upper arm with a cotton wad soaked in alcohol. She made room for me, but never failed to place her palm in a caress upon his eyes, as a blindfold, and I pinched up the skimpy flesh in one hand to impale it with the needle in the other, a moment I too disliked; the arm would flinch, as I thumbed down the reluctant plunger, then go lax. I eased the needle out, and my mother would stop the miniature wound with the wad, wipe the bloody drool from my father's lips, click off the lamp, and the two of us sat in the darkness listening to his breath, until its regularity told us he was asleep.

During the vigil I would go down again to the kitchen, and bring my mother up a cup of weak tea, with milk and sugar, which was her mainstay. Performing like an automaton, I did not understand her gratitude for that small favor, to be cared for in a year when all the caring was hers, nor how much she was leaning upon my presence in the house those nights. Yet I see one when I hissed at her—she never, till the year of her death, lost her capacity to irk me—and left her dumb in the dark doorway, but turned to go back three steps and hugged her tight, and remember in my hands her body so thin and forlorn in its cotton nightgown; some glimmer of her unillumined grief had veered me round.

Next day my mother scoured the wall clean, and over the washtubs in the cellar she scrubbed the bloodspots out of the bedlinens, and, despite her "weak stomach" for such things, scraped with shirt cardboards to loosen the clots of foul blood in the bucket, which reappeared at the bedside white and immaculate. And my father awoke, feeble but not hopeless, and recommenced his efforts to gain ground; it was October, and the goal by which he measured his improvement now was to reach the bathroom. Home from work, my sister or I would help him, and so learn some of what my mother's hands undertook in our absence. My father sat up in bed, his legs crawling out, and by lifting him under the armpits my mother stood him on his feet, his body every day more like a bagful of dry sticks, and he bent his head to her cheek, clutching her, as each foot in turn found its slipper; side by side they began to shuffle, my mother supporting him under an arm, getting behind at the doorway, and again at his elbow along the hall, while his other hand walked the wall like a third foot, each step a summoning of will, and if she stiffened her wrist to take more of his weight a flick of my father's eye would say no; the march down the short hall took them two or three minutes, and at the bathroom my mother sidled in first, backward, with her hands under both armpits once more, and he came to her as if drunk while she stepped him around, and lowered him to the john. My father was pleased to make it, because on bad days he could not, and my mother set a chair midway in the hall to break the journey, back and forth. Also, it was his only escape from the bed; he had given up dressing, and lay day after day on his pillow with his ruminations, pain, morphine dozings, and when in need of my mother he rang with a hand bell kept on the night table. It was one with a history, the iron cowbell they had bought to celebrate his brother Jim's survival on Armistice Day twenty years before. Its clanking brought my mother up from even the cellar; but her ear had grown so alert to the bedroom that whenever my father belched—he was living on ginger ale, the stomach gas was chronic—she was up the stairs in a hurry, in dread of the next hemorrhage.

Emaciated and bedridden, much of the man who had been my father was fading, but not yet the gist of him. Among the papers my mother saved in a ragged leatherette folder— embossed with a title, "Valuable Documents"—were two letters from her sister: one was the last note Minnie wrote, the other was of fervent thanks for the change in her domestic life effected by the radio my father had, it seems, bought for her and her husband. It was a benevolence I thought of as his grain, and it lingered in him still. One warm night my mother and her schoolmate sat on the sun porch and via the open windows heard the clinking of ice in highballs from the neighbors, and joked that no one had brought any over; next day my father sent me to the avenue with money to buy a bottle of gin and Tom Collins mix. It was his pocket cash, put aside twice a month from the pay envelope, delivered by his boys who every Saturday came from the bank to visit. The weather turned cold, and my mother wished for new cottonlace curtains on the sun porch, a dollar a pair, but could not afford them out of the food money; they appeared as a surprise, my father had given my sister seven dollars to select them. They were still fresh on the windows the night my mother, my sister, I, sat in the dark there with the burly doctor, down with his bag from the bedside to tell us my father was "terminal" and had perhaps three to seven days to live.

It was no longer unsuspected by my father; my aunt Minnie in her blundering way had cheered him up one afternoon with the news that "lots of times these cancers go away". My mother assured him that Minnie meant something else, after which he avoided the matter. It angered us that our goodhearted slob with the loose mouth had prattled out the word that for sixteen weeks we had so heavily carried within us; yet Minnie, deep in her sixties, was unwell too, and of necessity was forgiven before the month was out.

The image I keep of my aunt is from our summer together with the insecticide company, a weary figure in her organdy dress, with brimmed hat to ward the sun off her thin strawy hair and powdered face, her old shoes worn lopsided by the hurt of her feet, trudging with a satchel of samples down the baked streets of Brooklyn; the sight of her in our flat or hers had been a weekly event until my teens, and it was invariably Minnie who, in my mother's illnesses, took over our household. Some ailment now kept her in bed. The swart laborer who was her lugubrious mate—when my father "spoke to" him after his fistic attempts to get at the truth of Minnie's age he said his life was "an untold hell"—phoned our neighbor with the news. My mother wrote a letter, and my sister, stopping in with some flowers on a Sunday drive with her suitor, heard Minnie's complaints of stomach trouble and high blood pressure. Like me, my sister was as skeptical of Minnie's talk as of her hair, still dyed, and frizzed by hand with a "hot iron curler" held in the gas burner; the sloppy kiss of her life was on us, and in her gush of endearments, huffs, lies, tears, we saw only the histrionics of a coarse old woman; we forgot how as children we had run to her hands that were so lavish with bribes for a hug, and childless. That week, companioned by a cur and her goldfish, she lay in the clutter of the shabby flat she never kept too clean—my sister remembered the dog's hair in her meals—and awaited the daily calls of a niece who lived a block away, Ben's younger minx.

The day after she answered my mother's letter Minnie sat up in her old bathrobe for several hours, talking; for the first time she told the niece of her heartbreak over her "beautiful boy", dead of a broken skull in the cellarway four decades ago, of his young father lost in the Spanish-American War, of her parents Dennis and Mary Dore, rambling through story after story of the dead "like she wanted to get the whole family history out". Late in the October day she allowed herself to be put back in bed, exhausted. The niece was at the bedside when Minnie turned color, and having shouted at her in vain she fled out of the house screaming, "Aunt Minnie's blue! Aunt Minnie's blue!" until help arrived in the form of her boyfriend, neighbors, and at last a doctor, who pronounced Minnie dead; and the husband home for supper "went berserk, running around the rooms" till the doctor gave him a pill. At five o'clock in the morning the niece and the husband left the flat where Minnie's body lay, and after two hours of travel by foot, subway, bus, were at our kitchen door.

My mother, unlocking it to see them, exclaimed, "It's Minnie!" Incredulous in the kitchen, with its swingdoor closed to keep from my father the sound of voices and sobs, my mother heard their tale out; then at the sink she washed her eyes in cold water, and upstairs in the bathroom she powdered her face, and she went in with her smile to tend to my waiting father. Looking at her, he said, "What's wrong with Min?" My mother said nothing new, just not well, and my father with a pat on her hand said, "Don't worry, hon, Min'll be all right." Downstairs on top of the refrigerator Minnie's letter stood in its envelope, with the stamp upside down to signify love, postmarked eighteen hours before her death; the scrawl of her handscript—it began with "I am praying hard for Our poor Irv and hope he is coming around ok" and ended with "Sis *Please* do not worry about me as I will be alright very soon"—was a last word between the two sisters who, so unalike, had been inseparable for half a century; and how many times in the kitchen that day my mother's fingers were at it, no eye saw. Never informed of the death, my father knew only that his wife was off the next evening to visit with her sister. It was for a glimpse of her body in the coffin, and once home again she stayed within earshot of my father's dying breath, the funeral took place without her; poor Minnie had even died in the wrong week.

And my father a ninth time came back to life, or to his fretful intake of sickroom air for which we had no other word. His eyes grown larger in a face that was less familiar each day, unshaven and toothless—earlier he sometimes said he'd "love a good ham sandwich", though after my mother was back from the avenue with the ham to fix it he would vomit it up bloodily, and my mother among her other ministrations took his false teeth to the bathroom to wash, but now they sat untouched in their glass of water—my father lay staring at the ceiling, unable to die as predicted; we wished him the mercy of Minnie's end. The doctor said his heart, whose murmur at thirty had almost cost his hiring by the bank, was "too good". Indefatigable, it had less flesh daily to pump its blood to, or for me to nip up when I searched his bony arm for an inch unstippled by the bite of the needle; these days I felt the metal slide in under the skin between my fingers. It had become my chore to shave my father, two or three times a week. With his brush I lathered his sunken cheeks, and was awkward with the safety razor at the bonework of his face, literally skin deep, so too often I nicked him and saw blood; he was indifferent to it, not I. The hair grew ragged at the hollows of his nape, so frail, and we had a barber in, who then shaved him skillfully, with hot towels and lotions that my father took pleasure in, but it cost two dollars.

Yet in November his strength, fed by no one knew what, was on the rise, and once more upon some arm my father shuffled on the pilgrimage down the hall. Step after tottering step, he hoped only to avoid the bedpan; that his stool was habitually black with a leakage of stomach blood he saw as well as my mother. Crankier and morose, he kept no further count of the spindles in the hallway railing as a measure of his recovery, his eyes were on something remoter.

Surrounded by kith and kin, to whom could he speak of the spectre? It was no secret now, and of the women who visited us to help out—the schoolmate Nelie was living with us, but once a week Ben's minx would arrive with a bottle of brandy eggnog from a liquor-store gent of her acquaintance, and his brother Will's widow, working as a practical nurse in a hospital, spent her days off in the house, and all the faithful wives came with small gifts out of the neighborhoods of the past—not one but was cheerful, and evasive. If the large gift was to acknowledge his espial of the truth, we could not; instead the custom was to humor him, and when my father muttered he wouldn't "be here long" the minx said with a laugh, "Oh, yeah? Better stick around, I won't bring out your bottle." My father made a dutiful smile, surrounded by liars.

Acquainted with the doctor's word, two carfuls of the Jersey relatives—they had come before, but in ignorance—drove in to see him, not waiting for a weekend; he said to a sister's husband, "How come you're off?" and when the husband replied he was "on vacation", summer long past, my father said no more. My whitehaired grandmother, often at the bedside, was mute. To be an hour nearer, she and Ada took up residence with the cousin in Mt. Vernon; but even Ada, distressed that her brother was dying without religion, was incapable of mentioning it because she "commenced to cry". To the baby Ethel in leavetaking my father said only, "So long, kid," a lifelong epithet for her. But Milly would remember how, the day she sat in the bedroom with him, he "kept looking and looking" at her until it made her uneasy; at last my father broke the silence with, "Mil, what are you thinking about?" Milly said, "Oh, everything."

In a last chat with Ben's older girl—years ago this niece, planning on a room of her own while in training as a nurse, was put out of the Harlem flat by her irate mother, turned up at our door in tears, lived with us a time, and thought her uncle Irv "the most wonderful man God ever created"—he still kept the spectre to himself, except for a parting word. My mother led her aside to say, "I know you're smoking, dear, have you got some with you?" and at her request, because my father was unequal to it in his own lips, the niece lay across a twin bed with an immoral cigarette and blew out smoke so his nostrils could take it in; through the morphine my father smiled, asked, "How's the gink?" meaning her boy, and questioned her about his report card. The afternoon was passed in such talk until she kissed him goodbye, when my father said, "Always look after Flo."

Late in the month a minister came to prepare my father for death. Led into the house by Milly's son—at the urging of a Catholic neighbor my mother had suggested it to the sisters—this benign man knew of "a good place where the dead go", which did not add to my confidence in him, and spent a private hour in the bedroom with the door closed; when he came downstairs he told us not to worry about my father, he had "made peace with God", and my cousin took him back to Jersey. I never asked my father what occurred in this visitation. It was a solace to his sisters to believe that on his deathbed he had "made a decision for Jesus Christ", and their recollection that thereafter he was "more joyful" was one my mother would not have disabused them of; but it was not what we in the household saw.

I was in the midst of these comings and goings; with the doctor's prediction I had gone on a second leave from my job, and was hanging around the house. I ran errands to the avenue for my mother, like taking a suit of my father's to be cleaned and pressed, and three days later fetched it again to put in the downstairs closet, knowing it would next be worn by him in a coffin. I shovelled coal into the furnace, and fed the dog, and settled to work at my play, and wrote a letter to my teacher apologizing that I could not; I read until my head was dulled, and waited for my father to die.

Daily I was in the mahogany rocker in his sickroom to keep him company, but the talk was a trickle. I would ask could I get him anything, he would say no; I was not in his focus, another of the liars, and I sat in a misery of silence with fifty years of him to ask into, too late, my begetter was dying with the riddle of our life untold; I would ask was he comfortable enough, he would say yes; bedridden, his head awry to the window like a plant to the thin sunlight, he lay with eyes large as a child's and blank, lost in whatever a dying man thinks, why me, and I was of the enemy who would outlive him, tonguetied with it, too craven to say a word that would confess the last of our differences and let us share it for an hour; I would ask did he want the radio on, he would say no. Dumb in that bedroom with the alarm clock ticking, the cottonlace curtains moveless, the boudoir suite of twin beds with ruffles and chifforobe and mirrored vanity-table so feminine around us, every surface with its doily, I felt an ennui that would not let me breathe, and what was in my heart I hardly knew, so never said, that he was my true love and I could not forgive it in my mother that she was forever between us. I would fix the needle whenever he spoke for it now, and see the morphine lull his eyelids, suffusing in him, lulling his organs to sleep, but not the scatter of outlaw cells in them that had shrunk his flesh to this, so close to inhuman earth again; whatever flowering had been possible to it was at an end. One such afternoon he asked what time it was and I told him, he seemed asleep, two minutes later he asked again what time it was and I told him, and after some thought he said in a murmur, "Almost the same time." Interminably in the ebb of sunlight the clock ticked on, afternoon into afternoon, and I would think, Die, let me go.

Poor as it was, my father clung to consciousness. Downstairs at lunch my mother and I were interrupted by a dreadful thud in the ceiling; with her at my heels, I was up the stairs three at a time and into the sickroom, where on the floor between the twin beds I saw my father inert on his back, and knowing the scream I heard was my own, an oddity I had read of, I ran to lift, pull, push him onto the bed, but he was dead weight and I was too rattled; my mother helped, the two of us falling upon the blankets with more than a corpse, he was breathing. My mother nursed him back to an awareness of us which was confused, and after that he was rarely without a bedside watcher. In December he lay so skeletal that his bones poked at his skin, chafing it to bedsores, and these nagged him in every which position; my mother laved him with alcohol, and cut up rolls of absorbent cotton to tape as pads onto his shoulders, elbows, hips, and with pillows under the blankets kept their burden from his shins. Morning, afternoon, night, she "took wonderful care of him", her own face a wedge of worn flesh, pale and inexhaustible. I was not loth when, the leave up, I could escape my job; and after six weeks in Mt. Vernon my grandmother was taken home by Ada for Christmas in Trenton, not to see her son again, but it was a suffering to sit with him now. Yet my mother sat with him, and supported his head in her hands when every few days he retched over the white bucket until "all his insides came out" in great bloody chunks, and death would not them part.

It was my sister's habit, after frost killed off the backyard garden, to bring her father home a handful of flowers she bought in the subway, but toward the end his mind was too errant for such tokens; one evening he stared at me and asked who I was. I tried not to be hurt when for two days he would not have me in the room, yet I took it as the rebuke for my life. In and out of a half-delirium my father more than once called for all the lights on, the frilly lamps and the pink ceiling fixture, and required everyone in the household to sit where he could see us; abruptly then he would banish lights and family, to lie in the dark, and we heard him muttering to himself that he was "too young to die", the spectre was out now, and my father with his fist banged on the wall, intoning, "I don't want to die, I don't want to die," banged methodically on the wall till that hammering unnerved us. My mother, putting on the lamp to dissuade him, would be pained with the sight of his knuckles bleeding.

In the last week he went blind. Christmas was with us again, and in the sickroom—grown brilliant with the arrival of poinsettias, other plants, bouquets, and a hundred greeting cards propped everywhere, even atop the radiators—my mother set up a diminutive fir and hung it with a few of the ornaments that had been ours for two decades; my father was unable to make any of it out. Of that joyless day I retain little, but my sister remembers how our mother described each plant in the room to him. Presents too were there, a vestige of the old spill of plenty, and become a bitterness; we put into my father's fingers such things as the soft new pajamas he would never wear, and earlier he had instructed his chick to shop with his money from the vanity drawer, so my mother unwrapped the three or four packages he could not see, stockings, a waffle iron, a slip, his last gifts to her. Or not quite, for in that week when her face was gone my father held to her fingers, said, "Oh God, how I love you," and left her that too.

Two days passed, and my sister and I at the bedside each morning, kissing his brow and taking with us the word or two he murmured, saw no change; that he was sleeping the third morning was not unusual. Yet a few hours later my mother, seated in the rocker in the quiet sickroom, heard a break in the rhythm of his breathing. She called to her spinster schoolmate, and for some minutes the two women kept watch at the bed with its burden of skin and bone, which breathed, and faltered, took in a mouthful of air, exhaled, left off; my mother said, "Is he gone?" and the emaciated head on the pillow breathed again, and the spinster said almost but told her not to "cry or talk to him, you'll only bring him back," and so my mother stood over him, dumb, waiting for the next breath. It never came, and when she knew the discoloring body was at the end of its effort to live my mother said, "Now I can cry."

Around his unseeing corpse, the household which was his lifework slowly set about its business of survival. My mother went in to the neighbor's phone, and throughout the afternoon the front and back doors let in a traffic of doctor, undertaker and assistants, women of the family, neighbors, a houseful simmering with the suppressed excitement of death; at work my sister was interrupted by word her father was "very ill", knew, and travelled home, where she found my mother red-eyed over a cup of tea in the kitchen and the funeral arrangements in the expert hands of Will's widow, who had buried a second husband in recent years; upstairs in the bedroom with pails, scalpels, tubes, the embalmers were at their labors over my father's cadaver on a table, disembowelling it, draining off its corruptible fluids, and repacking its refuse of viscera, disinfected. My sister escorted my mother away to buy the first of the black clothes that she would wear for a year.

Inaccessible by phone, I knew none of this, served out my workday among storage bins, and, homecoming at dusk to the monotony of leafless hedges and stoops, saw the door to our house was hung with a lamentation of flowers. Inside, the downstairs was lively enough with others moving the furniture back for the wake, and after I talked with my mother I took my way up the carpeted steps to the hall; here all was still, and I stood in the doorway of the bedroom. The embalmers gone, nothing in the room was different since morning except that now on the twin bed my father, clad in his gray suit, pallid hands clasped, lay forever dead, and his good face which was like no other in the world was a stranger to me. I went no nearer, and I had no tears, something in me had become stony in those six months, and it would be weeks before I cried, but, once begun, was never quite done, for of course he never let me go. After a time I rejoined the living, and when later the coffin was delivered the men carried my father downstairs in a wicker basket, to create a flowery retreat of the living room with his corpse as its centerpiece, and my mother shut the keyboard lid of the piano; upstairs she stripped the deathbed, and remade it with clean sheets. It was occupied that night by the spinster in her dusting cap, and in the adjacent bed my mother for the first time slept without the sound of her husband's breathing in the room, or perhaps did not sleep.

In the morning the undertaker was at our door with his discreet box of cosmetics, to touch up the unstable face of my father, and so opened the wake. For three days and nights the little house was crowded with people, all the other faces of my life, the half-forgotten neighbors of childhood, my aunts, uncles, cousins, clerks by the score from the bank, each of whom stood his silent minute at the coffin and then lingered, in muted conversation, from dining room to sun porch; the sheaves of flowers they sent so swamped the house that everywhere they were

stepped upon, and were even hung on the walls. In the sickly
fragrance my father's mother for three days immovably filled
the easy chair opposite the body, hardly speaking, hardly eating,
sat. In the kitchen, with its swingdoor closed, the talk was more
cheerful. The coffee pot was always perking on the range, the
tablecloth was set with platterfuls of cold cuts, salads, cakes
brought in by the neighbors, my mother was in and out anxious
that everyone eat, and the visitors on chairs, or squeezed into the
breakfast nook, or standing with cups in hand against the refrigerator and sink, gossiped of other matters; I sat with them
chatting, nodding, smiling, until a sudden widening of my inner
eye saw what lay beyond the swingdoor, my father already
forgotten, and I contemned us all. Only once was my mother
somewhat beside herself, upstairs, when she and Ben's minx collapsed in a hysteria of laughing, excusable as "something Irv
must want us to do". I had asked one friend to come, and so at
the coffin my mother first received the girl who would bear two
of her grandsons, and led her from the dead man to introduce
her to the family and the food; the girl in wonder took in how
gentiles mourned. By ten o'clock at night the house was emptied,
save for a relative or two who slept over, ourselves, and the
body. On the eve of the funeral the bedroom allotments put me
downstairs on the sofa not far from the coffin; I awoke in the
small hours to lie with eyes open and breath held, listening, half
afraid of the waxen effigy that so unreasonably had befriended
me, and I had somehow let die.

It was an icy day when the hearse waited at the curb and
barren tree, with a black limousine behind, and from our house
in both directions the cars of relatives and friends waited one
after the other along the street. In the living room some folding
chairs had been delivered by the undertaker, but too few, and
the fifty or so who had come for the minister's valediction were
backed into doorways, stood against walls, sat two on each step

of the staircase that led up from the dining room; on the top step, unseen of all, sat my mother. I have no recollection of anything said by the minister, a stranger to us, but when the brief ceremony died into silence I heard from above me a scream, bullet-like, abruptly sent and broken off, and knew it was my mother. I was embarrassed by it, yet now realize she chose that step because from nowhere else could she see over heads down into the coffin and take leave of my father's face as the lid was shut upon it. So he disappeared finally from our sight, and was carried in the coffin out the front door, and was placed in the elegant hearse, and the sidewalk was busy with the dispersal of people to cars, and at the limousine a gathering of women in black—his mother, sisters, wife, daughter—was helped in, I joined them, and the headlights of the many cars came on, pale and dreamlike in the day; in slow procession we followed the hearse that bore my father's body out of the dream the four of us had lived in together.

The cemetery gates were a dozen miles away, and here, at a tombstone among others in a field patchy with snow, the grave was open. At the edge of this pit in the frozen earth my mother, with my sister and me at either elbow, and roundabout a silent party of watchers, saw the coffin lowered by straps until it came to rest, with something in it that was and was not her husband, and not in virgin clay; deeper were the remains of my uncle Will and his two children, in ground offered by his widow, and the women who stood in survival near that pit wept for more than my father, who was the oldest in it, having lived for fifty years, nine months, and twenty-five days; in her black half-veil my mother endured the last minute of rite and prayer, the flower tossed in, the first shovelful of dirt, and then turned away to the icy lane and the limousine. It drove us out of the gates, no headlights or procession now, a single carful of mourners going back to an empty house.

Yet it was late night before we were alone in it. Other carfuls returned to the street, and people again, food, a distraction of voices, filled the downstairs till dusk came, some of my mother's kin and her in-laws stayed for supper, and she sent my sister with her suitor off to the movies, common sense was the mood, but the hour was inevitable when all the dishes were washed, dried, put away, the comforters were gone, and my sister and I sat with our mother in a house which had disowned us. It was the last day of the year, and in the living room, so void of its coffin, the three of us with our tired talk saw the old year out, the worst we had known and good riddance, but with it came to another end; the decorum around our eyes, in chintz drapes, sofa and coffee table, console radio, easy chair, the upright piano and its stool, had been set to rights and was as before, only its heartbeat was done, the house too was dead, and not one of us but through its walls saw the reality of winter on the plot of earth under which my father in his gray suit was laid to rot. We had come to the end of our tale as a family, now each of us must find his own and other place in the world.

So in the first hour of the new year we separated for bed, upstairs, and thereafter lay not quite apart either, when in the dark of different rooms, and under a dozen other roofs, in each of our dreaming heads my father lived again, and died too, over and over.

35. To My Survivors

Tonight is winter's mouth
Haranguing
Our every window; I feel his teeth
Grate on the charmed

Roof, and his malediction
Moves
The doors; he wraps our house in his arms
And rocks it, noisy

With griefs. All he wants
Is in.
I make the rounds, and my resurrection
Is safe, two boys

Like beans we tucked in skin
Lustrous
In each dark bed, with sprouting hands
No comforter here

Will long contain; our care
I tuck
Again to their chins, and go to my rest
Under the boisterous

DIES IRAE

Huff of his rage. My bones
Twist
To that cry. Not if all night I cling
To my earthly hip

Of wife, or lock my fingers
Half
Grown in her hair with twenty years
Of grappling love,

Can I here, in the slip
Of wind,
Hold: tighter we hug in disbelief
But looser lie,

Knit in each other's dying
Limbs,
Breath by breath. I know who howls,
Wretch in my ear,

I never forgot. My boys
And better
Half of my life, listen, this curse
Within each skull

To keep my houseless voice
I leave:
When in my bed the sheets are staid,
And I elsewhere

Tucked in, the weepy stuff
I wore
All haircloth rags and sticks disjoined
May gladly dry

Wishless under its lid,
But I
Will not; hear, I adjure you, hear me
Ravelling out

Barbaric upon the wintry
Roof
In grief no fleshly lung has wind for,
Nightly my loss

To tell, and witless how,
When all
In heaven or hell I most shall want
Is in. Is, now.

agnus dei

36. The Green Is Back

Lambs, who take away the sins of the world, it is time to talk of the birth of children.

Hope out of hope, they do come again like leaves, and after so many deaths the tree is still prodigal; of the ten children brought forth by my aunts and uncles five lived and brought forth ten more, the three oldest of these have been fruitful with another seven, and my sister and I with four. It is half a century since a child in the clan died, and with every birth the tale, not yet finished, begins anew. Let my tongue not be prudent, it wishes to remember the vexations and ennui of that daily prose which is family life, but I am talking of salvation.

I mean, in a world where we are all damned, the absence of despair. Some cold breath of the void was on my neck, not always, but enough, in the fifteen years between my last sight of my father in the coffin and my first of the swaddling who was my newborn boy; the events of that interlude were a work of necessity, but it is not my history I have still to tell, and it must suffice to say that much of it in my mind is strung on two threads, a mourning of my father and my stillbirths as a writer. The two were not unconnected, and weighing in verse the pleasant and unpleasant contents of my life at the crux of thirty I wrote that its end would be no loss to me.

I had no place in the remnant of the family story. Or so I

thought, and I took myself out of it unsuspecting that in my new suitcase—lately my father's, a gift from the bank in his twentieth year of reliability and used by him once, to go to the hospital—was a ghostly collection of broken faiths like debts I had to work off. I was no worse than most, survivor, ingrate, renegade, self-server, failure, adulterer, and of restitution to the living I felt not much need; it never occurred to me that I should change to oblige anyone I knew. I was a given, take it or leave it, but the deposit in me of so many escapes from the claims of those who loved me was a good soil for bad dreams. For two years they rose in me nightly—perhaps not, I remember it as nightly—in one of two persistent fables, either my father was miraculously alive with his cancer years after the diagnosis or it was my mother who instead was dead of it; my bedmate would awaken me with a hand from the moan which in the dream was my guttural effort to scream, night after night, my body in sleep working to digest the stupendous fact of death.

Abating over the decade, such dreams never died out totally, and in those others which were the stories, poems, and plays I wrote I would come sooner or later upon the theme of resurrection, like an underground stream, always flowing. I had little but words to hide in against the wind from the void; minus a deity, I had substituted for a time a millennial faith in men as brothers, a subversion which indeed had warmed me and toughened my fiber, but it was half a hallucination wherein I confounded my pleasure in oratory with the world's pain, the other half was bombed out in the war which came to birth nine months after my father's death, and in the private ruins I had made of my marriage I saw how little in myself I could trust, for love, friendship, or family; I wrote I would nail the suave liar tongue to the table of solitude, and scrubbed at my poems with the assiduity I had seen in my mother scrubbing at pots. It was my sole act of belief or contrition.

To say those fifteen years were a long winter would omit much. Fallow and mellowing, I had nonetheless elected an occupation in which all choice was mine, not a light bondage, and if I waited so hungrily for thaws and shoots it was also for a witness that life was possible; mine was unjustified if words failed me, and I knew it in the coldness at my heart. I suffered some in my lack of worldly success but worse in my falls into dumb lethargy, and in such months of despair I more than once punched a hole in a plaster wall, my workrooms always bore those pocks like stigmata. I then so injured my fist that for two weeks I lectured on piano works I played with one hand twice the size of the other; but that blow anteceded the pregnancy of my wife and was my last, the winter was done.

It was a rainy dawn when I escorted my waddling wife into a hospital lobby, and three hours later I saw the tiny creature who had dwelt so long and anonymously in her womb: at the elevator a masked nurse bearing him from delivery to maternity waved me back, but lifted the cloth so I could spy the squeezed face and dark hair still matted with his mother's blood, and at last something in me found its pedalpoint. By what stumblings in the dark his mother and I had come to that beginning is another story, part and not part of this, but I had been a long way around and was home. Diminutive head, it pulled like magnetic bone at everything in my life, work, marriage, conscience, all was changed, and chiefly, whatever new griefs were in store, the oldest grief was gone under; a part of me dying as grown son was reborn, both as infant and as father resurrected, in a consciousness over three generations like the opening of a new eye. In so lengthened a perspective now the time between is shrivelled, and the two faces of death and birth swim up out of the darkroom fluids of the mind as contiguous as on a single snapshot.

And this very moment I spy him below me, homecoming from

school between the pines along our mud road, his younger brother tagging behind; each in burly coat and long pants, bareheaded, dangling a briefcase bulky with learning, is almost no longer a boy. Tall as my thumbnail, they halt, talking and pointing at what I cannot see, but not seeing what I can, a decade gone in a snap of the fingers and my voice cannot reach them, but is in them, as they walk on among the puddles and into the disasters of young manhood. All I relive of mine in this workroom is only in words, happily, for in fact nothing then stood between me and insanity except my good sense, and so my bowels yearn upon and follow these two along their muddy road to the pillared corner of the dark green house, in which they are less safe than I; and here I write for their eyes, dear readers entering into the bloom of youth, do not despair, it is outlived. Another hour and I will go down to them and my duties in the house.

For if I dare to say salvation I mean a state which is neither simple nor enchanted, but conditional, and paid for by the day in the commonest coin of domesticity. Two years before we were parents we heard a mutter of these boys pestering us to be born, and after half a lifetime of working only for myself I undertook to work for them. Seizing upon any offer that would make me a wage earner, a tardy ideal, I taught classes in music and literature, began a novel I saw would be publishable, sat with piano pupils, wrote to order an opera libretto and a pageant script, founded a theater group of psychiatric patients to direct, and on the run with my employments from breakfast to bedtime could not spare thirty minutes for lethargy; a feverish time, it was the most exhilarating of my life, and I lost the race to finish the novel only by a month; I scribbled its last pages in the hours after midnight in a rocker with my newborn son on my shoulder, a sleepless brat, and a writing board on my thigh. I had my witness, I wrote now in his service too, and I would never again fail to earn a living with a pencil, a revolution too timely to be luck. I took profound pleasure in becoming the provider to him, and later to his brother, that in another life my father had been. To be back in the human family was so long deferred a joy that for several years I was drunk on fatherhood; of every stranger I met I inquired into the number, sex, age, health, talents of his children, and could not but marvel at our skill.

Yet it was a dark mirror too, in which to this day I ponder reflections of me which are less than pleasant, the heart of the hope. I was a father not yet a month when at two in the morning our infant scrabbled on my shoulder in a refusal to sleep and, with my writing board blank, I shook all six pounds of him until he bawled in terror; my wife wept when I told her, and for days I was abased in that knowledge of myself. So it began, and though I recovered, confident that thereafter I would be the faultless father I had it in me to be, more than a decade later I am still making my own acquaintance with a painfulness no mortal other than these boys can evoke in me.

Now that they can breathe by themselves through the night their mother and I no longer hover so above a crib, nor do we sit a half-hour to jog it in rhythm to our lullabies; much of their innocence, and ours, is forgotten. Schoolboy faces, molded by purpose, they are not the babes we watched over when only the imagery of sentimentality, lambs, petals, angels, was apt. I understood heaven and hell at the cribside as I hung upon the face of our younger; it was his birth which had restored my mother to me, who now lay dying, and I knew that never in this world would I find a word to tell him the love that rose like a grace or perfecting in me as he slept, for every morning we awoke to a language muddied by the parting of our wills, and I saw why heaven was populous with cherubs; heaven was my moment of grace made into an eternity, as hell is the burnings of will. "You're a good boy," my father teased in my childhood, "when you're asleep," but awake I am flesh like him, alive and imperfect, and our cherubs are themselves not without faults, some being mine. Once when this three-year-old in helping me dig a ditch was unshovelling my labors I spoke sharply, and still see on his happy face the panic come at work he had thought was good and I thought was bad; what melted in me was some ignorance that my word mattered as it never had in other ears. Of all they and my wife and I have forgotton, little is lost, and much of my voice in them is error I would undo.

I cannot, and can. I sat at the bedside as my wife suckled our firstborn, and the meeting of blind mouth and great mothering breast was the point it seemed not of my life but on which the world itself turned; it was a glimpse of verity not without a mystical blurring new to me, and passed, but I knew I would have a part in no event more important. To these boys whom I invited into the world I am answerable for every item in my life. It never occurs to me that I should not change for their sake; I can do better, to overcome my nature is a vow I will break and make while I have breath, and so help me what am I back to but my father circling a day on a calendar in the year of his vow to master his temper?

Lambs, who take away sins, I mean not too easily that in each child born is the future, so much of it reiterates the past, but that I had no parents until I had children, and in the mirror of them I see my falls from grace, as son, as father, which must be redeemed. It is as undeniable a claim as a diaper to be changed; and in such small labors of love is our judgment on the past, to reiterate this, to outgrow that, a work that expiates some sins and lays some ghosts. It is how the future comes, is woven out of and seamless with the past, even in the enmity between the generations, for the child escapes, but the voice of his begetter is in him, and in him the begetter lives on, but having changed for the child.

So the coming of children is a birth in us also, of will in the service of grace; only hell is barren of children, and with every birth the tale, not yet finished, begins anew, never done, is all beginnings, like man, and in each it seems the past need not be unredeemable.

CREDO

37. The Wit Flowing under the World

One morning not long after my father's death the garbage truck that paused at the pail and ashcan under our tree found in the unlidded ashcan a mandolin in excellent condition, and carted it away. With my sister and me at work, no eye witnessed this small and bitter drama; time had not yet delivered us from evil, and what my mother in her winter coat thought when she brought in the empty ashcan she kept to herself. She was house-cleaning in the wreckage of her life.

My father's estate consisted of the furniture in the house, the car in the garage, and a life-insurance policy worth a little more than six thousand dollars; this money was in my mother's hands twelve days after the funeral, when she divided it exactly in half and opened two savings accounts. The first bankbooks in her life, they would in time be a financial history of her widowhood. She chose two banks in the city, for maximal inconvenience in getting to them, and the half she deposited far downtown in the district where her husband had worked was to sit, undrawn against by a penny, until the day of her death; it was her bequest to my sister and me. Indeed, she added to it the sum— $154.55—for which six months later she sold the car. Gone by then, I never gave its sale a second thought, but now know how many times, sleepless at night, she heard a voice urging her out to the garage to idle the motor with the doors closed; she sold it to get rid of a voice.

A touch of Dore theatrics or not, she confided such dark thoughts only to the spinster who had been her pal since they were schoolgirls of nine; in afteryears my sister and I would find it inexplicable that we entered so little into what our mother was suffering. Not unacquainted with it—the siege of the six months past had gutted us all—we were no doubt kinder than we remembered. Yet green and self-minded, my sister not twenty, I turned twenty-four, we were each on the threshold of a life to be built, love and marriage, family, work and fame, the promises that invited us away were common enough; and my mother in her black garb said not a word to keep either of us with her.

For a time after the funeral I stayed on with them in the house. Absent most days at work, and most evenings in a tiny office I rented to write in halfway between job and home, I was a token occupant, turning up in the kitchen at bedtime to kiss my mother goodnight, which I judged to be too much; half my years I had been backing out of her hands, still at my throat to run the knot of my necktie up, and even the mildest of her good cooking put my ulcer in a temper. It was my secret, she never knew I was tight of voice at her every other counsel, and considered her the flagbearer of the enemy. I was friendly enough with my sister, who on faith thought I "was wonderful", but the tableau of us as two children at night over a fire in a city lot, like orphans keeping each other company, was far behind us. A last straw, the kitchen was overpopulated by the placid schoolmate whose spinsterhood was dedicated now to sharing my mother's lot, and in the spring I moved back to a coldwater flat. Furnished with little more than my two necessities—an old piano, the third of four I abandoned to landlords in as many years, and a bed, in which I was awakened by the emaciated face of my father who left his grave each night to find me and was gone when I opened my eyes—it sufficed to entertain the girl who was my only intimate and help; I was tacking in on the decisions of my life.

I was on the move again by summer; I had finished my play, two years of work at night which revealed how ignorant I was of the stage, and the playbroker who had sold my story found me room and board at a theatre six hundred miles away. It was the first of the distances I was to put between me and my mother, disappearing out of her ken and most of what remains of her tale. I was off to an upstate city that fall after the girl, there for her doctorate on a scholarship, while the old world erupted in a new war which would kill half its young. I never went back to my eight-hour-a-day job, or held another; determined to be either a writer or a bum, with our marriage the following autumn I began upon a dozen years of becoming one disguised as the other, not always sure which was which. I lived on my wife, with an occasional bow to society and my conscience in such odd jobs as playing piano in beer joints or rewriting psychology texts. For most of those years my mother was to guess at my life behind the words on the postcards she awaited from Virginia, Kansas, Massachusetts, and with her nerves out in me guessed so sharply that I was no sooner in a hospital with my first hemorrhage than her letter came inquiring was I sick. I had fainted in the act of urination, and came to under the washbasin pipes to hear my voice explaining I "thought I'd lie down a minute"; if ever she spoke out of me it was then, and I should have learned how involuntary in my tongue was her dogma of volition, but my espial of our interfrettings of body and soul was in the future. To my knowledge, I had departed the city of our life with no luggage of sentiment, leaving furniture and mother and every familial memento behind, except my father's suitcase and the dreams.

In the suburban house my mother dwelt on with hers, mutely, and only years later wrote me—a sentence I remember out of the chitchat of five hundred letters—that "many a night and often I cried myself to sleep." It was unseen of my sister who, working by day, dating at night, "didn't talk that much" with her, but herself woke crying so inconsolably from dreams of the father she adored that my mother took her to the doctor in the city; he said it would pass. With the death my sister had put away her prayerbooks, doubting that any ear had heard, and desisted from all church rites. Not so my mother, who in the eddies of early widowhood found the rock she needed. In a phrase also memorable Ben's daughter told her "the coast is clear now to come back to the church", and she revisited the parish of her birth to kneel in the pews where she had knelt as a child, hard haven likewise to the knees of Mary Dore in her eighties; and at the altar of their common past she was received once more as a communicant. Thereafter she walked to mass weekly at a church a few blocks from the house, while my sister stayed at home.

It was not the major overturn in their lives. My sister broke off with the hothead who had wooed her for three years—her father had said she "would never marry him"—and went to the movies with other boys, still in mourning, until she wore a summerprint for a Catholic lad on whose arm she was escorted back to mass; an orphan, he sent flowers to my mother, who grew so fond of him that she and the spinster sat in tears over the news that he too was to be supplanted; a young Protestant clerk from the office, dating my sister, insisted on the dismissal of all rivals. Unwitting actors in an old script, my mother and my sister now relived the ceremony of Mary Dore and her Flo, with the young man drawn into the role of an earlier clerk whom he had never seen, but was not unlike. Disapproving of the suit because her daughter was "having such a good time" with a variety of beaus, my mother would lie awake in the dark upstairs until she heard his car at the curb deliver my sister home, and if they sat in it too long she would leave her bed for the hallway switch that lighted the dining room below and flip it repeatedly; the young clerk ignored this summons, and when my mother informed him she waggled the switch "for a reason" he expressed his worry lest she break it, which next time she did. Still, she was not discontent when in the second year of the courtship my sister, in her footsteps, read herself out of the true church to marry the heretic of her choice.

I drove in from Kansas to take my father's place in "giving away" his chick, and of all the tribe who convened for the wedding I, being the most intellectual, least knew that with it my mother was at an end and a beginning, the old walls were down; she knew, but I saw nothing of it on her brightest face. It was a happy event in an untrue church, festive with rustling gowns on bridesmaids and a flock of rented swallowtails, including mine, my mother in a front pew in her finery of blue velvet and plumed hat to match, all smiles and a tear for her daughter so pretty in white satin gliding out on the arm of a husband. The reception after was in the ballroom of a country club with a few musicians on a platform, and when they vacated it I filled my sire's shoe on the piano pedal for another hour, so the bride and her guests could sing and dance on. I heard from relatives there what I was to hear at every family encounter now, how much I "put them in mind of Irv", but surrounded by the strangers of another clan I could not but note how ours had thinned out. Of all the Dores only my godfather Ben was left, gaunt, seedy, uncertain with his small jokes, and I sat next to him that day in some pain at the fading of his personage; my mother and I would see worse before the end. Of my father's kin, on hand were Milly and Ethel—sister Ada was halfway around the planet in Africa—bringing the bride a vase bought with money put aside by their whitehaired mother, but their pleasant faces were not without a tear too, for she had been buried five weeks before.

Old and silent materfamilias, she had returned to Trenton from my father's funeral—her card on a coffin wreath was inscribed in her quavery hand "in memory of my two boys", one strangely forgotten—to sit in a ponderous melancholy until her death. Dutiful at her embroidery in Ethel's house, she took interest in little else and "lived in the past", and out of it had walked a visitor, himself in some way haunted, to be with her on the anniversary of her boy Jim's death; a middle-aged man, he was once the buddy at whose feet our young god had fallen with the bullet in his heart, and he brought her a rose for each year since. Inexhaustible, old sorrows die only like leafmold, enriching the new, and of her eighty-three years the matriarch who had suckled my father said wearily, "You're not good enough for the Lord, and the devil doesn't want you." She was enfeebled by pernicious anemia, and had been more than doubtful of her strength to journey to my sister's wedding; and one day in the doorway of her room she fell and broke her hip. Perhaps it was a slight stroke, for in the hospital to which she was taken she suffered five days later the stroke that killed her.

Always the "other" grandmother of my two, her death was remote from me, but the wedding was the first of the family gatherings barren of our ancients; the generations were turning, the children ripe, and the bombs that would drop on Pearl Harbor were being loaded. From the ballroom the bride disappeared on her honeymoon, my aunts travelled to the two houses in Jersey soon to be empty of son and daughter, Ben went back to sit in the childless flat he and his deaf wife occupied under the el in Harlem, and I took my mother home. In her fastidious house little was altered—the Horace Waters piano and stool were gone, she could not look at them, and a washing machine stood in the cellar where her husband had scrubbed—but it was a husk to be abdicated at last; for more than two years my mother, shovelling snow, mowing grass, stoking coal, had kept it without dipping into her bankbook, on some savings, five dollars a week from the spinster, and ten from my sister which now was at an end. To Milly she said with regret that my father and she "could

have bought the house for the mortgage, then I'd have something," but the bride heard no hint that her quitting work was of
any consequence to her mother, nor I that I should divert one
hour of my writer's year to earning a dollar. I slept in the house
that night for the last time, as my sister had the night before; in
the morning I was on a highway west to my wife and typewriter
in a university town seven states away, and my sister would be
back to live in a new apartment-and-garden complex halfway in
to the city.

In the weeks prior my mother had been looking for a modest
apartment in the neighborhood roundabout—she wished not to
leave it—and settled on a kitchen she liked in a two-story building near the store I had once rented to work in. During her
daughter's honeymoon she was packing, giving away or selling
all her furniture that would not fit into a small place, and scouring the house down for whoever came after; returning, the
newlyweds stopped in to see her and found it stripped, the
windows and floors exposed, and what was left of her furniture,
the barrels, rugs, cartons, ready to go. Next day the van was at
the curb to move my mother out, and into the three rooms
nearby in which she intended, for however long her widowhood, to support herself.

Neither of her children was with her when she last turned her
eye on the bare rooms altogether cleansed of us, and went out
the door. So ended our occupancy of the middle-class house I
had always hated, the lodestar of our morning together, and ever
after most bitterly loved; I would see it again only from the
sidewalk opposite, time gone by and the trees grown up in a
streetful of cheapwork dwellings run down, all needy of paint,
our lawn neglected and trodden back to dirt, and the house so
poor and narrow with the two mute windows upstairs behind
which my father had died, I believed by an effort that he had
died, and our lives had happened.

Of his three survivors, scattered now, my sister and I were each branching forth in another tale; this of our family would be done were it not that my mother, unhoused of the old keep, recreated herself in the new. If the promises which beckoned us ahead were in her world behind, she invented others, and I was to be grateful that, though I dreamed of my father, the bones in me had been fed on her milk. I never thought of her life as creative until I saw what she made of it, widowed, and so unforgetful that on her deathbed her tongue wandered to "my husband, my husband" as to a recent companion, but, even at the end, thankful; and that long coda of yea, like a distillation of our dogma, is what I have left to tell.

38. April Fool

Begin again.
Sorrow in us, now a mother's milk
Is in the mummied hands of bush that wooed us down
To rag and skull, or so I saw,

Begins again
In every leaf and wing to hold its wake;
Dead griefs I buried thaw, the airs my father sang
Rise in our muds, where bodiless

Faint air he lies
Unsung, and I am so skinful of all
Such earthy melt, come spring, in any jostling wind
I shake to tears as shrubs do buds.

Begin agains
Like bees I hear incite us to exude
Some profitable bead, when, in this round of thefts,
I see no rhyme or reason, sing,

Begin again.

39. Of Rag and Spit and Eye

Of the years when I was on the outskirts of my mother's life I have little enough to narrate, and it is not much more than the gist of it that I hope now to put into words. In among her treasures I find a diminutive gift card—"for your new home"—in her daughter's hand, and when I ask what the gift was my sister protests it "was twenty-five years ago"; I cannot believe it, the time of our own lives running out so fast, and the widowhood of my mother is like one long day of which I note a minute here, a minute there.

Six months after the wedding my sister was pregnant, and half a continent away I wrote to our dead father in a poem that he was "joined to the future", a mouthing of rote which eleven years later I would understand. That winter I came by train in wartime to see my mother, her newborn grandson, my sister, and some plays—I had written a second—but was feverish when I started out in a coach car spilling over with a clamor of boyish soldiers, many of them to be soon and forever quiet, crawling east on trackbeds jammed with a traffic of troops and supplies, all schedules off; I spent a night on a terminal floor with a hundred others, was succored by friends I visited in a Tennessee city I could not get a train out of, and ultimately arrived at my mother's with a strep throat which sent me to bed for ten days. Kept at a distance, I had a peek at my infant nephew's pate, and on my last night attended a play, but mostly I saw the three rooms in which my mother was establishing the daily rule of her widowhood.

Second floor rear, the apartment was one of four in a redbrick building on an avenue reawakening from the depression. The street door let into a vestibule not much larger than a closet, its slab of brass mailboxes gleaming from rag and cleanser, and the inner door unlocked to my mother's buzzer; the stairs up were dark and creaky, but at the landing her door opened into an airy kitchen and a glimpse of bathroom, daintily hung with "guest" towels not to be used. Immaculate as always, her kitchen with its white furniture and curtains, bright with one big window, was not a great comedown in housekeeping comfort, and only a couch along a wall—in which I convalesced, displacing the spinster pal whose nightly bed it was—lent a suggestion of straitened circumstances. Its space was augmented by the living room beyond, interrupted merely by our pair of chintz drape strips; here the furniture of better days was more cramped on the dark rug with its flower pattern; the dropleaf table, the upholstered chair, footstool, sofa with coffee table, the console radio, the mahogany armchair, were not untinged by a faint melancholy of objects going out of style. Two windows in the living room, with cottonlace curtains and floral drapes, let in good light, and the door that stood open to a bedroom with two windows let in more. It was in this tiny bedroom that the leftovers of the marriage were crowded against each other, twin bed, night table, bureau, vanity and bench, even my secretary desk, so that walking space was narrowed down to a foot around the bed; the closet was packed almost solid with cartons and suitcases, yet held all my mother's clothes. Little in the rooms was new, most conspicuously the linoleum on the kitchen floor and, at her bedside, a telephone for emergencies.

In the course of its footworn years the linoleum would be

replaced, but the apartment as I saw it first was hardly changed when I looked upon it last, and nowhere in it was she unreminded of my father. Downstairs the mailbox bore his name instead of hers—one of the printed namecards given to him by someone at the bank—which my mother thought, or said, protected her from burglars; in a corner of the kitchen stood the springy chair of white-painted steel in which he had last taken the backyard sun, and under the stove lurked a wooden box containing an old hammer, pliers, screwdriver, the other tools his hands had used in household repairs since their honeymoon flat; among the flower pictures in the living room were, framed in glass, two poems I had published in magazines, one on her valor in his illness and the other my deathbed piece to him; in the bedroom, placed on her bureau to meet the eye, sat his portrait, a grainy enlargement of the truest snapshot ever taken of his live face, with its self-deprecatory smile. I never walked in there but it stopped me like a greeting from him, and I think it served my mother so.

It was no surprise to see her vigorous in her new kitchen, cooking for the spinster who was with her for company; and that my sister also was fifteen minutes away by car relieved a good four-fifths of my conscience, though their relationship was less serene than I knew. Not a week passed but that her daughter visited or shopped with her, fetched her for dinner, picked her up for a Sunday drive or movie—long ago when Milly had protested that every supper was planned for the males my grandmother advised her that "the men you have to cater to, the girls always stick"—and the twinges of repentance my sister felt after her death arose not out of fact but out of what she too kept unspoken. Even she found her "not easy to be with", a little of my mother went a long way. Idealess, she was unceasingly talkative, and so repetitive of chitchat I saw she used words to ward off thoughts; under the politeness of her endearments she was insistent as a glacier, and her inquiry, "Would you like a nice cup of tea, dear?" could not be answered no because she asked it with such considerateness every two minutes that the tea was soon preferable to the question. She was unaware of this kindly erosion of others, and the shopping trips the two of them went on usually included a puzzling outburst of temper in her daughter.

The paradox in my mother was that so implacable a hand was so tactful of my sister's privacy in larger matters, and in these her errors of judgment were rare. One she committed before the wedding when the sweethearts, meeting in Brooklyn for a trousseau fitting, were vexed beyond courtesy to see my mother brightly enter the store to be of help; they argued her out of retreating by subway and bus, and drove her home when done, but it was an unhappy afternoon. Pride, love, an eye shrewd of her own independence, whatever, my mother thereafter was prompt enough in nipping her instinct to intrude. Her daughter had taken to cigarettes, my mother to a bedtime glass of port, and each was upset to observe so vicious a habit in the other; in the old house they sat to wine and cigarette in separate rooms, a shut door between, but after marriage when my sister lit a cigarette in her own apartment my mother said, "Dear, you know I don't like to see you smoke," my sister replied that it was her house, and my mother objected to it no more. In her visits to the newlyweds—perhaps remembering how my father said to have her spinster pal "come some other day, Sunday is our day"—she was most prudent, except for an extreme moment. One noon when she rang their bell to accompany them to a wedding in the city, and learned while they were still dressing for it that my pregnant sister had seen her "show" of blood, she simply ordered her child out of her clothes and into bed to await labor; it came quickly, and the birth was in a hospital instead of a hotel. Otherwise my sister remembers her as "never interfering", a feat for Mary Dore's girl, but my mother after fifty was again in growth.

Her principal asset was lack of money. Once satisfied that her household was speckless she travelled with a bankbook into the city, withdrew nine hundred dollars, and the next day deposited it in a bank fifteen minutes from her home. Three weeks later she took out $45.00; she was commencing now to live upon her half of the legacy, in withdrawals every few weeks—I wince at these careful sums—of $38.00, $34.00, $20.00, and over the next seven years her city account of $3120.00 would dwindle to $413.75 before it was rescued. Drawing upon it so frugally, she had to earn most of her living. Among her neighbors in the house was a family who owned a candystore nearby, and my mother introduced herself to wages by tending their children in busy hours, which led to cooking their meals and housecleaning; it was her only skill. Emboldened, she sat at her kitchen table to write out cards offering her talents to an unknown public, and dropped them in the mailboxes of the neighborhood. Soon she was doing the housework for a few women who, with business or club duties that took them away, came home and could not believe their eyes: my mother scrubbed at their toilets, floors, pots, closets, sinks, windows, with the obsession of a lifetime against dirt and disorder, attacking every crack in what to her was a religious war, a bargain at seventy-five cents an hour.

Far off, I lamented in a poem my failure to save her from the ignominy of her toil; it was hard work she got out of bed to every day, well or ill, but the fact is that when at long last I was inundated by royalties I could not get her to desist. Nor did I honestly try. In plain truth, as a houseworker my mother put every other to shame, and the word of her advent spread among the women she called "my ladies" until she was working in the city itself; able to pick and choose, she settled upon two or three in whose households she spent a dozen years, and with such attention to the troubles of the occupants she had little time for her own. It was a wisdom in her that, forever worried about her children, she so busied herself elsewhere she was no worry to us, earned her own money and respect, lived not a day but that her face was welcomed by someone, and persevered in a course of labor so athletic it may well have prolonged her life; with all the sickliness of her flesh, at seventy she was as lean of body as in her fifties, and looked not much older. She was always more than a cleaning woman to her ladies, counselling this one against a love affair, mothering the children of that one, testifying in court as a character witness for a third, and observing in all a variety of customs new to her, from bar mitzvahs to jewel smuggling. Clearly she was comforted by the birth of her four grandsons in a decade and a half, who brought my sister back under her roof and me once more into her world, but its daily business was long established, not on them and not on us; most of her time was spent among strangers to us, and the loss of her wonted self as wife and mother was a blight in which her life opened anew.

For years she rode the bus and subway into the city several mornings each week—the bulk of her housework was in an elegant apartment overlooking Central Park—and in spare hours she fitted in some of the errands which kept her so busy. Periodically there was the waiting room in the hospital uptown where she sat to undergo examination into and treatment of such a variety of afflictions that she herself thought it comical, quoting one of the clinic doctors, "Name it, you've got it." Always there were birthdays and holidays to shop for. The cream of her reading was still the newspaper ads of sales in the great department stores dominating the neighborhood where she had been born, and whenever there my mother took her bundles into the church in a side street to pray, light a holy candle, and promise Saint Anthony a few dollars if he conspired in my success. Less frequent were her calls on the savings bank in midtown to withdraw the money for her local account; she was at it more often in later years, when, spending sparely out of the checks I sent, she deposited every cent she could to return to me after her death. And, until she was sixty, there was Ben to visit in Harlem.

Clan loyalty brought my mother back once a week to a tenement that looked and smelled like a jakes; here, in a rocker at a second-floor window, her aging brother sat, unshaven, in a worn cardigan sweater and soiled shirt, tieless but buttoned. It was impossible to see in him now the strong sleek youth from the nineties, frozen by the camera in a handsome cutaway, white tie, white vest, "Gentleman Ben" standing with head erect and face boldly untroubled, his hand upon a five-string banjo. In his failure to discipline that instrument was foreshadowed all his history; blessed with good looks, his roughneck charm and joy in fellowship, the uncle I was fondest of found everything else a mite too easy. So opposite to my mother, perhaps he was unlucky in their sire, the song-and-dance man recalled by her from childhood mainly for women and whiskey, for like an entertainer Ben was most happily sure of himself when making others laugh; it was his talent and tactic. Always in my young eye Ben was on a platform tickling this audience or that—as barker, selling war bonds from a streetcorner van that contained my father at a piano, or as toastmaster, introducing with a chuckle of irreverent profanity the priests who orated at the beefsteak breakfasts we played for, or as father of the bride, reading to a banqueting crowd not only the proper telegrams he had in hand but the improper ones he ad-libbed from mayor and governor—and if I believed him rich, powerful, beloved of monsignors and policemen, it was as true as not. Yet in my mother's face I saw the worry that throughout his life followed after Ben like a shadow.

I have not much memory of him as drunkard, though her tales of how he drove home in the midnight streets while asleep were unforgettable, and I was in his sedan once when its fender picked up a traffic stanchion whose clanking accompanied us for a hundred feet without impeding my uncle's flow of genial talk; it dropped off, which was his solution of most difficulties. After Mary Dore's death, he was on the drink oftener, and longer. My mother disapproved of the wedding feast he threw for the older daughter—the fifteen hundred it cost might better have been given to the bride, she said—but no one knew it was to be Ben's last gesture. In the course of the two-year drunk he entered upon next the world of business came unstitched; Ben awoke from one phantasmagoria to another, his fleet of ice trucks gone, the old lady's seven rooms and the sedan gone, himself not familiar, a doddering man at fifty-five in a strange flat on home relief with his gut and mind half eaten away. Tammany pals, the exhausted daughters and sons-in-law, even the itinerant cousins, took themselves off to greener fields. Ben and his battered wife had ended alone in three coldwater rooms under the Harlem el at 119th Street, where my uncle dwelt in his rocker, listening for the footsteps of one faithful visitor; and week after week his Kate in bed with a broken leg lay for days in her own excrement, until my mother was at the door to clean both her and the house.

For a time their lives had been lifted to a kind of solvency when Ben was placed on work relief—one of the building projects which gave birth to such jokes as that of the foreman who requisitioned shovels and received a telegram, "No shovels left tell the men to lean on each other"—but my uncle was so hollowed he could not do even the half-hearted digging or carrying of bricks; for weeks he was in a terror of being fired, until some pitying hand wrote him down as night watchman. One winter evening in the thirties I had walked uptown to visit him on the job. In his shack, at the edge of a no-man's-land under excavation near the river, the two of us on broken kitchen chairs sat over a kerosene heater which was our source of light; we talked about nothing much, long silences, except for the buffeting of the wind off the river, and every hour we staggered out into it to make his watchman's round of dark derricks and sandpiles, and staggered back to the kerosene heater to sit another hour huddled in our coats; not a smoker, I watched Ben's shaky hands roll cigarettes to save money, so I went off to buy him a pack, and went two or three times after containers of hot coffee to warm us and help that night of our silence like a dumb sorrowing to pass, and eventually it was done; in the dawn I took leave of Ben in his shack, and walked home. With the war the work projects came to an end, and my uncle occupied his rocker again on home relief in Harlem.

Dating from this vigil a legend was born in Ben's head, and mine, that I "was always very good to him". In the autumn of every year one of my mother's letters to Kansas would remind me his birthday was imminent—"he's your favorite uncle dear send him a card"—and each time I mailed off a carton of cigarettes; in due course a note of thanks came back, purporting to be from Ben, but in his wife's scrawl. Ben no longer was capable of any act, the will had drained out of his body, and he simply sat at his second-floor window by the el from morn till night. I knew the flat, I was in it to visit him in the same rocker before the war and after, and could not believe that for six years while fifty million humans in a global madness had killed each other my uncle had stared upon a sidewalk traffic of colored folk as his only event. Ben and his wife were the last whites in the tenement, and my mother, unfailing in her calls, was afraid of the faces along the streets she had played in as a girl; I can see her hurrying past them, tightmouthed, always on her way home by nightfall.

In her own tidy household the war altered everything. It had plucked my sister's husband out of their apartment, and the bride, with her eight-months-old boy and a quantity of furniture, had been taken by our mother into the three rooms already comfortably full of the spinster. Like me, my mother worried much lest I too be drafted; that I owed my life to my country was a tenet I never subscribed to, and no one was under any illusion that I would make a soldier, including the government, which to my profound relief found me unfit in belly and soul; I retired to the Rockies for elbow room to write poems, in such a revulsion from the times that the invasion of Normandy was a week old before I heard of it. Happy at my deliverance, my mother throughout the war had smaller worries enough in her apartment where elbow room was extinct. She preserved its appearance and morale, kitchen and living room seemed none the worse, but behind the door to her bedroom—she had stored the twin bed and other pieces in the attic of a friend—was a jamming of her daughter's double bed, cedar chest, dresser, chest of drawers, baby's crib, and to get a vacuum cleaner in was possible only after piling furniture upon the bed, a weekly procedure. She and my sister shared the bed, with the boy in the crib alongside, the spinster in her dusting cap couched in the kitchen, and refugees like Will's widow on the sofa in the living room; so many hands divided the housework, and so many feet multiplied it, that little was lost or gained, and my mother surreptitiously redid whatever she thought imperfect.

My sister was allotted eighty dollars a month, which turned so quickly into baby foods, salves and medicines, pediatrician's fees, that my mother "wouldn't take anything" toward the household; but when her son-in-law was graduated from officer school as a lieutenant the allotment jumped. My mother then accepted ten dollars a week, a small act of deceit to be exposed at the war's end. Several times my sister rode south by train to be with her husband—barracksed in Alabama, Florida, Georgia, then shipped overseas, he knew his boy only in snapshots for three years—on travel money she earned by stints of sewing; my mother would bring home the work to be done, in part a gift, from the lady overlooking Central Park. During her daughter's trips, my mother suspended her daywork in the city and took care of her tottering grandson, who remembers her singing for his amusement, "Clap hands, clap hands till Daddy comes home, Daddy has money, Mommy has none."

It is a chant out of my own infancy, in another war; the round had begun again. Surely I was reborn to my mother in this boy, who, growing to her daily tune of how he resembled me, chose at nineteen to be the teacher of literature I at nineteen had half chosen to be, yet, unlike me, never felt her hand upon him as galling. She was grandmother now—and I hear the hoarse voice of my own, that bulldog who ruled so many sons and gave me buttered bread with sugar, scolding whomever it concerned, "For Gawd's sake, leave the boy alone"—and in my nephew's memories his Nana is the mild guardian who "never hit me at all"; she had learned forbearance in the lifetime since she bit her daughter's finger in a perambulator. It was the daughter who was "very strict" with the boy, and my mother also kept her tongue from butting in while my baby sister, suddenly in charge of another soul, invented anew all the hoary mistakes of childrearing.

Yet for seven years his grandmother was in the boy's eye every day. He took it for granted that she was "always sick, it never got her down, just part of her," and the energy I saw her put out with my youngsters was at his service a decade earlier. Regularly she romped with him on the swings and seesaws in a playground across the avenue; and took him by hand on bus and subway into the city, to show him the world from its tallest building or sit marvelling under the stars in the planetarium or stand on a sidewalk line before prices changed for a palatial moviehouse; and spoke of her dead husband who "would have you out to the ballpark" if alive, and in the kitchen with their heads together she read aloud the funnies in her tabloid, which he longed to read for himself; and commenced teaching him to read, and whenever he was ill bought a round steak to dice, letting it soak all night and simmer all day in its jar to become the "beef tea" my own mouth waters to think of, and partook of little meat herself throughout the war because her ration stamps went on lamb chops and bacon for him; and after the fish she broiled for all on Friday nights she led him through her weekly entertainment of "shopping" in the Jamaica stores—"I don't know if we ever bought anything"—where she did buy manly little clothes for him out of her earnings; and from the households of her ladies she came home to him with toy autos and soldiers no longer wanted by the other children she was helping to rear. In his boyhood and later, her grandson saw much more than I of her life as widow.

Summing it up, he thought she lived as though, insignificant in herself, she sensed her "only significance was in helping other people". It was unlabored, merely in her bones that at her neediest she must make herself needed by others, and her favorite prayer was one of Saint Francis that he "not so much seek to be consoled as to console". Devout in her churchgoing now after a quarter-century of abstention—of her daughter's in the war years she said without a blink it was "one thing to change your religion, dear, but you've given it up"—on many a Sunday she shepherded the boy to a pew, yet of his father's sect, not hers. The oddity is how much more catholic she was than the church she took shelter in, though on her deathbed she would ask the priest to forgive her children for leaving it; in the span of her life was a diversity of loves to conciliate, Protestants, atheists, Jews, and among the desiderata for which she prayed was always the "unity of religions". To which end she would mail to Milly's son in Panama, missionary, an occasional dollar to assist in his task, and in return get anti-Catholic tracts from him as part of it, and work off her ruffled feelings in the Central Park apartment where, as housekeeper in charge, she was impeccably kosher.

In the array of unfamiliar names in her letters to me—landlord, neighbors, new friends and their children, even a suitor—that of her Jewish lady was a constant for many years; after the war I met her at my mother's bedside in a hospital. She was a short dark woman with a very capable face, in her forties, the wife of an unbrilliant dealer in furs and mother of two children. The "brains of the family", she herself ran a clothes and fabrics factory which kept her occupied; when my mother turned up as a cleaning woman her vigorous work and kindness to the children were a boon indeed, and bit by bit the household was put into her hands.

As "Florence" she was there several days a week, vacuuming, scrubbing windows and making beds, shopping for meals, cooking, serving, dishwashing, and often, when parties continued late, slept over in a maid's room off the kitchen; in time she had a helper, another cleaning woman to oversee once a week and clean up after. Each day when school let out she cared for the children, a pubescent boy and his sister, separated by four years in a faithful echo of me and mine. Invariably in her workplaces were children whom she was fond of or sorry for, but it was of these two that my mother made a second family; I saw their photographs in her home, and they so took to her as half a parent that years later the girl, her own mother dead, brought her fiancé to mine for inspection. My mother lived in when business took the husband and wife abroad. She was on call in all their emergencies, the suicide of a sister-in-law, the sicknesses of the children, the trial of a brother for smuggling in jewels once too often, and favors were reciprocal, the woman came to visit my mother at home, bringing candy to her grandson, and to the husband's showroom sent her and my sister to buy their first fur coats of "let-out muskrat" at cost price, and on holidays welcomed them and their boy into her apartment to watch the parades from its windows. It was an orthodox household, and my mother learned to run it in a strict observance of the law. She bought meats from a kosher butcher to salt and rinse, mastered the cookery of such esoterica as kreplach and gefilte fish, kept the milchedike and fleishedike dishes separate, handled the money on Saturdays when her lady could not touch it, lived in a rhythm of ancient holy days and customs, bar mitzvah, seder, shiva, and, much impressed by Mosaic cleanliness, mailed to me in Kansas bars of white kitchen soap dyed with scarlet Hebrew letters; familiarity unbred contempt, and as she had washed my mouth of its childhood obscenities, so the word "kike" was forever cleansed from hers.

Thus it happened that the hospital in which I met her employer was named Mt. Sinai. As usual, my mother on her sick days worked and kept her own counsel, but was suffering a pain in her back that worsened; one day she "couldn't get off the sofa" at her lady's. Its origin was diagnosed as a stone in her left kidney, whereupon the woman took charge as though her Florence were kin, arranging for a bed in her hospital and a nephrolithotomy at a token fee by her Park Avenue surgeon. I undertook to drive east in a prewar car, which collapsed in Missouri, and the operation proceeded without me. It was on a Saturday morning; before my mother was awake her lady was up and, unable to profane the day in a taxi, hiked three miles across the park and uptown to the hospital; there earlier than my sister, she greeted the patient in her bed, walked alongside her as she was wheeled out to surgery, borrowed a mask from her doctor, and at the operating table stood holding my mother's hand until the anesthetic took effect; she stayed as onlooker to the end. I arrived two days later, to find her seated at the bedside and my mother pallid but perky, displaying to everyone her kidney-stones in a test tube. When after ten days she left the hospital, it was to convalesce for a week in the elegant apartment, forbidden to lift a finger, and waited on by her employer.

My mother of course was uneasy when cared for, and soon was travelling the subways again with her shopping bag—packed neatly with housedresses, medicines and toothbrush, comfortable shoes, it was her overnight luggage—en route to work, or home, or the invalids who were her own nurslings. Of these Ben and his deaf wife were her regulars, but her itinerary took in others from Brooklyn to Yonkers, nieces, former neighbors, new in-laws and old friends; busy as she was, much of her social life was in sick calls. Downstairs in her house was a couple I was shown to whenever I came, octogenarians on relief in a clutter of furniture, a birdlike man impaired of gait since a stroke and his wife with a skin cancer; my mother looked in on them almost daily, did some of their shopping and tidying up, bathed the wife, led her on the bus to her treatments in a hospital and home again, and brightened their poverty now and then with a half-gallon of tonic wine; they outlived her. Often back in the flat where her sister Minnie died, she ministered to the widower she had never been fond of, and when he married his ailing housekeeper my mother took care of the two of them, and when he in turn was buried kept on with her visits to see after the woman, all in the family. Days so spent were not a dissatisfaction to her, duty was pleasure, but what she most looked forward to was a chatty weekend in Jersey with one of my father's sisters; and there, the summer after her operation, she was introduced by Milly to a town on the seashore which won her back each summer following.

It was always to one house, and to the same room in it, that she returned. She saw it first when, the war over, her son-in-law came home from the army to my sister and found the small apartment was his and hers, for a second honeymoon; my mother had sent her spinster pal off and taken her grandson to the ocean for a week. With Milly, they stayed in a wooden hotel bristling with fire escapes, which was less to my mother's taste than a "nice-looking house" she spied in their strolls to the boardwalk, the home of a widow who rented out a few bedrooms to ladies no longer young. Before the week was done my mother struck up a pleasant acquaintance with her and the occupants, and upon her return to the city began a daily practice of saving quarters in a large glass jar as her "vacation money"; with them she bought a month next summer in the house she liked, and came back to my sister rested, tanned, and a pound or two plumper. Nowhere but under this roof was she content to let the work machine of her body be idle. To make her bed and wash out a teacup were her only exertions, and with the other "widowed ladies" who rendezvoused there each year my mother sauntered up and down the boardwalk, took meals in the crowded restaurants, swam her eight or nine breast strokes at low tide, sat on the beach to write her letters, bought the boxes of saltwater taffy she mailed to my sister and me, and each evening after the bandstand concert enjoyed a "good talk" over tea until bedtime. In this house, at her most relaxed, she turned a bathtub faucet off so conclusively it broke in her palm, which spurted blood, and she was taken in an ambulance to a hospital for stitches and bandaging; it was weeks before she could write, and she worked lefthanded while friends advised her to sue the landlady, but instead she went back as a guest for thirteen summers. Until she died it was her August nest, with the ocean as her neighbor for the first time since our season in the Staten Island bungalow, and not inconceivably the breakers washed in a long driftage of memories, for a witness to her vacations said she sat much on a boardwalk bench "without moving, just looking out at the sea."

If she was there the summer I flew east—my third play had won a $500 contest judged by a famous director, I came in a naive hope he would produce it—I see why my mind is blank of her, and what I recollect is my visit to her brother in Harlem.

Ben grown old at his window, hair still parted in the gay-nineties style, his cheeks gaunt and prominent nose jutting out, sat with a pallor of death in his unshaven skin, though his time was not yet; such a sadness had taken over in him that his eyes upon me were prompt with tears. Up from his rocker in a hurry he chuckled out a welcome over our handshake, but the old mannerisms of his bonhomie were like ghosts, tremulous, the muscles around his happy mouth and eyes asked not to be struck. I put on an air of cheer in the parlor with him while his slippered wife in the kitchen, grayhaired, unkempt, shouting through her deafness, heated me up some coffee, and for an hour or two the conversation crawled among items of family news. The upholstered chair I settled in was dilapidated, its springs broken, and the three rooms were badly run down, wallpaint peeling, linoleum worn through to the floorboards, sink rusty under a faucet drippage of generations, curtains on the open windows limp with city grime; I remember a standing victrola with a handle to wind it, defunct but kept for show, and two or three pastoral scenes from calendars tacked up among the wall cracks, a garish oleograph of the Saviour over the bed with a heart bleeding in his breast, a couple of photos of the neglected daughters now seldom seen, and a yapping poodle, dirty white, who came to masturbate against my shin. Ben doted upon me with the hyperthyroid eyeballs of my mother, saying in each silence, "Well, Billy," eyebrows up in wonder, "come to see your old uncle, hey?" Ransacking my head for talk, I worried about the greasy cushion under me soiling my good pants, and when they asked how I was and what brought me east I was loth to tell, my health and playscript and hopes seemed like insults in this flat of a decayed couple waiting to die. My aunt at least had the eggs to fry, swept the rooms, rasped out a few words at her colored neighbors, plodded after groceries up and down the avenue under the el; Ben left his rocker only for the toilet in the hall. Or once a day, when his wife gave him the change, he shuffled downstairs to a bar with his tin bucket. Beer was what he lived on, his stomach so intolerant of food that my mother suspected cancer, and half a glass on his windowsill kept us tepid company all afternoon while my uncle rolled cigarettes from a ten-cent sack, wet twists of paper around a few shreds of tobacco, his tongue and fingers so faltering I doubted he could manage. It was too soon when I stood to leave, as always, and I eased my going with a couple of dollars I put into his hand for what he called "real" cigarettes; Ben protested I "didn't have to" and commenced to cry. I made my goodbyes, and escaped downstairs. Crossing the street I sensed eyes still on me, and turned to wave to his stooped figure in the second-floor window; I eluded it in the traffic of Harlem, but not the thought that my father in his beneficence to everyone— Ben's girl said if there was a "saint in heaven and it isn't Uncle Irv, nobody's there"—was nine years in his grave while my godfather lived on, useless even to himself.

It was otherwise in the three rooms in Bellerose occupied by his sister Flo. With the son-in-law's homecoming, my mother turned over to him and her daughter a bundle of war bonds— accumulated with their ten dollars a week that for two years she had pretended to spend as house money—and the privacy of her bedroom; the spinster Nelie lived in a hospital where she was a cleaning woman, and my mother took her place on the couch in the kitchen. For half a year the small apartment was in effect my sister's. In it her husband made the acquaintance of their four-year-old, and in civilian clothes again travelled daily to his job in the city office, and on Saturdays repainted the walls while my sister cooked his favorite roasts, and their boy scalded his arm, broke the mahogany chair, fell down the stairs; their lives were back to the bliss of the commonplace. My mother, absent on workdays and off on Sunday visits anywhere, kept herself out of earshot.

In the scarcity of housing after the war the young couple looked in vain for a place of their own. Suddenly by good luck the apartment in front was vacated; my sister reclaimed the furniture she had stored with friends, moved it in, and so became the nextdoor neighbor. Invited back, Nelie said it was easier to room where she worked, and our mother, for the first time in her sixty years, was in a household alone.

She had only to bang on the wall if she needed her daughter's family, yet she schooled her taste to solitude; the boy's memories were of his Nana in her kitchen, rarely in his. In the small hours my sister, awakened by the storms which terrified our mother, would see in the areaway between their windows her lights go on, and visit with her over two cups of tea till the thunder died away, but it was her visit. Lonely at first, my mother was always adept at discerning blessings in disguise, and soon came to enjoy the use of her living room and kitchen late at night without disturbing a sleeper on the couch; the consequence of her new leisure was that she undertook so many tasks she had less time than ever to spare. With scissors and tape over the scrapbook she kept of my doings, or scrubbing the bedsheets on a washboard, or baking hundreds of cookies for her employers, neighbors, their kin in convents and barracks—the boy remembered them on cooling racks "all over the kitchen", and one tin that she shipped to a young soldier, travelling after him around the world, came back to her a year later—or putting up crisp curtains, scouring the floor, sprinkling and ironing clothes upon her board, and at midnight still awake, writing at the kitchen table the outpouring of unpunctuated letters which served her as conversation, my mother had no complaint other than that she didn't know where the time went. The phone was a companion and a respite while she sat on the bed with it, but, however happy she was to hear its ring, she also grew impatient when talkers kept her from the chores that "had to be done"; for the rest of her life no day in it was long enough.

I was a principal recipient of her letters, cookies, and the cartons in brown paper stuck with labels in her cramped ink-script, which turned up in Kansas on my birthday and every holiday for eight years. Punctual to the day—lateness in anything made her anxious, if some extraordinary circumstance delayed a carton I would receive beforehand a worried letter telling me not to worry—these arrivals, opened by me and my wife, were a delight to the eye: layer under layer of packages each in giftpaper gay with ribbons, snuggled together as cunningly as lovers, they contained everything a mother might send to a boy on a desert isle, pound cakes, socks and gloves, dates and figs, the kosher soap, underwear, raisins, pads of yellow workpaper, cheeses, slippers and belts, the catalog is endless, and in my thank-you letters I would report how each gift tasted, fitted, met a need, and reassure her, almost always truthfully, that not one cookie had been broken. Even I glimpsed the concern with which she shopped for, wrapped, and shipped these substitutes for mother's milk to a son distant from her by half a continent and a world of other interests.

I was present to her eye only in the scrapbook of my career, an imposing tome which must have cost her a week's pay. Its covers were rustic slabs of birch, bound by a leather thong; the upper cover, hinged with eight brass studs, was shellacked in a contrast of amber grain and blond, and on it was affixed in great cursive letters of wood the name I then used, *Will Gibson*, in echo of my dead uncle. Within, the black looseleaf pages began with the literary agent's note informing me of the sale of my first story. I sent my mother everything I could that was complimentary to my despairing life and she taped it all in, my only fan letter, programs of the community-theater plays in which I was acting, a congratulatory note from a magazine of verse awarding me a prize, rehearsal snapshots, a typed poem to my father's tombstone which she illustrated by a photo of him, a request from a university library for a sample of my worksheets, theater

347

reviews and publicity featuring my face, page after page that corroborated for both of us the rumor of my existence and evoked for in-laws a portrait of her brilliant son, who could not earn his food. It was my practice to mail her the magazines which carried my unintelligible poems—my sister's boy said it troubled her that I "always used words she didn't know"—and ten per cent of whatever I was paid for them, two dollars in the spring, three dollars in the fall; when I collected them in a thin book for publication, five years of work, I sent her ten dollars. Yet the scrapbook took a turn for the better with the handsome jacket of my book of poems. It was followed by a rash of news clippings on a local production of my prizewinning play, and my mother encouragingly wrote me, in an odd and persistent phrase, that "the ice is getting thin".

Indeed it was, for my poetry was no sooner in the bookstores than my mother was back in a hospital bed, cheering up the other occupants in her ward, and rather frightened; some internal bleeding had been spotting her underpants in recent months. Six days of examinations and a biopsy revealed its source in a caruncle on the urethral mucosa, benign, and she learned she had hypertensive cardiovascular disease as well. Discharged, she was a habitual occupant of the benches mobbed with outpatients in the waiting room, reporting to the heart clinic for follow-up, to the genito-urinary clinic for silver-nitrate treatments, to the endocrinology clinic for her thyroid, and each time sat with numbered tag in hand for several hours; she insisted on going alone because it made her too nervous to watch my sister waste the day if she escorted her. The bleeding ceased, but in the autumn of the next year my mother, washing out her undergarments nightly in the sink, was upset to see the evidence of it again, and said to my sister that "when there's bleeding there's something wrong".

Meanwhile her children were a source of happier news, my

sister heavy with a second grandchild, and I packing to move back east. Less solicitous than in the first pregnancy, when she would travel for an hour on two buses to scrub her daughter's windows, my mother was now no further than a cry away; the doors of the two apartments stood open to one another. It was an easy birth—her husband drove my sister to the hospital, was advised to wait at home, and hardly had sat down with his newspaper when the phone rang to notify him it was a boy—and only the christening was delayed, until I could come to be godfather. I was eastward bound in joy because my play had been optioned at last by a Broadway producer, in answer to my mother's prayers, and my wife was joining the staff of a psychiatric institution in the Massachusetts hills. Upon our arrival at the producer's country house as weekend guests, we were told that a reading of my play to raise a hundred thousand dollars had raised five thousand, the show was off; driving into the city to say hello to our families, I felt as though my stomach had been kicked by a horse. Sympathetic, my mother thought it over, and wrote me a few days later that God must have known success "wouldn't be good for you just yet".

I was still three plays away from my opening night; what I attended with my mother instead was the christening of her daughter's baby in a Brooklyn church. I held him in my godfatherly arms at the stone font, terrified lest I drop him in, and I too felt a sprinkling of some baptismal awe at the unfolding of our lives. Midcentury was upon us, and of the faces that once hung above me at my christening few were aboveground, and those grown old. In the next five years a dozen more deaths—wives and husbands of kin, friends, my father's sister and her own brother—left my mother lonelier over each birth; the past was disappearing.

In the flat in Harlem her sister-in-law Kate, half blind for months, her old body lumpish and blundering, was felled by a stroke, and carried in an ambulance to the hospital where four decades earlier she had borne both of her daughters. With her face twisted and one eye crooked upon Ben, she lay paralyzed, unable to speak in the voice no one understood was raspy with the complaint of a lifetime, the unwelcomed bride, never listened to, who lost her children to Mary Dore and throughout her womanhood tended a cash register instead; and after ten days she died of a second stroke in the night. My uncle Ben was led in confusion away from his window, to live alternate weeks with his daughters. The younger emptied out the flat, salvaging his clothes, the dishes and pots, whatever furniture was not junk, and the door was closed on the last echo of the footsteps of my mother's clan in Harlem; fifty years of that rowdy vaudeville had come to an end. In Yonkers Ben was querulous, uncomprehending, and like a child "kept wanting to go home" to the deserted flat.

So much luckier, my mother, visiting her brother now as a ward of his daughters, came back to the solitude in her kitchen which she could bear, and preferred. On the landing the two doors no longer stood open, for by winter my sister had moved away; cramped in the front apartment with their two boys—the firstborn recalled he "lived in the crib" until he was six—her husband had undertaken to buy a house in a new suburb, several miles out, a trim and pretty dwelling with garage attached. It was the first to be owned in our immediate family, and my mother was pleased by their prosperity, but declined to join them in it. She said, "Now I'll really feel alone," but only once, and made friends of the tenants who moved in; knocking on their door with a Christmas cake, and a toy or two, she discovered she was blessed again with "good neighbors".

In touch with her daughter over the phone every few days, she often travelled out by bus after work as a surprise, bringing in her shopping bag such goodies as a cinnamon loaf her grandsons liked; she had grown confident of her welcome. Once or twice a month she fed them in her kitchen with her Sunday cookery of their favorites, pot roast soft as bread in rich gravy and hot apple pie with hardsauce. Or she came for the weekend to baby-sit when the young couple stepped out on Saturday nights; she slept in the small upstairs room in which she was to die, and in the morning when all were dressing for church my sister would be vexed to see her hurrying to make up each of their four beds first; my mother said, "It only takes a few minutes, dear," and went in one direction to mass while they went in another to service, and after their reunion at lunch said, "I'll go home, so you can have the day together." Her loneliness was real—she confided in my wife it was "a lonesome life, dear, without a hubby"—but a condition she took for granted, busying herself with her spring cleaning every week in the year; in two and a half years she left a gleaming household behind her five times, off for her bouts in the hospital.

The bleeding was cancer of the urethra. In a semi-private room when she received word of the biopsy finding, it so rattled her that for a day or two she "thought she'd go out the window"; she asked to be moved into a ward. Once on her feet in that wing of the bedridden, changing the water of the other women's flowers, plumping up their pillows and chatting about their broken legs, looking out for whatever small chores the ward nurse was too harried to get to, my mother worked the edge off her panic. She had come to have a blind trust in the specialists who walked the corridors of the great hospital—she often said she was "only a clinic patient, but I have the best doctors in the world"—and the floor physician told her x-rays and lab tests showed no evidence of metastases; they expected to check the cancer.

My mother mustered up her faith in them, and after a week at home, scouring down the household she was uncertain she would see again, returned in dread of the knife. She was sixty-two and the strain imposed on her heart by the growth of her third goiter was being countered by medication because she was considered a surgical risk; to her relief now, the staff elected radiotherapy instead. She was in the ward for another week of observation before the tumor doses of radiation were begun. My sister visited her daily, and I drove down from Massachusetts to reassure her with the information my wife was obtaining privily through medical colleagues, all encouraging; the staff was not deceiving her. When after seven days of radiation my mother packed her suitcase and said goodbye to everyone she was in better spirits, her optimism irrepressible, and she left the hospital talking to my sister about the misfortunes of the other women in the ward.

Periodically now she rode the subway uptown to radiotherapy—another clinic added to her list—to lie again under the machine she detested because after it she "felt like an old rag, it takes every bit of life out of you"; still, on the next day she was at work in one household or another, unwilling to disappoint her ladies. In the summer she was back in the women's ward for nine days. The entire length of her urethra on the vaginal side was found to be necrotic, dead white tissue, and it was excised in toto for lab scrutiny. The diagnosis was dubious, leukoplakia or a malignancy, and she was discharged to be followed in the outpatient clinic; the stain of blood on her underpants was frequent, and that winter once more she was in a ward bed for a few days of routine tests and a third biopsy of the urethra; the diagnosis was unchanged. Ten months later she took her suitcase in again, and another wedge of her meatal flesh was studied and labelled as unmalignant.

Two years would pass before she would be hospitalized for a seventh time, for congestive heart failure. The bed in the ward cost her nothing, under an insurance plan which she said was "wonderful, you certainly get your money's worth," and she paid seventy-five cents for each clinic visit in between. The treatment for her goiter was a cup of radioactive iodine, which a nurse with tongs proffered her on a tray, and my mother sipped it alone in a chamber while her doctor peered through a window; she teased them, "You won't come into the room with it, and I have to drink it." She took thyroid pills also, and after the first episode of heart failure travelled nowhere without her bottle of digitoxin. Forbidden salt, she was intermittently on chlorthiazine and mercuhydrin for fibrillation of the heart, and visiting us for a weekend she would set out her variegated bottles of medicine like a "regular drugstore". Of the salt substitute so hated by others she said that "you get used to it", but she was apologetic about her cooking; she never served me a meal without two or three reminders that it "needs salt, dear, they won't let me cook with salt." Occasionally she felt a paroxysm of rapid heartbeat which alarmed her, and her ankle edema sometimes made her shoes hurt, and at work she was displeased by a shortness of breath. She spoke cheerily of her cancer which she was treating with "sitz baths" of plain water; a tub before bed was her habit, and to ease the soreness when she walked the doctors had advised her to sit in it for half an hour, twice daily, but workdays she was too hurried in the morning; nights and weekends she obeyed, for years, and said she expected someday to "shrink up and go down the hole". She kept a rosary hung on the spigot in her tub, and with it put the idle bathtime to a diligent use, praying to her maker, forever grateful "because he's so good to me".

My sister thought he was not "so good" to her, but our mother knew better. A middle-aged divorcée for whom she had worked came upstairs to her door one evening, in agitation, and my mother fed her and pointed out the brighter side until midnight, but, when the woman proposed she move in, had to say no; next day the woman hanged herself. Shaken, my mother much later asked me should she have said yes, and I said of course not. Like her mother, she had toughened with age, and it drew the helpless to her. Others with nearer claims whom she took in, sometimes for months, included an impoverished crony of the spinster with nowhere else to go and my uncle Will's widow, not impoverished—she had ten thousand in a bank—but incapacitated as a nurse because of "nervous hands"; it was parkinsonism. Watching her rattle a teacup on a saucer, my mother was never unmindful of her own chief blessing, she could "work and support myself, and I'm not in pain."

In her late sixties, this aunt out of my childhood had kept closer to my mother than to her blood kin, and lived sporadically with her. Over the years she had turned "odd", fitful, and so companionless that when my mother spent her month at the seashore she took refuge in my sister's house. There she was interviewed by two women from a home for the aged maintained by the masonic order Will had belonged to; his widow could enter it if she signed over whatever she owned, and the women, surprised by her stocks and money in the bank, advised her to spend it first on trips, clothes, good times, but my aunt "didn't have any interests". Soon afterwards she disappeared into the home upstate. My mother and my sister on a visit found her in a bed in the infirmary, so jerky she could not walk; she had written a note to the cemetery authorities—it ended with "excuse writing shake so"—bequeathing my mother the deed to the grave in which Will and their children and my father lay; her own wish was to be cremated. One day she died among the strangers in the infirmary.

Faster now, leaves off a tree, the contemporaries with whom my mother had shared her life were falling, not a year turned but it took two or three. In the prosperous house in Trenton the actuary who had risen "high in the state" came downstairs for breakfast, spoke to Ethel of a sharp headache, and fell dead on the kitchen floor; in the flat still haunted by Minnie the swart laborer who never liked work, and had been home from it ailing for four years, died of a stroke; in a Jersey bus terminal Milly's husband, the clerk reduced to odd jobs by the depression and now employed as a dispatcher, was found dead among his schedule sheets in the aisle of an empty bus. Widows together, my mother and the two sisters of my father exchanged visits, letters, memories—Milly in gratitude said my mother was "very understandable"—in a new intimacy, a holding of hands against time flowing out.

It was not the end of the news that came like a black frost, season after season, in my mother's sixties. Of all her good neighbors, the dearest was the hearty wife of the el gateman from the tar road who had been at her elbow in my father's last months with money and other kindnesses, almost a sister, and suddenly died of a coronary; the el gateman was fifteen years dead, and the el itself was no more. In a dwelling a short walk from the apartment, she watched the giant bricklayer who sang to her hubby's piano now shrivel in his deathbed, also of stomach cancer. The other bricklayer who "tickled the ivories", grinning from my mother's album in snapshots of the three newlywed couples swamped in old-fashioned clothes on picnics, was long gone as a widower into the sunny despairs of Florida; word came he had drunk himself to death. Further from her heart, the wife of her brother George in Larchmont, unheard from since his funeral, reappeared in a news clipping, dead. In her daily life my mother wept for a younger woman of her own fiber, the Jewish lady, who with bone cancer worked every day at her clothes factory until she collapsed; my mother moved into her apartment to be useful to the last, and afterwards returned to keep kosher house for the children and husband until he moved them abroad. And it was my aunt Ada's death that in the mid-fifties brought me back in touch with my father's family.

I had last seen Ada alive at his funeral; three months after it she sailed away to another four years in the jungle. She was at her happiest there, a stout spinster in her pith helmet teaching the blacks in the thatched hovels to "do Godway", but it was a rigorous life, and at sixty-five she bade Africa a last farewell. For a dozen years she lived at Ethel's in the bedroom vacated with their mother's death. Possessed and energetic—Milly called her the "bossy kind"—Ada ran her sister "a rat race" in the house-work to save her tasks, and was still devoted to church matters, lecturing, raising funds for the missions, persevering in a text she quoted, "Brethren, let us not be weary in well doing," but suffered again from asthma and angina pectoris; when in the week of her seventy-seventh birthday she was taken out of the house with a "worn-out" heart she said, "I won't be back." Two days later she died in the hospital. A totem figure I had always been at war with, Ada in the jungle half a world away had a weightier hand in my growing than either of us knew, but I was long indifferent to the battleground; old enough to see the loss of the past, I drove to Trenton for her funeral.

It was the first I had attended since my father's. At Ethel's house in an eddy of my aging aunts, cousins with children, remoter kin, I met my mother, lean and hardy in her best dress with the deft make-up that kept her indestructible, and an hour later I sat with her in the mortuary. In amber light Ada's body lay in an open casket; from its head the pastor of her church with prayerbook in hand addressed himself to us in a sermon which meandered into a bog of argument with disbelievers in the divine authorship of the Bible, whose origin he proved by citing above Ada's impassive face so many asseverations of its divinity from its own pages that my aunt Ethel whispered to me, "Ada always said his sermons were too long"; and when, having es-tablished the existence of heaven as Ada's abode, the minister consoled his listeners in a ringing voice, "I've never been in heaven, but I *know* it's a better place than Trenton!" only my ear was incredulous. Dismissed at last to the street and our cars, I saw my mother into the black limousine with the two sisters who remained of that family, and with a cousin followed in procession behind the hearse to the cemetery, stood while the casket was interred, and rode back to the house for coffee, food, talk. It was in the tales of the dead—I heard how Ada was indignant that "no man ever asked me to marry him" and Milly told her, "Maybe you don't want one," and how in Africa the kinky-headed natives came from miles to watch her when Ada let down her long hair, and how as a girl of twenty she mended the clothes brought "always to Ada" by the boy who was to sire me—that the past was kept ever so thinly alive; another bit of my father had died and been put in the earth.

And my mother, after a day or two with his sisters, went back to the city in which not one remained of her family; some months earlier Ben had been buried. For twenty years her brother had survived some death in himself and lived on as his own ghost, bewildered, in a body no one knew how to be rid of, and I learned there was something worse than death. I could wish him no other luck, and had shut my eyes on it; but my mother had not.

Soon after her cancer was diagnosed, she had written me three troubled letters. In the first, she said Ben thought the daughter he was now living with in Brooklyn—he "wouldn't stay put" in Yonkers—intended to commit him to an insane asylum; my mother had questioned her niece, who laughed and said the old man was "imagining things". Some weeks later, she wrote of a visit to the flat when Ben was missing half the day on a walk to the corner; a cab-driver brought him in from another neighborhood, lost, and the niece said it was always happening, out the window she'd see Ben in the gutter mindless of the traffic, he could be killed, and away as a nurse's aide she couldn't keep an eye on him; she'd asked the driver she "rode ambulance with" to stop now and then at the flat and tell her father if he wandered off the ambulance would take him to the loony bin. In the third letter, my mother was bitter at her niece; Ben was under lock and key in "the mental ward", awaiting final commitment.

I phoned my mother, learned the hearing to commit him was the next morning at ten, took an evening train down to the city, and was at the hospital in Brooklyn an hour early. I had made an appointment by phone with the chief psychologist, a man my wife knew, and I spent some of the hour with him, some with a social worker he led me to. The psychologist said it was a daily occurrence, relatives wished neither to commit these aged parents nor to keep them, and the social worker told me that private homes which were only run-down boarding houses cost forty dollars a week; neither of them saw an alternative to the state hospital. My mother had argued that Ben always knew who she was, how could he be "mental"? but the social worker—a pretty girl with milk-chocolate skin, competent in a tailored suit, one of the "coons" Ben had been lordly with in his days of precinct politics—said he was senile and disoriented, thought the date was ten years earlier, no longer quite knew what he was doing. For the rest of the hour, I sat as arbiter between the niece and her daughter.

I hardly recognized Ben's saucy minx, a woman in her middle years, become eerily like her mother Kate; and her own child—I had last met her in the Harlem flat, a small-boned girl who in a thin little dress looked fourteen but was separated from a husband and two children, reunited with the grandparents who had raised her—was a woman too, heavy and sullen. Neither would talk to the other. In a bustling hall we sat on a strip of metal chairs, I between the two, and waited for the hearing while mother and daughter each put a different story in my ear. In my left the girl said her mother had turned her grandfather in on a charge of "chronic alcoholism" only because she was sick of him, he was off even beer and drank sodas; in my right the mother said Ben had "spasms of raising the devil", threw dishes, slapped her and a younger daughter, yelled at her husband in the night to get up for work; the girl at a prior hearing had testified her mother was lying and been granted a two-week stay to arrange some care other than a state hospital for Ben, the time was now up, her last hope was a charitable home conducted by nuns where he wouldn't be at the mercy of maniacs in a violent ward; I said the social worker knew the home, it had no custodial staff, would refuse Ben unless deceived, and itself send him to a state hospital the moment he was difficult; the mother said he not only got lost but was incontinent, soiled his pants and the bedsheets, and the girl broke in to deny it, and her mother across me said, "Whatta you know, who was he living with, me or you?" She told me the younger daughter couldn't entertain her high-school friends in the flat with an egg-stained old character who buttonholed them in conversations nobody wanted to hear, was that right? I knew everyone alas was right, and the psychologist had asked me pointblank, "Do you want to take care of him?" I said no, and the granddaughter, miserable about an old man she had grown up with instead of a father, was crowded with her kids in a flat that had no room, and my distressed mother who on the phone said she couldn't leave Ben alone in hers was unable to voice the truth: nobody wanted him. Except a few children at the corner for whom, as in the old days, Ben with the money his minx allowed him for cigarettes had been buying ice-cream cones.

Muttering, the three of us in the hall—on the chairs were a dozen other families who stood up in turn whenever an attendant at a door read out a patient's name—came to a grudging truce. Ben's name was called, and we filed into a chamber with a broad table at which three men in business suits were seated, the middle one the judge. From a far door a colored guard dangling a key appeared with Ben in a hospital bathrobe, shuffling, skinny and weak, and when I went to take his arm I felt little but bone under the sleeve; recognizing me he wept, stammered what, what, did he "do something wrong" to be here, where were we, and the guard led him to a chair; I sat with his daughter and grandchild at the table, facing the judge. The hearing was brief. Our truce was that the girl would not ask for a second stay which seemed fruitless, I would put to the judge a request of my mother's, and her niece would no longer contest it; I said my uncle had a devoted sister who lived in Queens, it took her three hours by bus and subway to come to the hospital we were in, and she wished her brother to be committed to one called Creedmoor, a mile from her door, where she could visit him every Sunday. The judge consulted with the man at his elbow, who looked into his documents and said there were two beds in Creedmoor, the judge informed me my uncle would be transferred to one, and the hearing was ended. The guard prompted Ben to his feet and led him away; we filed out to the hall where, after a minute or two, the guard beckoned us to a heavy door with a barred vent in it too high for an eye, and his key unlocked it for us.

Inside, in a long white room without windows a score of patients in bathrobes sat on benches, wilted old men and women with straggly hair and a young girl, all dumbly staring at the floor or wall, trancelike; one of them was my uncle Ben. His gaunt face lightened at seeing us with him on the bench, and we undertook to humor him into feeling better. I told him it was country around Creedmoor, cooler in the summer, he would have sun and grass, they might even let him out for weekends with my mother; Ben blinked gratefully at us but, clear enough on the past, was hardly more than a word away from tears; it was on this occasion he told me with a quavery wink that he used to dress so spiffily he was known as "Gentleman Ben". It was not long before the guard tapped me on the shoulder, time to leave, and we said goodbye, with handshakes and kissing, and from the hall I turned to see the uncle in whose arms I had been christened, now frail and stooped in his cotton bathrobe, gawking at us as the heavy door locked him in.

I saw Ben once after that, in the senile ward at Creedmoor. I was with my mother, who brought him a cake, and we sat with my uncle among knots of visitors and inmates in a reception room made drab by a battered piano, our talk forced and gay; my mother encouraged Ben to believe he'd be out as soon as he "got a little better", but senility is not reversible, I knew her brother would die within the walls. I never went back. Sometimes I mailed off a carton of cigarettes when Ben's chuckling face came up out of the oblivion my mind drowned it in, merciful to myself, but my mother every week for three years walked through the gates of "that awful place" with foods to tempt his appetite; the granddaughter came, occasionally a daughter, and Ben, his cheeks "all scratched up" from what he thought were blows and the attendants said were falls, would ask in a plaintive disappointment, "Where's Kate? where's Kate?" and my mother kept up her cheerful chatter for two hours; on every Sunday, holidays, three of his birthdays, she walked out the gates with her grief, picturing her brother in the tiny room with cot and chair in which each night they locked him, and next week was punctual to the minute he expected her visit, with cookies, cigarettes, fruit, and gossip to brighten his day. In that cluster of deaths in a handful of years she was witness to none that bruised her so much as Ben's life in its endless twilight.

My godfather was seventy-four when he died in the ward of a "coronary occlusion", but the body delivered to his minx—one cheek, black and blue, had four stitches in it near the eye—convinced her he had been killed by an inmate, and she phoned the hospital to say they "had some nerve".

Ben was buried in the grave that had last been opened to receive Mary Dore, and earlier so many of her sons. For half her life my mother had "kept it up" with flowers, once or twice a year, in the footsteps of the old lady; in the few years left to her she was there on Ben's birthday too. It was part of her cemetery rounds, every few months, made easier since my sister had learned to drive and could take her. Yet often enough our mother travelled by bus alone or with the spinster on birthdays and deathdays to be with the remnants of her past, in this grave Ben and her parents, Willy, others, and in another cemetery her sister Minnie, and in a third, to which she came on her own wedding anniversary, my father; I was commencing to see in my mother, whose chitchat I thought so shallow, a retentiveness of mind which suggested a value other than intellect.

Two weeks before Ben died I published a novel, and my mother at long last, amid so many lowerings into the earth of her kin, saw my life on the rise. It had worried her much, she came home "upset" from infrequent weekends with us to tell my sister how I cooked the meals while my wife was at work; she knew better than I how unmanly I felt until, having achieved two more stillborn plays, a year of marital anguish, and my second hemorrhage, I sired a son. From the hospital lobby, ten minutes after I saw him bloodyhaired in the nurse's arms, I phoned first my wife's parents to assure them all was well, and then my mother. Still, as new parents leery of the malign influences of our own, we held the three of them off for weeks, while my wife nursed our puny scrabbler and bleater. Staggery for sleep, and anxious lest the miracle of her milk dry up, we divided the clock into shifts; in the night watch I joggled my heir on my shoulder till dawn, and, so manly nothing was beyond me, finished the novel with one hand. It was about then that we opened the door to the grandparents, who entered in the midst of further news that I had a book accepted for publication.

Oftener with us now, my mother in a snapshot taken that winter is radiant with our scowling babe in her arms. Outdoors, he is muffled to the cheeks in knitwear, but my mother—prosperous in her fur coat of let-out muskrat—is bare of head and of left hand against him; the hand with its wedding ring is sixty-five years old, the veins on it toilsome, but her face is fifty, hale, spare, unlined except for the laugh wrinkles at her eye which, behind the glinty rimless eyeglasses, is benevolent upon her grandson; her hair smoothed back to a faint net is still dark, an earring is decorative in her lobe, and her lipsticked laugh reveals a row of good upper teeth, all her own, since the partial denture she wears is of unseen molars. If I ask myself what I can read in that bold-nosed face—is it plain, brittle, insincere—my eye is too clouded by a lifetime to say, and I am certain only of its joy in the infant who has saved her son's life.

She has seven years left in her own, and they would be seven years of plenty. It was fitting that my mother—who believed in nothing more firmly than that tomorrow was a better day, but to be earned—should find her own twilight a blessing unlike her brother's, all in order, her children provident of her, and each of their houses established with grandchildren in fond hands; so proud of my success, she was humble in thanks for it after her twenty years of prayers. For once there had been time enough, and a second chance.

I subscribed in her name to a clipping service when the novel was published, and for weeks her mail was swollen by newspaper and magazine items from every city in the country with poor Billy's face in reviews, book notes, interviews, much of it syndicated; no matter how many duplicates, my mother taped each into her scrapbook. I had with a certain diplomacy dedicated the novel to "two mothers, mine and my infant son's, for their womanly strength," a bow to my predetermined choice of a helpmate. Once past that page, my mother was so taken aback by my handiwork that she "couldn't go to confession" until she had sat wide-eyed over it to the end; she then asked the priest's pardon for finishing a "bad" book, and loaned it to all her friends, quoting to me with a nervous laugh one who said it was "so sexy it almost gives you a sensation". She travelled out of her way in the city to stand at the windows of the great bookstores, gazing upon the scores of copies in displays. She was most impressed when her mail swelled again with a salvo of items released by a big movie studio to make known its purchase of the novel and its annunciations of star after star for the film. By the end of the year I was in Hollywood on an emergency summons to rewrite their script a few days ahead of the camera, and I mailed back to my mother glossy photos of myself on the set chatting with movie queens, who also went into the scrapbook; one photo granted her lifelong wish when the retouchers of the studio, anxious that even its writers be flawless, deleted the hair between my eyebrows. Undeterred by the hair, the producer invited me to introduce the stars in a coming-attractions trailer, and the next summer my mother, trekking with her friends to every moviehouse in the borough that advertised my title, but a week early, doted upon her son huge in technicolor on the screen.

I was not too dizzied by this whirl, my life had its ballast in my own yearling boy, but the money let us breathe. Though she could not comprehend my refusal to stay in Hollywood as a screenwriter—the glamor made me nervous, I flew home to the New England winter as to a familiar conscience—my mother was content to see us buy a serviceable house of thirteen rooms, with woods and fields, and a cottage for a workplace; in it I settled down to three years of playwriting paid for by the movie. I was able now, through her protests that I "had so many expenses", to send my mother a weekly check.

She worked fewer days as a cleaning woman, but never quite trusted my money; even when I had two hit plays she thought my sister's husband was "better off with a salary that comes in every week". Half of my checks she hoarded in a bank for the year I would be needy, and it was not mine that paid for her workless days but the monthly check that turned up in her mailbox once she was old enough for social security. She had been fearful to apply for it because each spring she ignored the income tax; though she said the treasury would not notice her mite, the truth was that the tax forms bewildered her, and she expected that on contact the government would put her in a penitentiary. Not sure she was wrong, I made inquiry and was emboldened to say she should apply, after which she was the recipient of sixty dollars a month. Serene with such sums, my mother was not altogether happy when I was more bountiful to her. Soon after the movies bought my book I mailed her for Mother's Day a check for a thousand dollars; at first glance she was pleased, imagining a mote of decimal point which made it ten dollars, but a day or two later discovered her error and in horror mailed it back to me; annoyed, I mailed it again to her, and my sister argued her into keeping it, but her bankbook in that month jumps with a deposit of eleven hundred dollars. To indulge herself in comforts worried her in the same way that Hollywood worried me, and I learned to obey her limits in both our lives.

I had a notion of setting her up in her own bakeshop, but my mother said she couldn't sell a cookie for what it cost her—"I use so much butter, dear"—and the idea alarmed her; she was satisfied with her day just as it was. One of the gifts she permitted us to buy her was a television set, a lively joy in her rooms every night. She was devoted to the wrestlers, whose overweight struggles she watched with a hand worried on her mouth; of that bizarre crew she knew each by name, and had an unshakable faith in the honesty of their confrontations between good and evil; on weekends when she sat for my sister, whose set was in a basement room, the boys in bed upstairs would hear their grandmother crying at it in passion, "Kill him! kill him!" Apart from the wrestlers, my earnings made little difference in the flow of goods between us, it persisted in my direction. The portion of my checks unsaved by her came back to me as presents—electric juicers and coffeemakers, and hand-embroidered pillowcases for my wife, who delighted in them, and "outfits" for our boys so tasteful I was puzzled, and a triple-jointed desklamp for my cottage and a two-beam searchlight to find my way back from it in the night—most of which I received sulkily as needless until they wore out in daily use, and I saw how alike we were; when my wife sent her a blender my mother thanked us politely, but it took her months to think it was better than her eggbeater. A boon of our prosperity which most pleased her was the habit I adopted of phoning two or three evenings a month, although five minutes of talking at long-distance rates would curdle her voice with hurry. Instructed to call me collect whenever lonely, she yielded perhaps twice a year to so costly a wish. In all our plenty my mother asked only two favors of me: one, when my sister's boy was old enough to have his eye on Princeton, was whether I could help pay the tuition, and the other, in her ninth hospital stay, was that I not lie to her if it was cancer.

In the voices of my friends who met her I heard a surprise that a woman of her years was so "self-reliant"; to them she was remarkable, and I began to notice it. Nothing was more telling of that strain of gristle in her, almost pathological, than the episode which at sixty-seven put her in the hospital a seventh time.

After a day with my sister and her family on an auto trip, my mother had been delivered by them to her door; alone in her three rooms she took her sitz bath, set her hair in curlers, and got in between the sheets for the night. Not yet asleep, she suffered her first paroxysm of heart failure, so acute she believed she was dying. At her bedside sat the phone that years ago she had installed for such an emergency, and to call me or her daughter or a doctor was only a matter of lifting it; instead my mother, unable to breathe lying down and seized by her old terror of suffocating, found a relief in sitting up, and when she could make her way through living room and kitchen to the bathtub spigot she picked her rosary off it, made her way back to the upholstered chair, and sat in it gasping, with her fingertips telling the beads; hour after panicky hour while we slept in our beds my mother said her rosary, until the windows were pale with the dawn. Dressing herself then, she removed the curlers from her hair, put a toothbrush into her purse, went downstairs to the streetcorner, waited for a bus, rode twenty-five minutes to the subway, waited for a train, rode a half-hour into the city, changed trains, rode twenty-five minutes uptown, walked a block to the hospital entrance, and said she was ill. At breakfast my sister answering the phone was incredulous to learn her mother was in the emergency ward, where later she explained that she couldn't phone her son-in-law the night before because he had "driven so much that day".

She was kept there a few days, on digitalis, while the doctors dehydrated her; she lost eleven pounds, never to be regained. Discharged with instructions to drink as little fluid as possible for the rest of her life, and to weigh herself every day, my mother for the first time appeared "too bony for her dresses", and suddenly the years were written in her face. In the next snapshots I took of her and our boy, seated on our porch steps, the boy is not yet two, intent upon a box of raisins in his clutch, but my mother in housedress and sweater holding him on her lap is older by several years; in one picture she bends with her nose in his hair, and her own so tidy in its hairnet shows a forelock of gray, the skin under her jawline is slack, and in another facing

my camera her throat is scrawny, her eyes pinched in the eyeglasses, and her mouth cannot quite manage its smile; for once the
camera has told the truth, caught the pain. It was an instant her
first movement would deny, and when at sixty-nine she went
back to the hospital ward for another week—the urethral bleeding had recurred, "quite profuse"—the doctors wrote her down
on the abstract as a "spry hyperkinetic white female" who was
"alert and cooperative".

In those snapshots on the porch steps she and the boy sit
among my wife and her parents, with whom my mother had
become friendly; grandparents together, they would drive up in
my father-in-law's car. En route the three of them picnicked
always alongside the river in Connecticut, which my mother
loved, unpacking her feast for five or six—years later I learned to
my astonishment she would also amuse her Jewish in-laws with
offcolor jokes she had picked up—and when in midafternoon
they arrived her first act was to hurry into our refrigerator the
tins of perishable desserts she had cooked for me, pies, hardsauce,
"icebox cakes", while at once she made tea for everyone. Somewhat overborne, my wife's mother would unwrap a shy jar of
chopped liver or chicken soup. Invariably my mother brought a
salami stamped with Hebrew letters for my wife, explaining its
superiority to other brands, and was wont to boast a bit of her
kosher lore. After the tea she cleared away and one pot led to
another, she took over the kitchen, scouring its objects with
apology—"I'll just give this a little shine"—as the housekeeper
who worked for us glowered, and my wife had to invent tasks all
weekend for her "because she could not sit still"; I in desperation
led her outside to the cellar steps, choked with dead leaves, and
she purged them down with scrubbrush and hot water, though it
was a chore she complained of with a laugh, too many "spiders
and things". Silence was worse, after her days alone my mother
was so tireless of tongue that in bed at night my wife would be

frantic, and hiss at me because I took flight into my cottage.

I had long been skillful in acknowledging my mother's conversation with nods and grunts while occupied with my own thoughts. Sometimes I guided her into talk about her past, which interested me, but she was interested in her present, and it was populated by a shadowy host of strangers I could not see; she described each as "very nice", except her landlord. Of the ladies each August in the seashore nest I heard much, down to the minutiae of their winter lives as exchanged in letters, but my mind wandered therefrom, I thought forgivably. I remember only the elderly gentleman who, at the ocean with his married daughter, proposed to my mother, and was serious enough to visit her at home; I said nothing, but I had a deep wish that she not admit a man other than my father into her life and her bed, and was relieved that she took it lightly. The landlord was a more persistent caller, forever popping in to accuse her of tampering with the thermostat he kept padlocked. I listened to a catalogue of his villainies; he was more than once haled into court by his other tenants, whom he hated as bloodsuckers, but in a give and take with him throughout her widowhood my mother wore him down; after ten years he surrendered to her cheerfulness, and granted a variety of favors such as cellar storage that he forbade the others. Of her inexhaustible tidings about the neighbors I recall nothing except her report of a baby-sitter who got stuck on the fresh paint of a toilet ring, the father while struggling to heft her off slipped, and a midnight ambulance carried them both away, the father with a broken leg and the baby-sitter with the ring affixed to her bare buttocks. The other neighbors were less lively, but my mother continued to sit for my sister's boys—of one his father said if the state thought him old enough to drive a car he was old enough not to need a baby-sitter—bearing to them her cakes and weekly allowance of a quarter each, and to me her headful of talk about my sister's family which was my chief source of brotherly information. She often relived her tours with them of the city sights, and romping with my heir on the grass she promised him too a trip to the Statue of Liberty when he was bigger, but time, kind to her in important matters, was not to permit her that. So much of her talking was an involuntary monologue repeated to any face she saw that I escaped it from one room to another, to outdoor tasks, to my work in the cottage; my wife submitted to rehearing it all, most taxed by her mother-in-law's passion for such topics as curtains. Two days of lending her ear for a third time to my mother's descriptions of everyone's curtains sent my wife exhausted to bed, with me at her heels. And downstairs, in solitude at a table, my mother talked herself out in the letters she "had to write" nightly before her sitz bath.

Courteous and evasive, I was not quite to open my eyes upon her until our second boy was born. It was a time of exigency —our movie money had run out, and a two-character play I had completed was again not finding a producer—and with my wife in her ninth month I undertook a television script to pay the bills; a proverb in another country says that each child brings a cake under his arm, and the script in a stage adaptation was to earn us enormous sums, but the gift brought to me at once by this newborn was my mother. Invited up to help, she ran the house while my wife was in the hospital, and almost overnight I saw her as my father must have seen her. In good measure I was living with his eyes in any case; I had become him as father, a restoral which perhaps enabled me to forgive my mother the indictment hidden from both of us, that she had been his love and between us. Now the exactingness in her which I had so long fled, and carried in me, she put at my service.

In the house with her and my three-year-old, I took note of how fond she was in caring for him, and I sat clearheaded with my script in the cottage. Every afternoon the three of us would drive to the hospital where my wife was nursing our new babe in arms, a jolly character, whom from a window we showed to his brother; not permitted in, he waited below us in a cindery yard, safe in my mother's hand. The sight of that pair gazing up, a gaunt woman in a housedress and a small boy overwhelmed by the sunglasses she had bought to divert him, was one that for ten days fed my homesick wife. Throughout she was reassured that the boy ate well on his grandmother's cooking, which no longer awakened my ulcer, and our kitchen sparkled into a cleanliness I beheld nowhere but under her knuckles. Aluminum pots hitherto dull gleamed out like mirrors, and our windows, each a latticework of fifty diamond panes too wearisome to scrub, were indefatigably scrubbed, and the linoleum shone as if new in the backtracking of my mother at work on her knees, readying the house for the homecoming baby; conscientious to a fault, she made it worthy in every corner while amusing our youngster all day, and I in the cottage debating each of my commas, conscientious to a fault, came across the grass to find my eye too was oddly cleaner. For the first time in my life it was glad of her despotic talents, and critical of laxer housework.

More, it was to divulge a buried news of myself. After I brought my wife home with our infant and took my turn changing his diaper—long ago, but my left hand retains the uphoist of his chubby ankles with my forefinger between, my right hand with a wad of cotton cleansing his buttocks and scrotum of the feces sweetly odorous as mother's bread—I relinquished him to no other grasp so sure as his grandmother's; and watching her with the safety pins in her mouth, snuggling the diaper to his hip with her finger in to ward each pinpoint from the flesh which was me, I discovered her hands and mine had made their peace. Despite a lifetime of war, I saw a gist in me was unquestioning of a gist in her, and something in my affections opened to her as not before.

Often thereafter she was in our house, and a weight had shifted, I welcomed her visits, and, proud of her competence and life, recognized I was in possession of another piece of my past. So I learned a certain tolerance of the differences between us, and it was mutual. I escorted her to a festival concert that summer, and not till after her death heard she was troubled that "poor Billy had a hole in his undershirt"; as a surprise she prettied our shelves with a paper which was a flowery eyesore, and I thanked her, living with it not too uncomfortably as a reminder of the story we shared. In such matters of taste she was on common ground with the sixty-year-old housekeeper who came to us daily. My mother made of her a friend, chatting over tea with her in interludes between their labors, and, home again, wrote to her too, mailed her small gifts, and invited her on trips to the city to sleep overnight on the couch in her kitchen; when this housekeeper took up residence with her mate in our cottage—a friend and I spent two months building me a light-filled workroom on our hilltop—I looked in at the furniture she crowded into it, and was painfully moved by its similarity to my mother's. It became a custom for my mother on visits to pass a social evening with the old couple in the cottage, where I think she felt more at home. Indeed, she was living out a fantasy of mine from my communist youth in which, as a playwright at penthouse parties, I would ignore the wealthy guests and be found in pantry conversation with the servants; in part the fantasy was of course a pledge of allegiance to my parents, and my mother kept a less witting pledge to hers.

Certainly I saw the ghost of Mary Dore in her, refined and pale, haunting the rooms of our house. She sat through the night at the sickbed of our boy, half delirious, to brush his imaginary bugs away; the patience of that mother of nineteen, incarnate in mine, helped us nurse our young through so many bouts of mumps, chickenpox, measles, that in one siege my wife in greeting her said, "The marines have landed," a phrase my mother took home like a medal; after her death my sister quoted it to me. Or in our kitchen I would come upon her fretting over the grocery bills we never looked at, she was always suspicious that the butcher was cheating us and waved a blithe hello to him at mass every Sunday that I drove her to the church in town; I spied one drop of Irish blood in her the old lady had not squeezed out. And two or three times I heard in the living room a sound I thought was lost forever, resurrected from our piano, and walked in to stand behind my mother while she played a fluttery song her fingers recalled from—earlier than my child- hood, earlier than my father—the ancestral flat in Harlem where Mary Dore had adored her for it.

In these years the uncanny round of life was to carry my mother, now with her own Willy, into a reliving of the old lady's heyday. First she saw my script enacted on television at my sister's and wept, spoken to at last by my work; and next she sat among an audience of celebrities the night I made my debut on Broadway, the two-character piece was a rousing hit, and she went home to place on display in her living room a clock- with-plaque awarded the same night to the best television script of the year, her son's; and next she took her seat in another theater to witness the opening night of my stage version, a new hit; in the spring of the year she died she hung in her living room a second plaque naming it the season's best. In her last years my mother was never without a play of mine on Broadway, shep- herded her friends to the choice seats I arranged so often she "could have taken any part", and in fact took the old lady's at the backstage door of show business.

It was like a crown on her threescore and ten. I escorted her to other theaters when I was in town, and if an usher greeted me by name I enjoyed her pride in me as a recognizable figure; I wished I was less recognizable when, in the aisle after the posthumous masterpiece of our greatest playwright, she said cheerily to all ears, "Dear, I like your plays much better." I thought it funny, in the balance between us the tolerance for error was in her favor now. Invited by me to whatever I hoped would interest her, a run-through, an audition of actors, a cast party, my mother in her wonted and self-conscious smile chatted with the theater folk so famous in her newspaper; not unfearful of embarrassing me before them, she told her nephew I had said we "all loved her", and she would bring her cookies to the star's dressing room after the matinees she attended. She promoted several of our careers with the holy candles she lit in churches. Of my first play she said it had "a good author, good actors, good director, and good prayers"—she was making a novena to Saint Anthony for it—and she prayed another producer into a hit after he agreed to "take care of Tony", a vow he thought facetious but not she; I delivered a flow of her reminders to him until, godless Jew, he walked to her midtown church with five dollars for the saint's box. I was both uneasy and satisfied that in the theater district, where my success was not unlike a froth of dreams, the mother whom I squired on my arm was still a cleaning woman. I thought what a scandal that item would be, in print, but truer than most of the trash that overflowed the birch covers of her scrapbook; with both plays in constant performance in cities throughout the world, the clippings that came to her now were accumulating in shoeboxes. I read hardly a sentence about me which was not in error—and learned upon what lies the populace based its judgments in matters affecting its life and death—but it was another pleasure for my mother to impart the backstage truth to her kith and kin.

I myself could not make sense of the rush of monies into our household—literally from the four winds, Broadway and the road, foreign lands, summer and amateur theaters, movie sales—but my mother knew her son was rich at last beyond all her prayers. Not much changed under our roof; in my forties, I was already living as I liked. So on her weekends with us my mother saw little that was new, a second Chevvy in our drive, a tennis court in our field, and never set foot in the cottage on Cape Cod we bought a few months before we understood she must die. It was in my face that she spied a difference.

In among her mementoes I was to discover a letter in my handscript, pencilled, thanking her twenty years ago for a loan which was "twice what I asked for", telling her she was "wonderfully tolerant of such an eccentric son" in whom she "must feel secretly disappointed", and promising that the world would come around to me in time; the words were smudged, the yellow page was cracked with her unfoldings, and she had seen it happen. To my sister she said she was glad I "showed them all" because there were so many who thought I never would. Yet if vanity lent a gayer color to her autumnal years its roots were deeper than the money; in my face success and fatherhood were one, and to read in it that I was happier was a completion of her own flesh. She said to me so many times that I went deaf to it, "How proud Daddy would be of you now." Or not quite deaf, when she said proud I heard forgiving, it was in my ear like her benediction upon my necessary forsakings of her and my father; the mistakes of my lifetime in thought, word, and deed were not mistakes.

So the penultimate year of her life came to its close, in a contentment which, fulfilling her, to me was not without a danger of complacency. I could not know how soon it would end.

40. Apology for No Poems

The birds are still.
Time was, when each wind at my scarecrow nose
Made my eyes fill
And my head was a loveless rag,
Cries

That I never chose
Would like an exaltation of larks in my bag
Of ribs be up
To breed in my tattered throat
Words;

Childless as sticks
Were my arms; my head was peopled with birds.
Now it is six
Years gone, love like a great coat
Wraps

My bones, and my rag
Is a riches and crown, of wife, infant son,
And friends; what claps
At me now is a windful of coins,
Done

Is my dance of lonely
Sticks. Kingdom is come in my fathering loins
And a summer is on
My griefless head; no wind is ill.
Only,

The birds are gone.

41. In Unum Deum

Children, I believe, as much as anyone you will ever know I believe, and the only question is in what. I mean of course something other than opinions, which come and go with the year, with the times, with the generations; those for which men think they kill and die in one century are matters of indifference in another. Of no greater weight, my own opinions are more easily told in the negative: I believe in no god, and in no country, not ours, not theirs, and in no cause. Yet in the scarlet woods of Valley Forge I came without warning upon a ring of loose stones, the grave of a nameless soldier, dead in that howling winter when the nation was coming to birth, and if I believe in nothing why did I weep?

I was not always so empty of creed. In my teens, I was a Sermon on the Mount atheist believing in the extermination of the unfit to create out of the divine spark in all a superman with free will to remake a universe inexorably determined by the laws of matter which I understood was sensory illusion. An apostle on alternate days of pacifism and the will to power, I walked unmoved through the knots of young radicals at college who thrust leaflets upon me; I deposited them in refuse cans unread, my own remedy for worldwide poverty was to make the masses listen to better music. It was not until my expulsion from college that someone put into my hands a booklet about two men seven years dead around whom all my scattered pieces of opinion and feeling were to consolidate.

This pair were the good shoemaker and poor fishpeddler, anarchists, who, under judgment of death for murder in a robbery, had lived in jails from my fifth to twelfth years, and then, after a world outcry that their sole crime was difference in thought, died in the electric chair. In our comfortable house, reading that crooked tale, I was brought to tears and outraged. Less omniscient now than in my youth, though better informed, I see that the one question I can put with hope of answer respecting them is why, on encountering a booklet whose smattering of half-facts I investigated no further, I was so prompt to believe these two were of necessity innocents, the victims of their malevolent betters. The truth was, their story supplied with dramatis personae a plot I believed in before ever hearing of them.

Under the thumb of my own betters, so unmalevolent, the plot was prehistoric in me. It was esthetic, and antedated my earliest memory of toddling to throw at a girl the horse manure I knew was beautiful and my longskirted keeper said was nasty; and it was glandular, budding into thought with the first itchings of sex like a tropical plant in me under the household frost, undeniable and forbidden; and it was ideological, it fed on the decomposition of the religious dreams my parents had wished on me, which one of them doubted and neither practiced; it was a hundred other things I was unaware of. Accretive as coral, this plot was in my bones, and its gist was that in such matters as beauty, instinct, truth, the teachings of elders—family, school, church, state—were a swindle.

This much was only personal, a chafing between parents and a child set on that obstinate innocence of vision, in the eyeball of every artist, which sees what it sees and can create nothing on hearsay; but I was hardly alone in my disbeliefs. The century I was born into had been introduced by a fanfare of scandalous proclamations—God was dead, capitalism was theft, sexual silence bred mental aberration—and I walked in the footsteps of a generation of intellectuals who, misled by their elders in everything, had then seen themselves decimated in the war which swallowed up my father's young and ever-mourned brother. In the twenties, the experience of that war was made literature, and in any novel I read was the huge and unforgivable betrayal; even my father, who rarely read a book, knew the war was a "racket". It was in the grain of the decade that betrayal was to be looked for. That the machinery of the state should crush the lives of a shoemaker and a fishpeddler for no reason other than their denunciation of the war was believable to many, with or without facts, and another kind of evidence soon washed away more old footings of faith. Two years after their electrocution the economy of the world fell apart. In the confusion of the thirties my friends and I saw on every streetcorner, where legless men in vestiges of army garb sold their apples for a nickel, that society could no longer feed its people in peacetime and would lead us back to prosperity only in a second war; the ring of the trap was closing, the betrayal was total.

Nothing in this tide of opinion impaired my capacity to believe. Caught by whatever morality works in history, I saw it as my business to join with others to change its course; within a hundred days of reading the letters of that fishpeddler I was on a stepladder at a streetcorner, a communist afire with faith, like him denouncing injustice and war; I was no longer the boy who a few months earlier had blushed whenever answering in class. I devoted a year thus to rectifying the society my parents had bequeathed me—with what success my sons may judge, if they survive the nightmare I bequeath them—before I was expelled once more. In that swirl of speeches, committees, studies, girls, leaflets, rallies, music lovers, picketing, I was in a more profound school, gay, grimy, invaluable, wherein I learned much and came into my manhood, but then could not thrive on its hearsay either; at the year's end I departed, in the echo of a trivial incident.

The band of young communists of which I was one, after borrowing four hundred dollars to sponsor a play as a money-making scheme, forgot to sell tickets; every cent was lost. Much put out, the party elders had our leader transferred to another borough, made me his successor, and invited me to air my views. I said our first task was to repay the four hundred dollars, and a thoughtful silence ensued. I was then gently told that my values were still bourgeois, in revolutionary ethics what expedited the revolution was good, what impeded it was bad, therefore to repay the money would be unethical. I perceived no flaw in this logic, but something in me heard it with incredulity; out of my father's house and a stranger, a chasm of ideology behind me, I assented to the tongues of my comrades, but believed with the bowels of my parents.

I left the band for other reasons—I was in love, a different faith—yet remembered that glancing collision with the ethics of dogma; mine was of a piece with all. Between borrower and lender, mother and son, killer and corpse, no transaction mattered in the adoration of the ideal, nor in its pursuit would the screams of the tortured and the dying ever be done. It was my last reach for a heaven; in the thirty years since I have lived without one, creedless and content, and still I believed.

In what, under the betrayal, what? Sacred and profane, out of a bleeding cadaver and the texts buried in the memory of a people had sprouted in my generation those wildflowers, lovely as any in the lineage of faith and revolt. For a story I wrote that year I took my title from an old lament, Jerusalem, Jerusalem, that killest the prophets, for even then I knew that not a fishpeddler or a shoemaker had made me treasonous, but a carpenter on a cross; and I was subverted by no manifesto so much as by the scriptures of my own country. It was sired by men so passionate of belief that their words—liberty or death, all men are created equal, I have sworn eternal hostility to every form of tyranny over the mind of man—are also holy writ. Such phrases were in the air I sucked in with my first bawling breath; in the history of our beginnings I saw my face as in a mirror, two ugly ducklings, born to one promise. So half of the world saw itself in our beginnings. And over the ring of loose stones marking a skeleton in the earth I wept for when I and the country were small, innocent, poor, and our adult deeds not yet on our hands.

Next year I wept for better reason over the cadaver of my mother, seeing it was all a dream and a diversion, opinions, betrayal, promise, history itself; death was the only fact. I was at the wrong side of the tapestry. Sadder but not much wiser, I understood it was no more than what I had long known, life was the only fact, and more miraculous after each defection; out of her glands my mother had made me the gift to be happy, I was thankful I could weep. And soon I was at my chores like her, with rag and spit and eye, keeping my book of the dead for the living. It is one of those daily acts of believing with the bowels that for forty-six years I saw in my mother, and cannot but emulate; all my disbeliefs are afterthoughts, skin deep. I had no other cause, simply life, for the declaration in our beginnings—of independence, tolerance, brotherhood of all creatures in bondage—was the avowal of growth, life's motion, and I was enemy solely to what aborted it.

Children, it was the promise I believed, of what we might be; and to this hour I know that the promise, not what we do, is the truth.

I write this in a time when there fell a great star from heaven, burning as it were a lamp, and the third part of the waters became wormwood, and many men died. In mountains and deserts the atomic foundries are roaring; I end as I began, in a fickle shadow that falls across the loins of every child born to the world; now perhaps life itself hangs by a hair. And I hear an angel flying through the midst of heaven, saying with a loud voice, Woe, woe, woe, to the inhabiters of the earth, but the hair is neither less nor more than the human tissue.

Of that tissue, who, having seen its failures, can say he believes in it? Yes and no and if, squatter in caves and voyager to the planets, all variant opinion of the animal who wants to live, to kill, to love, is indeed a matter of indifference now, for judgment is come, and man the starmaker will execute it upon himself, according to his guilt. Of that tissue I was born, saw what I saw, the betrayals and the gifts, take nothing on hearsay, and know the lives of my father and my mother, laboring to survive in self-respect; all that I see is true, and insufficient. History is another book, and its last page may be ashes. Yet the first page I read was the avowal of growth in eyes which, over me and my sister in cribs, made our survival their credo until from beyond the grave my mother said, "I loved you both dearly." Of that tissue, predicting murder or mercy, life or extinction, and allowed one belief, half tonguetied, what dare I say?

I believe in my parents. I believe in my parents, therefore, in myself, therefore, in my children. I believe in my parents, and in life everlasting.

GLORIA

42· Lullaby

Four are the corners of earth
Whose nightly turn
Is under my love in her sleep: and where
Grows a weed to wash our bone
Of ache?
Beneath our floor
There is wailing in hell, and devils burn,
But not her ear now wake.

Four are the horsemen of winds
Whose nightly brawl
Is upon us in chattering tooth and hoof:
And whom can I pray her soul
To keep?
Beyond our roof
There is war in heaven, and angels fall.
Sleep, be dark, so, sleep.

43. An Exaltation of Larks

I could not see her as I saw other women; she was a limb from the same hardwood as her own mother, and I never believed her capable of a weakness like death. I led her and the boys one October on a hike to a waterfall in a woodland gorge, sliding and slipping on a footloose trail that pitched down under great hemlocks among fallen rock, and below the falls we waded in the riverbed, scrambled along the lip of the ravine above it, risky enough, she helped me herd the boys to safety every third minute, and two hours later, tired and bruised, we trekked up the trail with the younger on my shoulders; my mother had not been in virgin forest before and said it was "beautiful, like no one was ever there." Only that evening she confessed she had felt so exhausted she doubted she could make it, and I realized she was a woman past seventy with a variety of ailments, including congestive heart failure, and a son who was a fool.

So I heard the little cough in her which commenced when my second play was in rehearsal, and forgot it. Throughout the autumn it was persistent, and troubled my sister, but she could not prevail upon our mother to "bother" a doctor, nor could I; first the painters were redoing her kitchen, next she was in a bustle of her fall cleaning, next she must prepare a Thanksgiving feast for my sister's family, then she was embarked upon her Christmas baking and shopping; "always rushing, always breathless," she had no time for physicians. By midwinter the cough was a nag, in seizures of a minute, and since my mother insisted on "talking and coughing at the same time" her daughter told her it was "annoying to everybody". Somewhat hurt, my mother made an appointment with a doctor in her neighborhood, and was informed she had "walking" pneumonia. With a low fever, she retired to my sister's house for a week in bed, on antibiotics; the fever subsided, the cough disappeared, and when she went back to the doctor he pronounced her cured.

Once more in her three rooms, my mother was not too worried about a pain in her chest, sharper when she breathed deeply; she understood it was a normal remnant of pneumonia. In any case, between goiter and heart, she was accustomed to a shortness of breath. Until spring I spoke with her dutifully on the phone—she would "go to sleep happy" after an I-love-you-I-love-you-too ritual which I was reluctant to mouth, but managed—and in our commonplace chats, to which I half listened, I heard nothing ominous of what the year was to unfold; I was hardly alarmed by her mention of a date with the hospital for "some tests", which were habitual. The cough had reappeared, a minor symptom, my mother was taking it to the doctors who never failed her.

Indecisive, they asked her to come back time and again. Several mornings a week she travelled two hours to the hospital benches, waited among the outpatients for a couple of hours, went in to this brief lab test or that, and travelled two hours home; it was her routine day. She was depleted by these trips, she no longer had the "pep" of her late sixties. Two years earlier, when in her sitz bath she had discovered a lump in her groin, the doctors said it was a hernia, not malignant, but told her to stay off her feet, a waste of breath; still, my sister and I had argued enough with her career as a houseworker that after ten or twelve months of assent—"I can't keep doing this forever"—my mother let the work peter out. She was grown thinner, so bony in a dress with a scooped neck that my sister advised her "not to wear such bare dresses anymore", and now was losing weight on the hospital benches in a round which left her not only worn out, but irritated with the doctors. I urged her to go to a private physician without fretting about the money, but she would not hear of it, and in June a staff doctor looked into her face as well as her hemoglobin; the clinic suggested that she enter the women's ward for further study. It was the thirteenth of the month when she took her suitcase in, and my sister noted it as an unlucky day.

I came into the city next week to see her in the ward. Out of the elevator, I walked into a spacious room with a bleak odor of medicines and disinfectants, a dozen beds, a busy nurse or two, and relatives at every other bedside; at my mother's I joined my sister, there with a couple of her in-laws, and for two hours we took turns on a single chair, making conversation. Wan, on her hip in a hospital gown, my mother felt better than she looked. The chest x-rays had shown a right pleural effusion, and on her fourth day a thoracentesis had been done—a syringe impaled via her back to withdraw a few hundred c.c.'s of "yellow foamy fluid"—which was painful, but freed her breathing. Of the tests in progress she said most were repeats of those done in her weeks of outpatient visits; she thought it odd but "very thorough" and said, "I hope they find something," meaning a muscle impairment or perhaps emphysema; a young doctor on the floor had told my sister that an x-ray shadow might be tuberculosis. Often summoned to the tests at mealtimes, my mother had small appetite for hospital cooking to begin with, and was underfed, drawn and weakly. Yet she was in good spirits, chatty with the wardmates to whom she introduced me, and confided that one of them who was skin and bones made her realize "how fortunate I am". It was almost incidentally that on my visit the next day she said if the tests revealed a cancer she wanted me to tell her, and I promised I would, neither of us—certainly not I—expecting it.

I drove home again, and a week passed. The tests went on, of her liver, colon, urethra, intestinal x-rays, another biopsy of her thyroid, a bone series for spine and pelvis; all were so remote from my mother's complaint that she was perplexed. I talked with her once on a public phone in the corridor, and her daughter visited her each afternoon or evening. Still not eating, she was weaker by loss of a few pounds, and weary of her imprisonment in the ward; my sister was anxious to bring her home to some tempting food.

Late in the month, on a night made hectic by a tornado warning, our phone rang; my wife had hurried the boys into the cellar with blankets, and on my way down I picked up the receiver in hope of a word on the weather. Instead it was my sister from the hospital, her voice shaky, telling me the floor doctor had just led her aside with "bad news", our mother had cancer of the lung. From the cellar my wife was shouting up at me to hurry and I shouted down at her in a rage to shut up, and my sister said it was inoperable, the doctors gave her less than a year. Instantly, after twenty years like a day, I felt upon us the monstrous weight of my father's dying, and I said it would be a long year, and we talked on until my wife came upstairs to hear; I told my sister I would drive to the city, and hung up. The tornado blew itself out somewhere, forgotten, my wife and I were numb. In bed that night, speaking of my wish to be truthful with my mother, I tried to say I didn't "want her to be lonely" but could not get the word out; some floe of pity in me, unsuspected, was breaking up in tears, the first I ever cried for her.

In the next few days my wife was on the phone to influential colleagues in the city. I learned the floor doctor was a resident, unauthorized to speak for the staff, and the diagnosis was not final; a possibility of error like a fool's light flickered before us.

Leaving a housekeeper with the boys, my wife and I drove down in our convertible to meet my sister, and confer in the hospital with a "big doctor" not usually seen by clinic relatives.

An elderly surgeon, he received the three of us in a rich wood-panelled wing of offices, together with a young doctor who was in attendance on my mother; with a patient factuality born of a lifetime in the presence of death, he told us what they knew. Cells in the fluid withdrawn from my mother's lung were malignant. The tests were a search not only into the extent of metastases, but for a primary site; they assumed the lung cells themselves were metastatic, and were pursuing the tests. I asked why, and he said the determination of a primary site would influence the therapy. Yet his voice, kindly enough, suggested no hope in treatment by irradiation or chemotherapy, nor in surgery, which he judged would be fatal. To our inevitable question, how long would my mother live, he replied that a doctor who predicted would be a fool; he could only say that it was "not a matter of weeks".

From his office, the three of us in silence descended by elevator into the poorer reaches of the hospital. In a basement hall we kept an appointment with an empty desk; awaiting its occupant, we sat on a strip of wooden chairs and debated my promise to tell my mother. To me it was catching at a straw, I had withheld most of my life from her, to be honest now would open us to each other at last. It meant an hourly commitment to her while she was looking the spectre in the eye, and was conceivable if she lived in our house; my wife said my mother's ease of mind was more to be desired than mine and was likelier if, ignorant of the facts, she spent her days with a daughter she was already close to; agreeing, my sister doubted she herself could see it through if our mother knew she was dying. The occupant of the desk, a young woman, returned to greet us. For a quarter-hour we talked with her of aftercare, nurses for hire, readmission—a doctor had advised my sister they took no terminal cases but "if your mother ever wants to come back we'll find a place for her"—until we had no questions; we thanked her, and looked again for the elevator. I saw by now that my sister must carry the load of our mother's death, as my mother twenty years ago had carried our other, and with the same smile of false cheer, it was her legacy. At the elevator I said I would not keep my promise, but do as she wished.

Upstairs, in the ward past the beds astir with patients we came to our mother in hers, inert, her eyes closed. We settled to wait in a sun room beyond, but on my way back to the corridor I gazed again at her bed as I passed, and stopped; in a sleep of exhaustion, the woman who had borne us lay on her back with her head fallen to one side, hair limp with summer sweat, her face starved and without make-up, mouth half open, and I saw her as dead. For a minute I stared, experimenting with the sensation. In the past when a rare image of my mother's dying had crossed my eye I foresaw myself as calm to it, if not indifferent, I thought even it would simplify my life; rid of my duties to her, I would have less guilt and more money, a notion not in me now. I was on the brink of a loss and a liberation of a different order, but it eluded me, the figure was only that of my mother sleeping. I knew the corpse I had recognized must be, but like my emergence out of her vulva it was not believable, the most elementary realities of birth and death are untenable in the mind. And in that minute, with my promise forgone, some expectation in me was already turning from her; it is the last image I keep of her face in the ward.

Once she awoke we sat with her until nightfall, but of all we said I recall only our lie that the tests showed a "chronic inflammation" of her lung. Otherwise it was small talk, unreal even then; what I remember is irrelevancies—my plateful of chicken cacciatore in a restaurant nearby, the ballpark with a nightgame where we dropped off my sister to join her husband and sons, a movie my wife and I walked to from our hotel in midtown—like intermissions of fact in a bad dream. Sometime that evening we arranged for a consultation the next noon with an internist known to my wife. Listening to us over lunch in the cafeteria of another hospital, the one place he could fit us into his day, he judged that to subject my mother to such dubious therapy as nitrogen mustard would only turn the remnant of her life into a misery; the chief aim must be to "make mother comfortable", and at my wife's request he agreed to find us a humane doctor on the staff of a hospital near my sister's house. Grateful for a small solace, we spent the afternoon at my mother's bedside in further chitchat, but of that visit too I retain nothing; my wife remembers how my mother introduced her to a woman in the next bed as Jewish also, spoke proudly of our careers, and played hostess with her sprightly talk and smile until, quite suddenly, she paled out in fatigue. By early evening we were driving home again, and from a phone booth on a parkway I called the dressing room of the star of my play to say that if she could visit my mother in the ward it would enliven her face, and so she did.

In the mirage of those two days I cannot pin it down, but for an hour I was alone in the convertible and drove it into the past; the distances of the city, so vast and alien in my boyhood, had shrunk, and the throng of buildings in which my mother lay was hardly more than a mile across the Harlem River from the tar road where I had been born. Parking the car, I walked among pedestrians and delivery trucks from one streetcorner to another that bounded the old neighborhood of my innocence, heartbroken at how forty years had changed it for the worse. So lovely in memory, the road was now an asphalt street, empty of the poplars, and the charm of the shady sidewalk with its slabs of slate, on which the smallfry of the block had scratched with stones a history of who loved whom, was gone under a merciless flow of cement; the field of vegetable gardens had grown into a parochial school in concrete behind an iron fence, and the rollicking hill with its ballfield and sled runs, the communal oak in the dell, the ledgy corner which hid my father on his way to work, had been levelled to make way for a huge apartment house; others with stores crowded around me in all directions, and everywhere the green of the earth, grass and trees and even the primal rock, was no more. In this hive and pavement litter, the band of narrow three-family houses with bay windows still stood, preserved in tarpaper of simulated brick, mean and ugly. Passing a porchlet once fashioned of wood—on it had hung a black tin mailbox bearing our name in my father's large clear hand—but now also cement, I stared up at the second floor with its trio of windows, unforgettable, where lurked in the gaslight of my childhood the ghosts among furniture made of dreams in the five unheated rooms which had warmed all my life, and eyed the same window in vain, my young mother would not again be half out of it to wave and cry her "I, L, Y!" after the jaunty figure who long ago had disappeared around the corner and out of the world, for here was no continuing city, and I walked on back to the convertible, homeless, in the midst of a thousand families who had made strange the place of our past.

Homeless I hardly was, for my mother invoking "the old days in Highbridge when we were all so happy" meant a household lively with her small children, and it was to ours that my wife and I drove back; next week we were to take possession of a second house for summers, a Cape Cod cottage in a pine woods overlooking the ocean. I thought my mother might convalesce with us there, but when I invited her via the phone in the hospital corridor she said it was "so far, dear," and she looked forward to the familiar room at my sister's. In July the staff came to the end of their tests for a primary site, fruitless, and discharged her "to be treated symptomatically". Called for by her daughter in the ward, my mother said goodbye to the other patients, and took her last leave of the great clinic which in the infirmities of her flesh had for thirty years kept her alive; my sister drove her and her suitcase out of the city, across the river and past the cemetery where whatever was left of her husband lay, to the trim and pretty dwelling in the suburbs twenty miles beyond. I was in touch with it by phone from our cottage three hundred miles farther on. Here along the stretches of solitary sandbars the boys and I broadjumped as naked as born, my wife in the salt foam arose feeling "tall and beautiful", and we scrambled up to the headland dunes for a gull's view of dipping moors and long beach and green ocean in its lace of breakers, the four of us tan and lucky; only my stomach, never free of its tie to my mother, was digesting itself in a new ulcer. I was loth to let a month now go by without a visit, and one morning in August I set out on a day's drive to my sister's.

I found my mother in a housedress sitting under a little apple tree in the backyard. It was a moment to put me in mind of my father in his last summer, and indeed the neighborhood was not unlike that to which he had raised us, the houses more prosperous and varied, but inhabited by clerks like him who commuted to the city; my sister's was white, two-storied, with two redbrick steps and an iron handrail to a screen door of aluminum scrollwork, and the six rooms within were spick-and-span, as smartly furnished as the alcoves on display in stores; my mother was always at home in this household born of her own. For a time each day she sat in a corner of the backyard under the apple tree, peeling vegetables, and was content, if less than brisk.

She had been taken by my sister to the doctor found for us by the internist. In his hands for a month, our mother had regained a half-dozen pounds, and felt she was on the mend; she was invigorated perhaps by his injections of a vitamin complex, and certainly by her daughter's cooking. My sister coaxed her appetite back with favorite foods, and regularly in the backyard served her a thick "cocktail" made of fortified milk, raw egg, malt, and other nutrients, which my mother swallowed dutifully. Not entirely a docile patient, she resisted the young doctor's instruction to take what she called "pain pills" every six hours, nor could she be kept from helping in the light chores of the household; they also fed her. The pain had put her in a hospital nearby, the week preceding, for withdrawal of another syringeful of pleural fluid. Again it relieved her difficulty in breathing, but the true bill of her health was in the abstract which described her as a "small cachectic woman"; no one had ever thought her small before.

Never fleshy, she had lost eighteen pounds since the onset of her cough, and when my sister fetched some of her clothes from the apartment "nothing fit her"; as we sat my mother spoke with much interest of a dress worn by one of her friends. It had been bought in a town a few miles out, and late in the afternoon I drove her there in the convertible. We spent an hour or two in the stores searching for it, my mother picking others from racks, putting them on and off in booths, thanking the saleswomen who at the mirrors urged them upon her, and she would let me buy none; all looked identical to me, and I knew she would not live to wear whatever she chose, but her heart was set on a particular dress. It was a joy to both of us that finally in a long rowful of sleeves she discovered it, the very print and style, in her size. She tried it on, I saw its distinction was a flounce of bosom ruffles, and when my seventy-two-year-old mother with a flutter of fingers at her flat chest said rather shyly, "It fills me out here," I could have wept.

The bright face of my sister was commencing to be etched—she too would lose twenty pounds by winter—but nothing in the house was out of the ordinary. I was host at dinner in a restaurant dear to my mother, one of a chain throughout the city that she said served "clean food", after which we returned to sit in the living room over gossip and small jokes until yawning time. Lights clicked off at ten o'clock, for my brother-in-law arose at six to commute; all went upstairs, and I went down to a couch in the basement. I was undressing when my older nephew in pajamas appeared on the steps. Seventeen, tall, about to matriculate next month at Princeton, he had remembered or been reminded to thank me for helping pay his tuition, the favor my mother had asked of me, and in a moment of awkward duty we played out again the scene in which I thanked my affluent uncle Ben for maneuvering me into a brainier highschool; a reticent boy with intellectual interests of whom my sister said, "I don't know what he's thinking or even feeling about things," he then withdrew to take up his original life. I retired to ponder mine, and overhead my mother, who had not finished elementary school but taught him to read on her lap and me to spell in a highchair, lay ignorant that her own life—so unintellectual I thought it empty until I learned that love was the substance, and could rise to fill every crevice in her as amply as in me—had come to its end.

I drove back next day to the Cape, and the mirage of her improvement grew; in September she was strong enough that my sister, by way of a deep breath, spent a week alone with her husband in a resort not too far away. My mother stayed in the house with the boys. To help out, their father's mother also arrived with a suitcase, a jolly woman who a year earlier had undergone a breast removal for cancer. Sympathetic when this in-law passed the days on the sofa with a back pain, my mother cooked, served, kept house for her and their grandsons; my sister came home to a neighbor's tale of "your skinny mother waiting on your fat mother-in-law", but in fact she had enjoyed one of her best weeks, "useful and happy". She then insisted on moving back to her three rooms in the redbrick building on the avenue, she had "so much to do". For two weeks I heard some of it by phone, how our mother shopped and housecleaned and walked a mile to lead her half-blind spinster pal out of a furnished room home to the kitchen couch for a stay as in former days, and "did everything" for her too; she could not sustain it. Tenants in the front soon told my sister that after church she "could barely make the stairs". Driving down for her and her toothbrush, my sister escorted her out of the streetdoor of the building, and my mother never again opened it to climb to the three rooms on the second floor rear in which she had lived out her widowhood, independent of us; the mirage was over.

I think something in her was coming to know that leavetakings now were for keeps. The last snapshot I have of her is on our lawn in early October after my wife and I had driven her up from the city for what we, and perhaps she, suspected would be her final visit. Glinty with eyeglasses, she stands in the sunlight in a gray housedress too loose upon her, and beside her is our four-year-old, fondling a toy she has brought him; her right palm, cupped around his cheek, draws his head to her hip. She admires his big brother—amused, she has told my sister how at this age over crayons he would say, "Go away, Nana, you bother me in my work"—but it is the younger who always runs to her hands; together they have been under every bed in the house playing "squealy pig", and a year ago at a theater rehearsal it was her lap he climbed into, content in her arms for two hours, and on this visit, when floor play is beyond her strength, they share a table over his favorite game of "merry milkman" with its toy truck and toy milkbottles; on her deathbed ten weeks later she will sigh of "my boys, my two boys," and mumble to my sister's question the names of her first grandson, at college, and of this boy, her last. Behind them is the dark green house with its white windows whose host of small diamond panes is an aggravation to her, some flaw in the old glass has survived all her scourings, and she never arrives without a new brand of cleanser to "get them", but this time is unequal to the challenge. She wears her "hiking" shoes—flat low-cuts I bought her for country use, which between visits she keeps in the guest closet—and around them the grass is still green, with a few autumn leaves; in her left hand she carries a basketful of zinnias, red, yellow, white, gathered for her in the garden by my wife's father. If I lay a thumb over her head I see a body straight and slim, thirtyish, stiffnecked as ever, but in her scraggy throat and sunken face, unsmiling, despite lipstick, brown hair, pearl earrings, her brow and nose and jaw so bony now, is the coming of a death's head. And on this lawn she says to me, lightly, "I think I must be dying, everyone is so good to me." It is winy weather, and she will sit in it for a few days before she hugs our boys whom she is not to see again, goodbye dear, goodbye dear, while I put her suitcase and shopping bag in the convertible; and with the top down I drove her for the last time out of our amber hills, back to the city.

Two days later on the phone my sister reported her face was "all windburned". I said in pain I could as well have put the top up, and so my sister had observed, telling her it was silly not to ask me; my mother said, "Oh no, dear, Billy likes it down."

Later in the fall she undertook one more journey. The summer gone was the first in fourteen years she had not vacationed in the seashore nest of widows, and now, though she "looked so dreadful", she made plans to go; unable to dissuade her, my sister and her husband drove her through Jersey to the deserted town with its boardwalk and surf, and left her in the hands of her friend, the landlady. For a week she lived in her old room, and sat solitary with her thoughts on the boardwalk, looking out at the sea. Because her son-in-law could not come back for her—his own mother was in a hospital with her lumbar pain—the landlady kept her company on the long bus ride to the city, where my sister met her; she was haggard. It was a shock to all when next month the other mother, as plump as when she so recently had come to oversee mine, died in the hospital of the cancer which had sprung up anew in her liver and bones. Fond of her, my mother by then was too fragile to travel even into Brooklyn for the wake; she consoled their tearful twelve-year-old grandson, and out of his earshot said, "One down and one to go."

I was alone with her an evening of the wake. I undid the orderliness of my sister's living room by pulling a chair to the sofa where she lay with a pillow under her head, and we talked of old days—she said, "Where there's dying there's fighting," but it would not be true—until I saw it was an effort for her, now that I had time she lacked breath; by nine-thirty she was in need of bed. I bent to kiss her goodnight, and with her thin arms around my neck, clinging, her lips at my face three or four times, I felt something almost amorous in her, I think it was another goodbye. But she said nothing again to suggest the imminence of her death.

She passed most of each day on the sofa; she was so fatigued even by the auto ride to the doctor's that he was now calling on her. Once more he had arranged for a thoracentesis in the nearby hospital, a stay of two nights made unhappy by a blunder about her "pain pills". On the second evening my sister discovered our mother was suffering rather than complain that the pills were not on the tray of medicines the nurse bore on her rounds; my sister went to inform the nurse a pill was due every six hours, the nurse refused it because she had "no order", and my sister in a rare loss of temper said, "It's all you're doing for her and it's the least you can do," and marched back to dig a bottle out of her own purse, but our mother would not take it without the doctor's knowledge, whereupon my sister phoned me, from two states away I phoned the doctor and reached a colleague on call, the colleague got word to the doctor, and the doctor called the hospital; it had taken all of us two hours and more than three hundred miles of telephoning to move a pill a distance of twenty steps to a dying woman. My sister brought her home the next morning—the third lung tap, less of a relief, showed "clusters of malignant tumor cells"—and a week later escorted her on a last outing. It was to an endocrinologist who, after testing her for thyroid activity, administered a dose of radioactive iodine. Leaving his office, my mother was so exhausted her daughter with difficulty seated her in the car; she rode with her head lolling back, and had to be helped into the house to the sofa.

Thanksgiving came, and with it her grandson home from college; my mother said, "I'll cook a dinner," and made the pot roast he loved. It was her last family act—and of a kind I never knew mattered to me until after her death I awakened from a weeping dream of the recipes I had typed for her in my teens, there was nobody left to feed me—but of that feast she herself ate only a mouthful, at my sister's urging. She was emaciated, her weight unknown because the news on the bathroom scale was worse each week and my sister hardly encouraged its use; if our mother weighed herself when alone, she was silent afterwards. Without hunger, she sat at the table with the family each evening but soon asked to be "excused", too tired to be up, and made her way back to the sofa. In the afternoons she dozed a good deal. When neighbors and friends visited to chat she made an effort to sit up, but the conversations sapped her; she no longer wrote her letters or travelled to the basement to watch television, and the one entertainment in her day was the tabloid her daughter went out to buy for her. Yet she continued to put on her lipstick and rouge with a deft touch—she never liked to be seen "without my face on"—and when I visited she took pains to be at her perkiest.

I heard her testy once when she said, "I can't *do* anything." It was not literally so, she made up her bed until the last and on her knees she scoured the tub with cleanser after her bath, to my sister's despair, but over the episode of her Christmas cards she lost heart. To mail out two hundred or more was her habit; working from an address book which in her inkscript contained the name of every acquaintance in her life, our mother by three envelopes at a sitting, with rests between, reached the C's and was helpless to finish; my sister took over the task. Glum, she kept to the sofa in a mood so alien to her that my sister spoke to the doctor, who prescribed "some potassium medicine", an antidepressant. Its effect was a worse humiliation, my mother lost control of her bowels; hurrying to the lavatory off the kitchen, she refused to let her daughter in to help, and scrubbed out her soiled clothes in her hands. Thereafter she spread pads on the sofa to protect it from the treacheries of her body.

Unaccepting of them, she made it a daily rite to walk three times around the table, for "exercise". She was no less stubborn about the analgesic pills; my sister and I argued with her to forestall the pain, but she resisted until it was unbearable. She was of old "not a medicine taker", and when the doctor to circumvent her wrote out a more potent prescription it so nauseated her he cancelled it. The worst time in her day was when she first awoke and sat on the edge of the bed endeavoring, mutely, by cough, wheeze, gasp, to loosen the clotting in her lungs; each morning it was thirty minutes before she could breathe enough to walk. My sister could not watch that effort, and went about her housekeeping with ears alert until our mother, clutching the banister, came downstairs to a sip of breakfast. It was an expenditure in vain; the next week when I visited she was not on the sofa, nor would she be again.

Upstairs I found her in the bedroom which had been vacated for her by the younger boy. It spoke of him in the gay pennants on the wall, a cozy room perhaps twelve feet by nine, with bookcase, desk, chair, but his narrow bed with a night table filled

403

most of it; the table held a small crucifix my wife had sent. Here my mother lay, too enfeebled now to manage the stairs or even to dress herself. She no longer ventured to the bathroom after bedtime. To get to it meant traversing a landing where the stairhead opened, and my sister, worried about a misstep, had furnished her with a hand bell to summon aid in the night; she refused to ring it. My sister then set at the bedside a "potty" of enamelled metal—an heirloom, we had both used it in childhood and been succeeded on it by her own offspring—but it proved too low for our mother to squat upon in comfort. My sister substituted a bucket made of plastic. Deceptively apt, it had no weight or stability, and in the small hours my mother in urinating on it fell to the floor, and sat in its spill unable to get up; in the next bedroom her daughter awoke to hear a weak voice calling, "Please help me," and with her husband ran in to lift our mother back into bed. The work machine of her body was at last abandoned by its demon of energy.

Not of will: the next day she stood under the shower to shampoo her hair. It was a weekly ritual—she would accept no help, never permitted her daughter to see her undressed, and with her own hands put her hair up in curlers afterwards—and although my sister now argued that someone be called in from a beauty parlor my mother said no, they "wouldn't wash it clean enough", and closed the bathroom door on her. My sister waited outside it in dread of a fall. None occurred, but she came back to encounter our mother on her knees mopping the floor, and with a touch of hysteria screamed at her, "Don't do my work!" Unoffended, my mother let herself be tucked back in bed; she had confided to her daughter, bearing meals upstairs on a tray, that a "good thing that came out of this sickness is I know how much you love me." The meals were liquids, she had no appetite but thirst.

She was also wasted in interest. I sat with her off and on

throughout two days, our talk desultory; she asked after my family, I said all were well, she said good, but my news no longer engaged her. So wan now, without cosmetics, the skin on her bonework of face had a clarity almost girlish, only her lips were cracked and dry, and when I kissed her I was surprised at how unfouled her breath was. She was dying rather sweetly, not in much pain—the doctor was injecting morphine into her—except for difficulty in swallowing; the bloody death of my father was not to be hers, but the grief of it was sufficient.

I was at her bedside when the doctor came up the stairs, a man several years younger than I, and she introduced me to him as "a good boy". Shy for a moment, the doctor murmured some mercy about "a famous man now", and my mother, to whom that fact was bread in her last seven years, said with indifference, "Well, famous," and more firmly said, "But he was always a good boy." I left the room while he ministered to her; later he joined me downstairs to discuss the necessary matters of terminal care, from medication to undertaker. Getting his overcoat on, he asked me where she "came from", I said the city, and in some surprise he said, "I see mostly weak people, she's like a pioneer." And he informed me how in receiving him yesterday my mother, too tired to reach, had said, "I'll give you the left hand, it's nearer the heart"; he thought it "beautiful".

I had arrived in the wake of a talk between him and my sister; she was of a mind to sleep in a beach chair at the door, the doctor recommended a night nurse, and my sister was worried about the expense. I said of course we could afford it, but the choice implied was one of where our mother should die. I hoped not in a hospital. My sister was mulling it over with her husband, and was troubled; our mother had detested the hospital nearby, the city was too distant, yet they wished to spare their twelve-year-old the memory of his grandmother's corpse in his bed. In mentioning it to the doctor I was struck by his saying offhand,

"If it's done right it's done right forever," and quoted it to my sister without further effort to impose my sentiment on her bedding. She and I had a more immediate decision, whether to protract a life become so unsatisfactory to our mother; the doctor judged he could "take her through Christmas" with blood transfusions if the holiday mattered to us, and we said no. I was content to see, when my sister phoned the agency for a night nurse, that the other choice too was in the making.

I told my mother I would be down again soon, and drove home with her last greeting and gifts to my wife and sons; it was a week and a day before Christmas. Seven and four, the boys were in a simmer of expectations, as innocent of my pain in the loss of their grandmother as I had been of hers in the loss of Mary Dore, and next morning in our woods we cut the young pine they were to hang with ornaments. In the night a blizzard whipped in, and by afternoon the county was deep in snow, still falling; outside our windows all was whiteness and wind when I answered the phone. It was my sister to say our mother was weak and incoherent, had rambled on for a day and a night in a monologue like a caricature of her talk, and now, quieted by sedation, might or might not be in her dying hours. The roads were undriveable, so I took a suitcase to the only train out, and after six hours of glancing at my wristwatch every fifteen minutes I was picked up sometime before midnight by my brother-in-law at his depot. I was set to hear of a death; he said there had been no change. My mother was still in a drugged sleep when I stood with my sister in the dark bedroom.

In the morning she awoke clear of mind, but feeble, and in the kitchen my sister and I talked over the matter of a priest. The two of us were alone in the house with the patient—with her males away at work and at school my sister had been so for four months, durably cheerful, but in fear of the hour when she would sit with the face of death—and now were at the edge of the unknowable, it lurked under our practical talk of arrangements, and the reality of the kitchen was less solid; I knew how easily we were in tears when unseen of each other, but in me a fluttering had opened, as of a small eager bird. It was not a question of whether our mother would wish a priest, but of when, and not to alarm her too soon with the ritual of the last sacrament we put it off for a day.

Yet my mother, in touch again with the world of her room, saw she was on her deathbed and was without fear. Complaining only that her mouth was dry, she moistened it often at a tumbler of water in her daughter's fingers or mine; more than that she could not drink, and the bedpan now at hand was not to be used, the workings of her body were done. To care for her in her dying, as in her living, was no task. My sister bathed her skin with alcohol, and I took my turn on the chair at the bed, held her left hand, conversed in murmurs, watched her doze off; sleep was a surcease from the drought on her tongue. And in the enigma of whoever in past weeks was pretending for whom, my mother came first to the end of it. In my attendance on her bony face with its large eyes awake, I bent to catch her low voice, "Billy, was it cancer?" and was ashamed to hear my quick word, "No."

The day passed without event—the doctor came, a neighbor stopped in, I phoned my wife, the twelve-year-old ran in from school, the afternoon darkened—except that I notified a mortuary. My sister said our mother had always spoken with approval of the looks of a funeral home a few blocks from her apartment, and when in a heavy sleep of morphine she could not hear I phoned it; they recorded her name, and said they would come for the body at whatever hour I called again. It was a simple evening, supper in the kitchen, dishwashing, the boy and his father with us at the bedside for two words and a squeeze of my mother's hand, until the nurse rang the doorbell and took charge of the sickroom for the night.

With breakfast, my sister and I sat again to our vigil, and saw our mother was aware both of us and of other presences in the room, but so was I; if her eye detected a perturbation of butterflies in a corner, mine was widening on an iridescence in me. For the most part, she spoke to us intelligibly. Of her money in the bank, she said each of her grandsons was to have five hundred dollars for college; that year I had declined three-quarters of a million for my play from a movie star I did not want, and put aside a trust fund for my mother of some thirty thousand, and her legacy—twice she told us, five hundred for each boy, the rest for my sister and me—was insignificant until with a lift of her starveling head she said, "I scrubbed and cleaned for seventeen years to keep it there." Yet her eyelids were feebler, and at times her talk sidled off to unseen listeners in a mutter I could not follow, other than to hurt when she said with a sigh, "All my flowers died. They were so pretty." I held the fingers that had worked so long, and earlier throttled in me the capacity to give myself into the hands of a woman, but escape at last—surely it was there—was not all the quickening in me.

Late in the wintry morning I walked several blocks to the parish house, to find the priest gone; I wrote out my sister's number for his housekeeper, and walked back between the heaps of snow past fifty dwellings that also could not hold in life, but the misery in me was strangely eager as spring. I took turns again with my sister at the bedside. Despite the dreamlike fragments of talk my mother was in touch with each of our small attentions to her, remarking idly, as my sister washed her limbs, "Your Daddy always said I had pretty legs." While she dozed I picked up a book of common prayer on the night table, and read in it; at once it was like food, a voice from heaven saying unto me, Write, blessed are the dead, I thought yes and no, but the burial service spoke to me more than as solace, it was the only truth, and I knew that in the valley of the shadow of death was no evil.

I heard it too in the voice of my mother when, in the twilight, her uses in the world done, she said to no one, "Why doesn't the Lord take me?" It was a puzzlement her tongue was to wander back to, twice, like a child thirsty and fretful, and at her ear I said as a promise, "Be patient." The fact is that half of the fluttering in me was of the dead, darkling, near, live, I almost did not doubt they were live, a mingling of faces and hands waiting to receive and comfort her, and me, and all of us; the distinction between life and death was dissolving in the grave, and at its edge I saw I could invent immortality, but others had been before me. At nightfall the priest phoned, and on my judgment that my mother would be rational said he would come in the morning.

Soon after daylight the nurse took her leave, and our mother was rational enough that in mentioning the priest's visit we said it was for confession, not extreme unction. By her head the night table was dressed with a white napkin, two candles, a crucifix, holy water, a spoon—brought in a communion box by a devout girl, on hand to guide us in the sacrament—but my mother was without curiosity in the preparations; she lay with her eyes big in a stare at the ceiling, her cracked lips parted to each breath, and to speak or swallow was an effort. When the doorbell rang, the girl covered her hair with a handkerchief, asked my sister to cover hers, told me not to talk to the priest while he was carrying the host, and bore a lighted candle down the stairs to usher him in.

It commenced like a comedy, she could not unlock the door; I hurried down after her, and both of us worked at the knob in vain under the gaze of the shivery priest just beyond the glass, to whom we could utter not a word, and by candle we conducted a search of the lock for its release until my sister too ran down, losing her handkerchief, and the three of us let the priest in. Silent, he followed the girl and her candle up the stairs. Last in to my mother, I saw her eyes were brighter and attentive upon the priest, and I knelt on the floor with him, my sister, the girl, while he adored the crucifix; muttering in Latin, he sprinkled holy water on my mother and on us, and presently sent us out. The door shut on her last confession.

Of what pale sins she had to unburden herself I could not imagine, but after the priest reopened to us she told him she must not be a good mother because—uncertain of eye, not of charity, she asked if my wife was in the room—both her children had married out of the faith; she had it in her head for twenty years, and we never knew. The priest consoled her that God had his reasons, and the four of us went again to our knees around the narrow bed. Murmuring after the others the confiteor which came back to my lips, I confessed that I had sinned exceedingly in thought, word, and deed, and the priest stood to the crucifix; in his fingers he elevated the wafer which was the body of the hanging Saviour, and showing it to my mother—I supported her while she sat upright—he intoned three times the non sum dignus, I am not worthy, and laid it upon her tongue. My mother could not swallow it. Twice she tried, gasping, but the wafer, which I knew disintegrated at the touch of salivation, reappeared entire in her parched mouth. Retrieving it, the priest fed her a spoonful of the holy water, and soon she tried again, hungering for it, but gagged, coughing in such a shortness of breath that my sister hurried to the window, raised it, struggled with the storm window to no effect until I joined her to pound, and loosened it to the winter air. My mother with her eyes closed said, "Oh, God, let me take it." Disturbed, the priest said it was not necessary, he could give her a spiritual communion, but my mother shook her head, and we waited; after a moment of inward summoning she once more offered her tongue to the wafer, it was the last chore she set herself in this world, I knew she would manage, and she swallowed it whole. For a few intakes of breath she sat, resting, seventy-two years of workaday bones, and then she said clearly, "I thank you, God, for everything."

It was a sentence that shattered me. She lay back on her pillow, and we knelt around her while the priest with a hand above her head invoked the archangels against the power of the devil over her, but I heard and still hear the voice of my mother dying with thanks on her tongue for everything she had seen, blessings and afflictions, toil, love, tears, pleasures, the pinching, the plenty, the ills of her body, the births and the burials too; she meant the gift of her life. More, she meant even the gift of her death, and with her affirming of it the fluttering in me rose, I was filled with a joyous taste of myself as I watched the priest at the candles moisten his thumb in holy oil. In the sign of the cross he anointed her eyelids, praying aloud for forgiveness of the wrong she had done by the use of her sight, dipped his thumb and anointed her ears, praying for forgiveness of the wrong she had done by the use of her hearing, dipped his thumb to anoint her nostrils, and I saw he was purging her body of the deeds of its senses, it was a rite that for a thousand years had made peace with the defects of the human material, and the thumb of the priest anointed her mouth, for the wrongs of its taste and speech, and her open palms, for touch, and lastly her feet, for the wrong done by her power to walk. Mute, our mother lay in exhaustion, all her strength had gone out in the offering of her little gloria. At last the priest joined us on our knees, and we muttered with him the prayers to keep her from the enemy, the eleison, the paternoster, others ancient and wise, but none that opened the gates of my being like her words, always known, in my ear from my birth to I hope the day of my own death; with them my tale began, and is almost done.

I led the priest down the stairs to the door, where I gave him ten dollars, and not long after my sister unlocked it again to the doctor. She and I hovered near while he sat beside our mother, taking her pulse and temperature, and only his shot of morphine put her thirst to sleep; I asked him to leave some. It was a busier day, the older son was back from college for the holidays, and later the half-blind Nelie was brought to the door by a crony. Sole survivor of their schooldays when my mother had befriended her as a stricken girl, she sat at the bed through the afternoon until the daylight failed and the lamps in the house went on; they spoke seldom, but old ghosts were in the room. My mother dozed, or flopped a hand, or mumbled; once she said, but to no one, "Let me look pretty." To me at her flank with alcohol and needle she sighed, "Oh Billy, you have to see everything"—with reason, my glimpse of the lean groin wherein I was conceived was not innocent of a flicker of the erotic—and I thumbed the morphine in. After a time she murmured, "My husband, my husband, no one could play piano like my husband," and drifted into sleep. I was to drive Nelie home for supper but she lingered, would neither eat with us nor go, sat, could not be budged, and I was impatient but suddenly knew what she knew, to rise from the bedside was to take leave of my mother forever.

Next day she died. In the hours before dawn she awoke and attempted to crawl out of bed, the nurse restrained her, but she babbled of a trip, she must get dressed and pack for a trip; reporting this at breakfast the nurse said it was not uncommon in the dying. When I sat to my mother's hand it was too cool, and at the blanket's edge her foot was gross, purpling around the heel. With her jaw hanging and eyes adroop she was conscious half of the morning, breathing over her caked tongue in a distress neither my sister nor I could suffer. I injected her thigh with morphine, and once again—often, in those four days—said in her ear, "I love you"; I had said it many times in the years preceding, that dutiful lie in my mouth, and it turned out to be true. She slept until after lunch, with my sister at the bedside, and when she awoke to more distress I emptied a second needle into her thigh. It may have been the load she could not carry into another day; she fell into a sleep like a coma.

Late in the afternoon, no change obvious, I buttoned my overcoat and went for an hour's walk; it was the shortest day of the year, cold, the light gray on ice in the streets, and somewhere unseen the sun had reached its furthest point, would creep back now through all of the winter that lay ahead; when I returned it was almost dark. I recognized a station wagon at the curb, and upstairs found my wife seated with my mother. Caressing her knuckles, my wife, who would always pay a price for their scourings in me, told her over and over she was "a good girl"; she thought the gaunt face, its eyelids closed, smiled. After a family supper we rejoined my sister—she kept watch alone while we ate her cooking—to share her vigil in twos or threes, sat, gazed, waited, the talk subdued and fragmentary, and pondered what our lives meant. Still no change was seen, and we vacated the bedroom when the nurse returned to duty; in the midst of her ministerings, she found a moment to tell me she doubted our mother would survive the night.

I was on my couch in the basement with a letter my wife had brought—from my young worldling, middle-aged, divorced, unemployed, asking for five thousand dollars so he might write a play—when my sister called that the nurse wanted me. I ran up the two flights of stairs to the bedside where the nurse made way from the pillow; I saw my mother's face had come to life, her eyeballs wide and bulging, her mouth open as in a despairing cry, mute, and out of that cavity I then heard an exhalation which was not human breath, low, even, long, it was air leaving a crypt. The others had followed my run, and before our eyes the miracle went out of my mother. Something altered less than a shadow, the eyeballs simply died, her dropped mouth was the gaping of death; she had abandoned her body to us. All that had kept it flesh was soul, and within a minute of the stilling of the blood it was a corruption, yellowing, a great haggard doll of evil in the bed, unclean and sickening. I could not take my eyes from it. My sister, I, the others stood in silence for some minutes over a carcass of which we must be rid, once our good mother, who had made us the last gift a parent owes to children, a good death; and for what was in us speech had not been invented. Yet from this moment a spacious quiet was in the house, and in me too, as I went downstairs to phone the doctor and the mortuary.

It was almost midnight when the drivers rang the doorbell, two men in black like ministers, and I showed them up to the waiting nurse. Downstairs, my sister was boiling water in a kettle and setting out tea cups, and we all took refuge in the kitchen, out of sight and hearing; I thought better of it, and moved into the dining room where I sat at the table in the dark, the stairway in view. Down it the two men soon came with a stretcher. It was of black canvas which, overlapping its contents, was strapped and buckled, although what rode within was of such negligible bulk it seemed the canvas held nothing but itself; and in that airless bag, too ugly for eyes, the thing of bones, skin, hair which had been my mother was carried out of the house.

I watched the door shut, and suddenly my sister thinking of rigor mortis remembered her mother's plate of false teeth. I ran upstairs while she hurried to call to the men, and in the small bedroom—the bare mattress was a shock—I located the teeth in the drawer of the night table; I ran down with them, the driver stood at the door with my sister, and I put this relic of our mother into his hand so that, her last wish granted, she might look pretty.

44. Ending Work

　　I was born
Like a stone let cry,
　　And began
My day with goodbye

　　To earth
That held me back
　　But forth,
My handful of folk

　　In the hug
Of time, and I kicked
　　Like a frog,
So slow its tick,

　　Till I rose
In a shatter of flesh
　　And ties,
The wind all my wish,

　　I was loose
As a bat let fly
　　And my house
Shrank down to a pea

GLORIA

With folk
And their earthly rot
        In my wake,
And time I forgot,

        I was gull,
I was sun, I was man
        Let fall
And my time was noon

        As I dropped
Plumb in my sprawl
        Past the hip
Of earth, and a whirl

        At my eye
Of its workpatch lands
        Into night
Far out of my hand

        In a turn
Was gone with the house,
        And I heard
In my fingers a hiss

        All day,
While my halfwit years
        Flew by,
Of souls I dearly

        Unloved
Spectral and clutching,
        And dived
Like a stone into dusk

Crying oh
For the years when time
Ticked slow
In my footholds of home

To boys
Who out of me kicked
And rose
Where I fell in a crack

Of doom,
And earth took me back
Dumbed
With its dayless folk.

45. Et in Terra Pax

Starting in the thick of Harlem, it is a mile to the bridge that connects the three boroughs in which my mother passed her years, two miles in the traffic of cars by the dozens over the forking river at Hell Gate, and a mile to the tall ironwork fence which shuts out the bustle of life; the gates stand open to peaceful roads, trees, tombstones, and at one lane a walk of thirty steps leads to a level of earth whereunder lies the boxful of bones of which I was born.

It is a route I sometimes take, driving in from a hundred miles to the north, and before I am within sight of the city I have entered the geography of my origins. To my right a roadsign points me to Hastings, the village where the infant who was to be Mary Dore was diapered a generation before the emancipation of the slaves; a few minutes later I view the house-littered hills of Yonkers where one of her grandchildren is now a grandmother. Nowhere in the city am I out of our soilbed. If I leave the parkway to the left I come into Mt. Vernon, where my great uncle George Jennings retired with his books, and a short ride beyond is Larchmont, where my uncle George Dore retired with his money; I was bequeathed neither, but something else, the places are meanings become flesh in the folds of my consciousness. In the upper Bronx I pass the park where as a toddler I was taken by my father to watch his brother Jim play football, and again to say goodbye to him in an encampment of soldiers, and somewhere in the woods is a little river toppling over a falls in which a rowboat is caught on the rocks, lifeless and rotted, an image of fear I have never forgotten. I drive into uptown Broadway where at Dyckman Street no ferry runs; in the water the upright logs of the slip are remnants, that forty years ago saw us embark to visit our Jersey kin the day I doted upon a gift from my parents, a living watch in my hand, I am in love with time, and who is to tell me it is the enemy? I drive in the convertible with the backsides of apartment houses climbing the rocky rise to right and left, and high in one I spy the fire escape on which my mother would hang a tablecloth as a signal to my sister and me, come home, come home, wherever you are. I turn east again, and cross the stagnant river. I am in the neighborhood from which the garden has disappeared, though I bring it with me, and on the lost hill sit as a chortling babe in the lap of a grave young uncle in a dark tie with white dots, surviving in a snapshot my father has captioned "big and little Will", and slowly out of that ghostly street I drive on. Now I am following the footsteps of my mother, a darkhaired and longskirted girl pushing me daily in a baby carriage southward along this very avenue, thirty blocks into her own past, over a trolley-car bridge and under the shadows of the Eighth Avenue el in Harlem, where aloft in a window the old lady on a cushion waits; and the baby carriage vanishes, the old lady is peering down for her other children, Frank, young Minnie, Gentleman Ben staggering around the corner of the century, and Willy too with his banjo, one of fourteen sons lost to my eye; seven blocks on I drive past the street where my father was born to another clan. If the pavements could sing it would be of all their feet who were flesh before I was, and in this ghetto of black strangers I head east to the bridge that leads over Hell Gate to the cemetery.

I stop on my way to my sister's, for we are closer now; in a note among our mother's effects was her posthumous appeal to us, "Please dears try to keep in touch with each other as there are only both of you left and at least you have in common blood & love if nothing more." To the sod above the hand that wrote it I bring no flowers, never come on the day of her birth, marriage, or death, an infrequent visitor, and yet this strip of earth in which she lies next to my father is of me like no other in the world. In the twenty-eight years since I first was at her elbow here it has become a gentler retreat; then it was a field of sparse tombstones, but they have multiplied, and around them has grown up half a young woodland; where I park the road is overhung by black oaks, and I pick my footsteps in a snowy lane with an occasional maple, cedar, sycamore among the granite slabs.

It is the wrong lane. I cross into the next, and for ten minutes am lost in a host of headstones incised with names that are nothing to me, though I know each stands as a massive last page in a family tale identical with mine, and I cut between them, backtracking, here, there, not without panic; then, in a row of inconspicuous letters on the base of one, my surname jumps at me. A wreath of hemlock conceals the upper half of the polished gray stone, and below it two inscriptions are visible, *Geo. I. Gibson*, with his dates, and *Florence A. Gibson*, with hers. I notice it is by her name that my throat is gripped, an oddity. On this slab the two inscriptions are afterthoughts; above them in bold letters hidden by the wreath is the patronymic not ours, with the names and dates of my father's half-brother and his son of five; the one-day-old girl who was the first occupant of this grave lies in it unrecorded. The foot of the stone is bedded in a decor of fir sprigs and red leaflets which like the wreath is fresh, newly laid, my sister's doing. Its foreground of snow is patchy with blades of grass, I see the deep wound in the earth is healed, though not in me.

Six years ago tonight the body of my mother reposed in a coffin in a mortuary parlor, looking indeed pretty, or better, austere as a duchess; her head was of a greater dignity than in life, and I was not unglad of it, for it was also a truth. I was not in attendance each day of her wake because my wife and I drove home to spend Christmas with our boys, living flesh, and saw them scramble among their gifts, including a few from my dead mother—on her instructions my sister had shopped for them—of which I remember a plastic locomotive whereon our younger sat and heeled himself about the house. Years later the older boy confessed that our news that day of his grandmother's death meant he was rid of her, and after a breath I thought it was permissible, to living flesh everything this side of murder is permissible. To me as someday to him an inheritance of self not possible while parents live was come, but I knew my grief, and the iridescence in it was not riddance, it was discovery of love; that I loved her was the joy I felt at her deathbed, I was trustworthy, and more, could trust his love of me as much as mine of her; I was less afraid of my death. Returned to the coffin in the city, I did what I never in my life had wanted to do, kissed a pair of dead hands before the lid was closed.

The frozen earth under my shoes is of course unconsecrated. In a procession of cars we followed the hearse to a church a mile away; here my mother for twenty years had come with her missal and eyeglasses, and I had prevailed upon its priest to ask his monsignor in Brooklyn—her marriage and heretic children were an impediment—to grant the body a mass for the dead, a rite that mattered to a fraction of her mind in us. Sealed, the coffin sat for an hour at the altar rail while the requiem mass, a solemnity of priests in black vestments with tinklings of bell and burnings of incense and besprinklings of water, was intoned in Latin over it, ancient and stately, and a mite too long. Carried from the church, the coffin was then taken by hearse a dozen miles to this grave. Raw earth, that icy day it was apparelled in mats of artificial grass, unreal as our lives; my sister and I in a score of friends roundabout saw only the faces of our old aunts Milly and Ethel, and understood that all the kin of our childhood were dead; and the coffin went down on straps, inch by inch, into the pit. The dirt was shovelled in without a benediction, no priest would accompany the body, the cemetery was not of the true church. It was never a question, my mother's wish in death as in life was to be with my father, and the two armfuls of bones lie here together in unconsecrated ground forever.

Seldom out of mind, in the posthumous note to us her husband appeared in the last sentence she penned, he "would have been proud" of us. Undated, the note was in effect her will, and its first sentence was, "My grand children are to get $500 each toward their education." To her daughter, nieces, my wife, she bequeathed her rings and "braclet", all scintillant with a few small diamonds; these stones, gifts from my father in early brooches, he had asked the bricklayer-become-jeweller to reset in modern pieces, and thereafter a glint of paranoia in my mother's eye saw them as diminished in luster; she suspected their pal had substituted tinier gems. To her schoolmate she left a hundred dollars, and the remainder to my sister and me, writing, "I have tried to save as much as I could for you both." It was a practical note, and apart from her last words to us—its next sentence was, "My darling children you have been so kind and good to me and I loved you both dearly"—was concerned with items of monetary value; unmentioned is the boxful of trifles, her mementoes of my father, which waited in her apartment.

It is a little box, originally of notepaper, and contains the odds and ends she salvaged from his drawer and pockets. Into it she placed one of his namecards, a duplicate of that in her mailbox, of no use otherwise. It rests on a toenail shears older than I, scissors size, which as a small boy I often borrowed from his top drawer in the bureau; then it was rich with its ivory-clad handle, sallowed by time and the oils of his palm, but is rude steel now, the ivory lost. She put in his medal "for excellence in piano playing", black with age, dated 1903 when he was fifteen. Under it are two snapshots of my sister, and one of a skinny gawkling dressed to the teeth, with a downward smile; and to this photo of him as suitor my mother added a news clipping no larger than my thumb announcing the funeral of Mary Dore, "mother of the widely known banjoists". She saved three of his stiff-collar buttons, and from his business suit in the closet the mother-of-pearl knife, with two blades, used by him to sharpen his pencils to deft points. Scattered in the box is the money— two one-dollar bills, folded, and coins dulled by disuse, three dimes, five nickels, eleven pennies—which she found in the pockets of his pants. And in a twist of wax paper, dried as a little mummy, never lit, is the last cigarette he held in his lips.

For six years, since the day my sister and I left her in this grave, these relics have been mine, and in my workroom keep company with those I in turn salvaged in the three rooms of her widowhood. Still in fastidious order, the apartment so conjured up the image of her I could not unbelieve that, if I sat and waited, I would any minute see her brisk in the cheery kitchen, urging lunch and tea upon me; but her bedroom, with its enlarged snapshot of a husband on the bureau, and its made bed, and the missal on the doily of the night table, was doubly bereaved. In her scrapbook there I came upon her keepsakes of the opening night of my first play, two ticket stubs—the seat beside her was empty, for my father—and the treasured corpse of an orchid my wife had sent her in my name. It was part of the legacy I collected. I picked out her leatherette folder of such documents as my father's death certificate, old letters of condolence, and her bank-books; across a century I fingered and kept her two souvenirs of Mary Dore, the black-oval earrings and the tintype of a young head firm as a tulip; from the drawer in the kitchen table I took one of the spoons I had eaten her cooking with in my boyhood. I claimed three pieces of furniture, the secretary desk at which I had entered my hidingplace of words and the two armchairs that remembered the tale around it, the one her hubby's last summer and the other their wedding. The rest of her leavings, furniture, dishes, linens, rugs, clothes, were borne away by this cousin, that friend, and within a month the portrait of her constituted by the rooms was gone. Only, in the tiny bathroom with its skylight, the twin faucets of the washbasin had been scoured by her over the years till not a fleck of the nickel plating was left, and the true brass shone forth; she had transmuted them into something quite like gold. In the empty flat nothing except these told of her existence, but I was by then sitting to her missal, note, eyeglasses, my handful of relics that kept the leaf of misery green, beginning work.

And now in truth I am at the end. In the snow here at the stone that above the two names bears my sister's wreath of hemlock, I think my wreath of words is as real, but poor, and itself a hallucination; what more have I told of her than the faucets? It was not a voice from heaven that said unto me, Write—if I could raise the dead, and choose between writing of and talking to her, what then?—but I have kept my word, such as it was, my joyous and mournful time as the family bookkeeper is done. I have let no fact go unwritten that in my eye would illuminate these echoes and apparitions, but brings no face back; and is dumb to impart the miracle of each face, alive and imperfect, never to recur, for who is like unto thee, my father? or thee, my mother? All I have summoned up is a shadow of the resurrection of a shadow of the body, born, lived, died, but no other trumpet will call their bones together; doomsday has been.

I have not even made my farewell to the past. I tell myself now I will think no more of these things, but something in me that knows nothing of time refuses to believe in death. In the dusk when three miles from this grave I stand at a corner in the winebrick colony of my teens to stare up at a lighted window I will see upon it the shadows that an hour ago were ours, but no longer are, the four of us are vanished into nowhere, and my adult wits stammer in me like a bewildered child, how can it be, how can it be, how can it be? and I have no moment worse, the meaning I have made of my life is as idiotic as a match that winks and is out in the spin of a dark planet toward its extinction, uninhabited and senseless. It is a moment of truth, upon which philosophies are built, but will pass, a child's bleat of despair.

My foot standeth in an even place, headstone, grass in the snow, the earth healed over their remnants of rag and skull, and on what may still be a finger of her hand is a ring of plain gold. I remember it in her housework, never taken off since the day of her wedding until in their middle years my father replaced it with one of engraved platinum, then fashionable, which she wore to her death; my sister searched in her rooms for the original, and it went back upon its finger in the coffin. I took it for granted at my lips when I kissed her hand. To both of us it was a ring of some import, for within its circle we had been born, fed, clothed, and sheltered in a house which was safe and faithful, and all the later currents of the world in my head— clamorous of evil and impotence, that tide of unfaith I know by hearsay is my time—could not wash away that which I saw with my eyes, I mean the lives of this ordinary woman and man who, now become the ground I stand upon, kept a pledge to love and to cherish.

Into Paradise may the angels in whom I do not believe lead thee; at thy coming may the martyrs long decomposed take thee up, in eternal rest, and may the chorus of angels lead thee to that which does not exist, the holy city, and perpetual light.

ite, missa est

Is, Now

It is the end of summer in this site among the climb of the pine overlooking the ocean, and the open light of the afternoon is upon us where we sit in silence outside the cottage, reading. Here a circle in the hogberry has been cleared, and a floor of flagstones laid in the sand, on which are a few chairs and a glass-topped table; the circle serves us as a living room out of doors. Behind us is the cottage, all shingles of cedar, sea worn to a silvery gray. To the simplicity of life in it we come for a part of each summer now, escaping out of the harassments of routine onto the sandy moraine of this cape, even to its fingertip. I escape the past too, for this landscape and the cottage are new ground; none of my dead ever set foot in this place.

Go, ye are dismissed, saith the missal: but I am mindful of old of another voice, which comforts me.

To be quietly alone is at the heart of our time here, and today the spell of it in the late afternoon is almost sorcery. At my left, two pines a dozen feet apart support in their shade a hammock and our younger boy, a trayful of toys in his lap; in the sunlight to my right our older boy sits with a book on his up-drawn knees in a reclining chair; outstretched in another on the far side of the coffee table my wife, in swimsuit and dark glasses, is intent upon books and a notepad. No one speaks. I am in a rocker, my bare feet up on the table, not quite reading, now *and then attentive to the sorcery.*

It is a cloudless afternoon, no stir in the branches, no sound except of gull, and the everlasting voice of the sea. From our high ground the pines in a stunted matting descend the slope, and die out in meadow; beyond is the irregular dune, of beach grass and sand, which holds out the waters. At two dips in the sand the vast level of them is visible, intensely blue, but not the white breakage of their attack under the dune. I hear their voices gather, break, roar and boom, recede, hissing and tumbling, never singly, for along the beach the breakage upon breakage is everywhere, voice upon voice, the old, the new, never done with saying the former things are passed away. All else is still.

The other voice said, I saw a new heaven and a new earth.

I am facing east, where this morning the sun stood out of the ocean; to the north the moors and few housetops are mute with the vacationists gone, and to the south a hill of pine woods is not enough to deprive us of the huge sky; in it now the sun is behind me. It is the openness of the earth so wide to the light which is its charm here, and the serenity of barren moor and the inexhaustible voice of the sea, but the sorcery is something else.

The light in which we sit is that of early fall; the nights have turned cold, and in the shadows the air is chill, yet of such clarity that the sun upon three of us is still hot. Under the pine branches our boy in the hammock is cozy in a blanket. Idling with his toys, he is unaware of what is extraordinary in the day, like his brother rapt in a book, but my wife's head is up as if to drink the afternoon through her opaque glasses. I know she knows, and I go back to my own page, wiping the eyeglasses I have this summer taken to, my first for reading; I am on the wrong side of fifty. The two pines cast a dark shape which lengthens across the chairs. I note that one of my bare legs in sunlight is warm, the other in shadow is cold; and though the rare light with its marriage of warmth and chill is also what holds me, it is not what I am loth to leave. I would not sit here alone.

It is an afternoon with no event, and the sorcery is the stillness upon us, as though time is not, nothing will change, we will always be thus; if I rise I will break the spell. Into it drifts a touch of music, two or three sweet notes blown to us, poignant, very faint. I lift my face for its source in some other and far house, and see my boy in the hammock is the player, with a toy harmonica an inch long cupped in his hands to his mouth. I listen to each slow note he breathes into the stillness; I think this sound, so small, sweet, brief, is not unlike that of us and our happiness, and its poignance is in how commonplace is the substance each of us hardly looks at, and, once lost, cannot forget. It is the last day of our summer here. The sun is already in the west, and the shade of the cottage at our backs has begun to move outward to us; soon we must leave this place.

And the voice said, Behold, I make all things new.

WILLIAM GIBSON

William Gibson, poet, novelist and playwright, was born in New York City in 1914
and now makes his home in Stockbridge,
Massachusetts. His plays include *Dinny and
the Witches, Two for the Seesaw, The Miracle Worker, Golden Boy* (with Clifford
Odets), *A Cry of Players, American Primitive,* and *The Body and the Wheel.*